GEORGE MACKAY BROWN

NO SEPARATION

George Mackay Brown

No Separation

Alison Gray

GRACEWING

First published in England in 2016

by

Gracewing
2 Southern Avenue
Leominster
Herefordshire HR6 0QF
United Kingdom
www.gracewing.co.uk

ISBN 978 085244 883 0

Typeset by Word and Page, Chester

Cover design by Bernardita Peña Hurtado

CONTENTS

*This book is dedicated to the memory of George Mackay Brown
on the twentieth anniversary of his death, 13 April 1996*

ACKNOWLEDGEMENTS

I would like to thank all those who have helped and supported me in my research, especially in granting permission to reproduce copyright materials.

George Mackay Brown Estate
Ernest Walker Marwick Estate
Archie and Elizabeth Bevan
Morag McInnes
Lucy Gibbons Orkney Archive
Edinburgh University Special Collections
National Library of Scotland
BBC Permissions
Orkney Print
Ignatius Press (original publishers of
    Hans Urs von Balthasar)
Pluscarden Abbey
Hugh Gilbert OSM, Bishop of Aberdeen
Mario Conti, Archbishop Emeritus of Glasgow
Inga Croy Kirkwall
Sarah Drever Kirkwall
Isla Holloway, The Pier Arts Centre Stromness
Bryce Wilson, Sylvia Wishart Estate
Joan and David Peppitt Twatt
Anne Marie and Maurice Ward Dounby
Doreen Wake Redland
Monique Webb Stenness
Mary Heddle Stromness
Gabrielle Barnby St Andrews
Jane Coll Dunnet

PREFACE

This is a book that is needed. Just as George Mackay Brown himself re-opened the Orcadian memory, readjusting it, recalling things beyond surface modernity and, among them, the islands' long Catholic centuries, so Alison Gray—New Zealander and Orcadian all at once—has made it possible for us to recover the fuller truth of Mackay Brown, Orcadian and Catholic Christian.

She has not done this by crude apologetic or any kind of hectoring one-sidedness. She simply knows her subject and her man (they conversed and corresponded over many years). She is familiar with unpublished material. She writes persuasively of an 'Orkney Poetics', of which George was as much inheritor as practitioner. She respects the concepts and language of literary criticism, but does not allow herself to be confined to psychological and sociological perspectives. With the help of John Henry Newman, Gerard Manley Hopkins and the Swiss theologian Hans Urs von Balthasar, she is able to move beyond the usual constrictions and shed as distinctive and compelling a light as that physical light which can break through the clouds of an Orkney day and transfigure the archipelago.

'No Separation' is a deftly chosen title. The natural and supernatural, the cosmic and the human, outdoors and indoors, land and sea, past and present, local and universal, life's long stretches of suffering toil and sudden gashes of glory—the inseparable interweaving of all these are the mark and genius of Mackay Brown. But at the same time—via a fifth-century Church council—the book's title alludes to the unity-without-confusion and duality-without-separation of Christ himself. It is impossible to understand Mackay Brown as person and as poet without the Eucharist, where that very Christ entered his own life and that of the islands for which he sang.

This book needed to be written. Dare I say it? It tells the truth. And as Orkney prepares to celebrate the 900th anniversary of St Magnus's martyrdom, it deserves to be read.

Hugh Gilbert OSB
Bishop of Aberdeen

Introduction

One must be passive, often, to let the swarming delights of the world in, and things beyond.[1]

A Swarm of Symbols

The sun pours into Hamnavoe Bay and splays its radiance across the waters. Points and petals of silver water-dance, drawing in those who perceive and see, those reaching for the enlightenment that is Orkney, a place where symbols swarm. Orkney, theophany, a magical place, like no other. George Mackay Brown naturally engages with the abundance of primary sources of which Orkney is the 'primer'. His reading of Orkney, as 'a swarm of symbols' is a communal space, a deep shared reality. He is not a theologian or philosopher. He, as poet, is a master of symbols—'In the fire of images, Gladly I put my hand'[2] emerging with texts that are sparse, taut, detached and highly reasoned, as they joyously speak to an aesthetic of beauty and truth. Orkney is read as a forecourt to theology, where a pre-theological perception becomes his path and technique.

The poetics of George Mackay Brown are 'prior' to a professional theology. The Swiss theologian Hans Urs von Balthasar provocatively asserts:

> Now it is primarily laity who, out of an adequate theological culture and with a more powerful vision and deeper creative insight than the theologians of the schools, carry forward the concern and guarantee of its effectiveness with a breadth and depth that escapes the professional theologians.[3]

Orkney, storehouse of symbols that 'swarm', is made intelligible by Mackay Brown, who is 'interested in facts only as they tend and gesture, like birds and grass and waves, in the gale of life'.[4] This intelligibility emerges in a craft that is lucid, taut and pure, never private, always a communion that invites but does not impose a religious assent.

Mackay Brown does not craft a religious literature or a Catholic literature, and it is not synonymous with theology. He includes all the subjects of literature pre-theologically, treating facts, birds, grass, waves, life 'as a Catholic would treat them and only could treat them'.[5] It is his distinctive perceiving and seeing, his creative insights, that unfold a shared vision between poet and other poets and poet and reader. 'Never forget: in silence is the movement of purer deeper thoughts, that words only stain and obscure, mostly'.[6] Mackay Brown has an interior space that early establishes an attunement that determines decades of effort through texts packed with images and symbols that swarm. Mackay Brown's literary experiments always go beyond a searching retrogressive primitivism, resonant of a nostalgia or a cult of purity or the creation of a private world. The search is not autobiographical, with poet-author placed as its central point. It is not bourgeois. This early existential attunement is evidenced in early writings that went through much re-finement over the years. It is these early drafts that declare the intensity of his psychological turmoil and religious experience. In the Orkney Archive there is much evidence of his experience of Orkney as the glory of the Lord. They, Orkney and the glory of the Lord, are one and the same; there is 'No Separation'. It is here in these unpublished writings that a contemplative attitude can be seen to emerge, fortifying Mackay Brown to enable him to 'put his hand into the swarm of symbols'. This creative path was not without its suffering or passion that was intensely personal, and that others have documented in published biographical details.[7] Yet there is more to be said on the basis of other relationships of those who knew him over many years through letters and dialogue, through Orkney Catholic parish seasons and religious duties. These are best related now, while the chance to record them lasts.

The Glory of the Lord

February snow surges across the Bay of Birsay. The island of Westray backdrops the penetrating snow clouds against a steely blue sky. The sun enraptures the ice crystals, refracting light in prismatic forms, and swings in on the wind in an uncontained splendour. Inscape, Gerard Manley Hopkins would say. Mackay Brown also, without which he cannot understand Orkney, or himself. The instress is the glory of the

Lord, a radiance and splendour breaking forth from a veiled depth of being. Splendour breaks forth and is recognised or realised as the love of God which gives itself without remainder. Everything of beauty found in the world is drawn up into a relationship with the glory that is God and moved by a faith that must go out onto the stage that is the world. The relationship is one of a theological aesthetic, that has a theological drama and a theological logic. The intelligibility of the 'swarm of symbols' is ordered to these contours. Mackay Brown reads and writes accordingly, in a pre-theological language of beauty. In Orkney and twentieth-century preoccupations and themes, he sees God; he finds God in the mystery of Form. This seeing and finding shapes his poetics and literary experiments.

His 'spiritual eye' sees what is true and reaches piercingly through the desolation of everyday life, of sham existence, to the Absolute. The best of his writing resists the temptation to slide back from this absolute, primal form into derived secondary detail. Putting one's hand into the swarm of symbols to have intimacy with the Primal Maker of images with courage raises everything in the texts into the light towards the true the good and the beautiful. Mackay Brown is directed in this special way of seeing by Hopkins and his intuitive absorption of the philosophical method of Duns Scotus to see Orkney as a set form, a cruciform, with its land, sky and sea scapes. This of course is not without precedent in Orkney poetics, with the writers Edwin Muir, Robert Rendall and Ernest Marwick and the artist Sylvia Wishart expressing in their own ways and sympathies this special way of seeing and understanding and reading Orkney, but none went so far as to embrace the Cross as did Mackay Brown. The role of the artist is to seek an opening through which a special way of seeing finds expression in different types of media. The writer will master the art of word-pictures to make known what has been seen. Mackay Brown writes 'We should be grateful that magic casements opened once in the dark tower, and showed us things rare and unimaginable.'[8]

Contemplative Attitude

What is really said, what is really presented to us, what is really meant through the pen gives a likeness of the original image, and it has to have a level of correspondence that mediates between what is primal and what can be shared. Orkney poetics demonstrates an overlap, a mutuality, a convergence and particularity true to both the difference and the similarity between Orkney writers. The literary and artistic processes of each go their own way. For Mackay Brown the contemplative attitude becomes his imperative when an early rapture takes hold, when there is a moment in which the bursting light of the spirit makes appearance in the unpublished 'Summer Day', quoted in chapter 2, that can be tracked and traced as he works and reworks the origin of this 1947 transfiguring experience through his body of texts.[9] The contemplative attitude is fortifying as he glides seamlessly from the natural to supernatural worlds, examining the subjects of literature pre-theologically. Mackay Brown brings a pre-Reformation time and place and vision that shows awe, thankfulness, admiration, submission, joy, pleasure and delight in God and His splendour. His readers, too, can be caught up, even though they may not be aware of it, by that first joyous attunement of the 1947 rapture. The time of this first encounter has a special dignity about it, a special power to open up the depths of the Orkney mystery.

From this encounter and its formal documentation, even though it proved a draft of the later, finely honed, poem 'Hamnavoe',[10] comes the contemplative attitude, the imperative by which Mackay Brown follows a pattern of faith that is quite prototypically feminine as in the Virgin Mary, Our Lady of Orkney. John Henry Newman preaches the attitude:

> Thus Mary is our pattern of Faith, both in the reception and the study of Divine Truth. She does not think it enough to accept it, she dwells upon it; not enough to possess it, she uses it; not enough to assent, she develops it; not enough to submit the Reason, she reasons upon it; not indeed reasoning first, and believing afterwards … yet first believing without reasoning, next from love and reverence, reasoning after believing.[11]

This is the Catholic contemplative attitude, for the learned and the unlearned. Mackay Brown is in harmony, as is Hopkins and Duns Scotus. The literary processes that have manifested themselves in Mackay Brown before and after the 1947 'Summer Day' experience now have an ecclesial fortification for his endeavour: 'In the fire of images, Gladly I put my hand'.[12]

This contemplative attitude is robust enough not only to grapple with the Maker of images but also with the historical forces special to Orkney in its various timely formations. Mackay Brown's technique is never an empty vessel. There is always an attentiveness to an accepting, dwelling, developing, from the Mary-pattern of 'reasoning after believing'. So doing, Mackay Brown takes his literary experiment 'back before Scottish literature' until we see 'a recognisable mirror to our modern, multi-cultural, hybrid-identity literary scene'.[13] Mackay Brown consciously stands or falls on the edge of a medieval Christendom and within his writing is contained an implicit theology that can be uncovered. Theological learning is on display as a derivative of a theologically rich culture that is inquisitive and aware of the questions that drive theology. Mackay Brown's Orkney pre-theologically investigates the multi-lingual texts, monuments and buildings that define Orkney in its languages, its chronology, its cultural and political realignments, and a 'trajectory'[14] emerges that comes forward into his twentieth-century work. The contemplative attitude finds a 'quarry of images' in a pre-Reformation sensorium within which Mackay Brown embraces not only a wild beauty but also vanished communities; 'the old wals of Churches and Monasteries, the defaced ruines of altars, images, and crosses do cry with a loud voice, that the Romain Catholique faith of Jesus Christ did tread this way'.[15] This snippet of local gossip in 1654 holds good for Orkney as it does for its English origins. Mackay Brown re-opens a previous time to explore what was lost and where his literary processes can experiment with the 'swarm of symbols' that are about the future as much as they are about the past.

Mackay Brown's alertness to local topography as well as to the subjective states they elicit make Orkney's medieval past impossible to forget; his writings take up a host of voices that are never merely a retrospective rallying nostalgia. This host of voices that well up into literary contexts is a form of social correction, muted sacrilege narratives that take up a blend of linguistic expression that has the power to re-open a 'world-view belonging to an earlier stage of development'.[16] Theological grievances need not always be voiced in theological terms[17] and one wonders if Mackay Brown is Orkney's Piers Plowman, articulating a discontent through defiant literary contexts that long for a reversal of worlds.[18] A re-opened world view is in keeping with Clancy's 'back before Scottish literature' until we see 'a recognisable mirror to our modern, multi-cultural, hybrid-identity literary scene'.[19] Other writers from different disciplines converge in their inter-disciplinary thinking, giving considerable ballast to the re-opened world view that mirrors a pre-historical, pre-theological forecourt that takes up the 'swarm of symbols' that overflow into literary contexts. Mackay Brown is understood in this book through writers and thinkers who resonate one way or another in their research with a magical Orkney poetics.

Mackay Brown lived on the edge of Christendom, on a geographical periphery that never became a bourgeois habitat for him. The margins are a good place to be. His margins were geographical and psychological. Orkney was his interior and exterior. 'Summer Day' in 1947 records a religious experience from which there is much development. From here the symbols swarm in Mackay Brown's texts held in form and space energised by a faithfully consistently literary technique, not always applauded and understood, unless there is engagement with the embedded assent that takes up the contemplative attitude that reasons after believing. In his novel *Magnus* Mackay Brown platforms the sacrilege narrative, 'This crucifix is the forge, and the threshing floor, and the shed of the net-makers, where God and man work out together a plan of utter necessity and of unimaginable beauty'.[20] Swarming to the death-call of the 'catafalque',[21] Mackay Brown seamlessly moves to 'April ditches teaming with Resurrection'.[22] Mackay Brown is Passion-Partner through Magnus. Theo-dramatically he reads Orkney as a transitional place, firmly rooted in its natural physical formations, that elicit a supernatural demeanour. Of the Stations of the Cross poem 'Stone to Thorn'[23] he wrote: 'Those 14 couplets condense everything I wanted or want, or will ever conceivably want to say'.[24] As the 'symbols swarm' what is said entwines Orkney, storehouse of the sacred and the profane into which 'In the fire of images, / Gladly I put my hand'.

Notes

[1]   George Mackay Brown in a letter to the author, 2 September 1983. See Appendix.

[2]   George Mackay Brown, 'Hamnavoe', in *The Collected Poems of George Mackay Brown*, ed. Archie Bevan and Brian Murray. London: John Murray, 2005, p. 25.

[3]   Hans Urs von Balthasar, *The Glory of the Lord. A Theological Aesthetics. II. Studies in Theological Styles: Clerical Styles*. San Francisco: Ignatius Press, 2006, p. 15.

[4]   George Mackay Brown, *An Orkney Tapestry*. London: Quartet Books, 1973, pp. 1–2.

[5]   John Henry Newman, 'English Catholic Literature', in *The Idea of a University*, ed. F. Turner. New Haven and London: Yale University Press, 1996, p. 179.

[6]   George Mackay Brown, in a letter to the author, 1 March 1984. See Appendix.

[7]   Rowena and Brian Murray, *Interrogation of Silence. The Writings of George Mackay Brown*. London and Edinburgh: Steve Savage, 2008; Maggie Fergusson, *George Mackay Brown. The Life*. London: John Murray, 2006.

[8]   George Mackay Brown, 'Suddenly there were Penguins', *The Scotsman*, 15 June 1985. Orkney Archive, The George Mackay Brown Collection, D124/2/1/1.

[9]   George Mackay Brown, 'Summer Day', 1947. Orkney Archive, Ernest Walker Marwick Collection, D31/30/2.

[10]   Mackay Brown, 'Hamnavoe'.

[11]   John Henry Newman, 'Sermon XV The Theory of Developments in Religious Doctrine', in *Fifteen Sermons Preached before the University of Oxford between A.D. 1826 and 1843*. Notre Dame: University of Notre Dame Press, 1997, p. 313.

[12]   Mackay Brown, 'Hamnavoe', p. 25.

[13]   Thomas Clancy, 'Scottish Literature before Scottish Literature', in *The Cambridge Companion to Scottish Literature*, ed. G. Carruthers and L. McIlvaney. Cambridge: Cambridge University Press, 2012, p. 23.

[14]   *Ibid.*, pp. 13–14.

[15]   Edward Frances Eyston, *A cleer looking glass for all wandering sinners*, cited in Alison Shell, 'Abbey Ruins, Sacrilege Narratives and the Gothic Imagination', in her *Oral Culture and Catholicism in Early Modern England*. Cambridge: Cambridge University Press, 2008, p. 23.

[16]   Clancy, 'Scottish Literature before Scottish Literature', p. 52.

[17]   Alison Shell, 'Answering Back: Orality and Controversy', in her *Oral Culture and Catholicism in Early Modern England*, p. 83.

[18]   *Ibid.*, p. 92.

[19]   Clancy, 'Scottish Literature before Scottish Literature', p. 23.

[20] George Mackay Brown, *Magnus*. Edinburgh: Cannongate Classics, 2000 (orig. published 1973), p. 65.

[21] *Ibid.*

[22] George Mackay Brown, 'Why live in Orkney?' Orkney Archive, George Mackay Brown Collection, D124/2/4/1.

[23] Mackay Brown, *The Collected Poems*, pp. 178–9.

[24] Note held in Essays and Articles 2 May 1983, Edinburgh University Library, Special Collections, MS 2846.1.

Pre-theologics

> Heraldry is the mysterious signs, deeper than art or language, by which a family or a tribe pass on their most precious secrets, their lore of a kingdom lost. It is a stillness into which the torrents of history are gathered, like an unflawed mill pool. In the silence an image out of the past stirs, and illuminates things in our present circumstances, as individuals or as citizens of a country or as members of the human race, that we do not understand. Heraldry is the fury of history made wise and formal; from its hands we take at last the wholesome images—the heart's bread—that our ancestors sowed for us in passion and blindness. That quiet pool turns the millstones of religion, and of art, and of the simple graces and courtesies of daily living.[1]

Mackay Brown sets out *An Orkney Tapestry*, but in the first instance is it more of a northern mosaic, with compositional borders and frontiers that startle the reader out of a conventional and static view of a remote and peripheral cascade of islands? The weave of the tapestry, the patterns of his literary composition become a *lectio divina*[2] of Orkney as he lays out his path towards an enlightenment that is a communal deep-rooted responsive attitude that is intensively crafted in the philosophical manner and method of Duns Scotus and Gerard Manley Hopkins. Catholicism is therefore integral to Orkney and so to Mackay Brown, but never in an exclusivity that does not pay homage to the realism of the entwined 'no separation' of the sacred and the profane. A way of seeing 'the gale of life' becomes a way of living. To read Orkney, meditate Orkney, pray Orkney, contemplate Orkney, is the Mackay Brown *lectio divina*, the evidence of which is his literary endeavours. From an 'adequate theological culture and with a more powerful vision and deeper creative insight,'[3] the layman Mackay Brown, poet, reads from below 'the gale of life' and a heraldry emerges, 'a swarm of symbols' seamlessly moving from the natural to the supernatural with a technique that argues for 'no separation'. There is no theological analysis in this forecourt of 'facts only as they tend and gesture, like birds and grass and waves, in the gale of life'.[4] The message or reading of the natural world is one of a beauty that is no less audible for being unwritten. Expression is made manifest in the 'swarm of symbols'. Here lies the ground of an aesthetics that liberates Mackay Brown, who moves and works within the re-opened world view of the pre-Reformation sensorium. What emerges is a convincing expression of 'swarming' phenomena, crafted as symbols within a pre-theological Orkney poetics that never stops the process of thinking, or learning how to think.

Von Balthasar: The Glory of the Lord

It is significant that Mackay Brown, although not a formal reader of the twentieth-century theologians, is in accord with the same Catholic instincts that are indignantly reactive against the prescriptive rationalism of the neo-scholastics. The 'ressourcement'[5] or 'back to sources' is the restorative theological understanding that underpins Vatican II realignments. While Mackay Brown was crafting his prose poems in the 1940s, von Balthasar, 'widely regarded as the greatest Catholic theologian of the century',[6] was embarking on his project to overcome the struggle with 'the dreariness of theology, with what men have made of the glory of revelation' as he rediscovered the Church Fathers and their patristic heritage. A 'close reading' of Mackay Brown reveals the many-stranded threads of the Orkney patrimony but also a presiding intellectual spirit where the world is read as a system of sign and symbol with a meaning beyond itself in the inseparable 'particular' and 'universal'. This 'close reading' is in accord with the 'back to sources' ethos wherein Mackay Brown is crafting a path in a shared deep reality where 'gladly I put my hand into the fire of images'. This deep reality is documented throughout von Balthasar's multi-volume theological project: *The Glory of the Lord*.[7]

With patristic and medieval sources von Balthasar shows how Jesus Christ relates to the particular and the universal in a cosmic dimension. His Jesuit formation and understanding of John Henry Newman and Gerard Manley Hopkins in particular find a profound synthesis within the tensions of the twentieth century and its preoccupations with world wars, the rise of fascism, Soviet communism and the subsequent Cold War. Just as the twentieth century swept into the turmoil of relativism, philosophy showed a special concern for theories of language, evolution and phenomenology. Mackay Brown provocatively embraced an intimate working relationship with the mystic Adrienne von Speyr and through their 'complementarity' was enabled to restore a theological aesthetics that is 'fit for purpose' not only in the twentieth century but beyond. His rich encounters with the Protestant theologian Karl Barth also brought a certain command and authority into the heart of Christianity as he searched towards an authentic unity. Von Balthasar was a ploughshare with a rich literary formation who worked with authority to review and synthesise the great bodies of knowledge—sacred and profane. He was able to plough furrows in an earth that had become intractable, re-opening ancient well-springs that others will be nurtured by in the years ahead.

What is of importance here is von Balthasar's articulation of the form and shape of the 'glory of the Lord', which Mackay Brown simultaneously gives expression to in a pre-theological manner in his literary endeavours. There is no evidence that Mackay Brown read Balthasar (although he had a deep sympathy for Germanic literary and Christian figures such as Thomas Mann, Bertold Brecht and Dietrich Bonhoeffer). Mackay Brown nevertheless actively participated in an ecclesial communion that gives expression to Catholicism as a religion ancient but ever-new, with a persevering freshness that draws in the 'gale of life'; literature becomes an apostolate to reach out to others. Whether Mackay Brown is deliberately conscious of this is open to debate, but he has left a record of glimpses into his manner of life and method which demonstrate a concern for language, a mastery of sign and symbol, a historical frame of mind and a cosmic appreciation of the 'particular' as inseparable from the universality of God. The 'swarm of symbols' that Orkney is home to leads to an interpretation that holds the classic kenotic self-emptying of the divine Logos in the Bethlehem manger, the maturation in Nazareth, the Galilean ministry and the death on the Cross, and the invincible nature of the Resurrection and deep consciousness of the Parousia. All the particularities of Orkney, in the Mackay Brown interpretation, lead inseparably in a cosmic sweep to the universal, the divine Logos.

> In my first rootless days in Edinburgh ... and reading Bede's History
> of England, one of the set books, there was an image, in the foreword,
> of the old monk sitting in the bitter cold of his monastery writing on
> his parchments by candle-light. The image enthralled me: and yet I
> felt as isolated and cold as Bede.[8]

'Enthralled', 'isolated' and 'cold' mark the contemplative path that is
so dominant in Mackay Brown, and for all the particularities of his
literary compositions they are contextualised here in this timeless
ecclesial image.

Von Balthasar had taken up the view that after Aquinas theology
takes the form of commentary, and the authentic quest to express the
glory of revelation, of the Lord, passes to the laity. The laity who take
up this challenge perceive that 'the run-of-the-mill-clergy'[9] are no longer
able to defend this quest. The poet and artist engaging with Primary
Form (God) make it accessible for others through secondary form—
through words, concepts, images, patterns. But the secondary form
must be able to make the Primary Form present as a source of the inner
radiance that is original and can break forth anew from its centre into
a specific historical context. Herein lies an ecclesial instruction 'set into
ways of thought and the forms of speech of the epoch and it is in this
way it finds its uniqueness'.[10] 'The sensorium for the glory of Creation
passed into the hands of poets such as Dante, Petrarch, Milton, Keats,
Hopkins ... to name but a few', according to von Balthasar's 'alternative canon'.[11] The test of their authenticity is what lies at the centre of
their literary endeavours that animates the whole, where a theological
aesthetic occurs most centrally in the heart, in the original vision and
in the middle point where the basic (secondary) forms crystallise.[12]

There is also an immediate relationship to biblical revelation.[13] As
Mackay Brown wrote in *An Orkney Tapestry*, 'from its hands we take at
last the wholesome images—the heart's bread'.[14] The 'dialogues' of the
poet, the artist, do not form an 'overall system'. Their inherent discor-
dancies in style and content are for von Balthasar able to work as for
the orchestra, whose various instruments blend well with one another
and play a mutual harmony from the same score.[15] Von Balthasar's
articulation of the pre-theological status of literature and especially
poetry is deeply underpinned by John Henry Newman's thought and
writings, as he takes full account of Anglo-Saxon and certain features

of later English literature that are animated and ordered to a Catholic reading and understanding. How we come to faith through a principled and sensed journey to assent and realisation by means of the conscience holds a special place in von Balthasar's twentieth-century convictions. He also had a strong empathy with the Catholic poet Francis Thompson, as did Mackay Brown, using his words to inscribe his volume of *Glory of the Lord, II, Studies in Theological Style: Clerical Styles*:

> The Church which was once the mother of poets no less than of saints, during the last two centuries has relinquished to aliens the chief glories of poetry ... she has retained the palm but forgone the laurel ... What you theoretically know vividly realize: that with many the religion of beauty must always be a passion and a power, that it is only evil when divorced from the worship of Primal Beauty.[16]

The 'pious laics' re-open the path to the Primal and do not fall into the trap of mistaking a closed secondary literature for an original source. Newman assented to an understanding which many 'pious laics', including Mackay Brown, were able to take as their model of life and work. The 'living minds' of an ecclesial Catholicism were the kindred spirits within which Mackay Brown found ballast, sanity and nurture and from which he could craft his own path, having the freedom for his literary endeavours. An ecclesial patristic and medieval patrimony was able to give to a twentieth-century 'modernism' that was lost in the 'particular' its rightful connection to the universal.

> Some kind of ancient wisdom whispers always, 'Stay where you are. What is good and necessary for you will be brought or you will be led to it. Wait. Have patience. What has been written down for you will happen when the time comes' ... The minds of writers work in a different way, in pulsing controlled image sequences, which are no less strict than the workings of music or mathematics or philosophy.[17]

Mackay Brown found himself most fully in this rich depth of reality, which he came to understand as Catholicism, to which he surrendered. Like John Henry Newman, his conversion was a gradual one, but not in an Anglican England. Mackay Brown rejected the severe Presbyterianism of Reformation Orkney and Scotland but like Newman he had much to lose socially. Whether, like Newman, 'I should have been a Catholic sooner than I was,'[18] his surrender to Catholicism was to its deep reality, so resonant in the wild beauty of Orkney, and its shared world of sign, symbol and sacrament.

John Henry Newman: Contemplative Attitude

Mackay Brown's awareness of and relationship with John Henry Newman is autobiographically documented in *For the Islands I Sing*. In his teens he adopted the Catholic path from Francis Thompson:

> Our English master one day read Francis Thompson's 'Hound of Heaven'. I think, looking back after forty-five years, that the poem has many flaws in its pure gem-like flame; but I could not have enough of that wonderful discovery. I read it over and over, until I had it by heart. And I knew that the man reeling from delight to vain earthly delight was a Catholic—a very sad and weak and fallible one—and that the Hound in relentless pursuit of him was Christ, or the Church. And for some reason, these facts gave to the poem an extra relish.[19]

Mackay Brown embraced the model of classical conversion laid out in Newman's *Apologia pro Vita Sua*. This is described by Mackay Brown as a journey through 'luminous prose'[20] to the point where the experience 'made me catch my breath'[21] and to an identification with Newman's experience of 'astonishment'.[22] The realisation that he too, was caught up in a 'current in the direction of Catholic truth, when the waters are rapidly flowing the other way' was compounded when he got hold of the *Apologia* and was transported by 'those passages, all exquisite and soaring as violin music, that rise clear above all his own dilemmas and difficulties'. Furthermore, in a letter to Ernest Marwick in 1947 Mackay Brown wrote: 'Have you ever read John Henry Newman's *Apologia pro Vita Sua*? I have just finished it and, as always, it has shaken me to the core. There is a magnificent devastating logic about it.'[23]

Like Newman, Mackay Brown was embedded early on in his life in the counter-current. The maturation of religious experience was forged on the biblical paradox: first the seed must die, then the shoots emerge, until finally the fully grown plant is brought to harvest. Mackay Brown's Orkney peers and mentors would travel with him only so far in his contemplative attitude, that ordered the many strands of the Orkney experience according to a pre-theological swarm of symbols. But these symbols would not be accessible without Mackay Brown's realisation that they are appearances of a higher reality, where the conflation of the sacred and profane seamlessly move from the natural to the supernatural. The experience of 'transporting rapture' is a Christian marker well documented in the Bible, and in the Christian life. Mackay Brown writes:

> Cardinal Newman was quite right: we ought to rest in faith and trust. I myself don't have one iota of Newman's marvellous power of reason—but I do have a certain measure of the imagination, and I seek out my way by that light[24] … One must be passive, often, to let the swarming delights of the world in, and things beyond.[25]

Clearly from the Catholic point of view there is a communal convergence in and between writers, clerics and 'pious laics', and Mackay Brown consciously works this interior space. This ecclesial shared community includes those that Mackay Brown knows about and clearly relishes and also those he does not, who are living through the same times and in their cultural context have a similar responsiveness to a shared deep reality. In my view, Mackay Brown was explicitly conscious of this and would be comfortable to be seen as such now, even if at various points he struggled to live and work through personal difficulties that might be interpreted otherwise if detached from the Christian struggle. He saw that struggle as his Christian credentials. In conversation with me in 1996 he made it clear that the *Autobiography* was essential in order to get across what he wanted to be said about his life and work rather than lay himself open to what others would say about him.

Newman was his model in these matters as in many others. The contemplative attitude holds and orders personal subjectivities, the messy life of skewed emotions to be interpreted and recorded by others, the conflation of the sacred and the profane, to find realisation and a Catholic enlightenment always more than mere consolation. The faint shadows and tracings brushed aside by irreverent minds were prized by Newman and by Mackay Brown. The strong and physical evidence laid out in a many-layered Orkney was understood by Mackay Brown's 'reverent mind', that interpreted it with a deep sensitivity to the delicate fragilities and evanescent intimations that supernaturally elevated a vision that would never be complacent and satisfied with a bourgeois art divorced from the worship of a primal beauty.

The universal categories became for Mackay Brown a core ballast. These 'universal categories' for him cannot be seen, perceived and understood apart from Orkney. The intensive rigour through the contemplative attitude embraced the northern traditions of the sagas to counterpoint and make his literary experiments especially strong and distinctive. What crystallises at the centre of his literature is also his personal centre, as fulfilled as it could or ever would be. His personal difficulties, recorded as such in the Ferguson biography and other interpretative works and accounts, reveal a debilitating depression that was never far from the surface. Yet I can say that, surprisingly, others were never dragged into it—my personal time with him was a time when I saw a nervous disposition that inevitably collapsed into laughter and an intimacy in religious matters, which one never left without being filled with a great sense of cheerfulness and joy. That was my experience in correspondence and in conversation and dialogue with him. The added dimension of a shared Mass attendance also signified the experience of a shared Catholic community, both in the local parish and also in the wider Church. Being picked up en route to Sunday Mass in the John Broom[26] days added an extra bonus of other passengers. Mackay Brown had many Catholic friends and visitors. These were important and life-sustaining for him. Yet while he did have kindred spirits in the local parish and wider Church, it is true to say that he kept his work private. Certain letters are testament to this.[27] One always wanted to know more of the 'man' but as one learnt over the years 'more is less' when knowing the 'poet'.

Newman's legacy and enduring influence give a special prominence to the ecclesial concept of the 'living minds' of the Church Fathers. Equally, one can argue that the concept of 'living Orcadian minds' emerged in a venture increasingly communal, where the many-layered ethos of Orkney is catalogued, sorted, classified, distributed, harmonised. This sharing was a searching for patterns beneath surface features and beyond personal subjectivities. Symbols became an encoding of the world of Orkney phenomena, working to convey to the mind the reality of features which Mackay Brown argues are of the pre-Reformation world, where the visible was a manifestation of the invisible. His writings and experimentations demonstrated a yearning saturated with memories of this world. Just as Newman entered the Oxford

Movement and became an integral part of it, Mackay Brown entered an Orcadian movement, in which he had a special part to play, the fullness of which was yet to find its greatest expression. His contemplative and introspective literary journey through which, and by which, he was able to convey to others an intense consciousness of the reality of the spiritual world was not a vague journey towards an unknown destination. It was marked by clear literary and spiritual directions through a diligent, patient working-out of the many materials where faint shadows and tracings found a distinctive maturation. It is also clear that Newman was instrumental in Mackay Brown's conversion, as he was in so many other people's.

The Oxford Movement was a many-featured dialectic, spurred on by the romanticism of its age in reaction against the complexity of ideas unleashed at the Reformation. One can assert with confidence that Mackay Brown, influenced by Newman and the legacy of the Oxford Movement, was spurred on with a degree of vehemence in reacting against the suppression of Orkney's Catholic past. Certain features of the Oxford Movement appealed to him—its sacramental spirituality, its blend of romanticism imbued with moral strength—and most certainly he was reacting against the Reformation principle of private judgement. Like Newman, Mackay Brown was more than comfortable in the letter-writing genre. On 15 November 1991 he wrotes to me:

> No harm in studying the scriptures, so long as one knows what one is about. It is such a richly poetic-symbolical body of work, some people read into it (especially a book like Revelation) all kinds of meaning. The Reformation happened because people were making private inferences. The Church is never tired of saying 'this and nothing else, unless the Holy Spirit unfolds some new meaning … it shouldn't be forgotten that the Scripture we have is a translation of translations— and meaning alters subtly with each translation.[28]

Mackay Brown was, it turned out, firmly opposed to Bible groups on the basis of the principle of 'private inferences' as recorded here in this letter and also in response to the group in the local parish of Our Lady and St Joseph, in Kirkwall.[29] He was aware that it is not only Protestants that make private inferences, but Catholics also. In a letter of 15 March 1992 this can be seen when he writes:

Catholics everywhere, it seems, are great at squabbling. The wonder is they haven't torn themselves apart many times since the Reformation. I suppose the wind of the Holy Spirit keeps the ark from the rocks … I'd never belong to that Lefèbrist lot … It is all a great mystery. Cardinal Newman was quite right: we ought to rest in faith and trust.[30]

The Newman legacy is an iconic one and is keenly felt and adhered to by Mackay Brown. Maturation of the Mackay Brown vision created a dialectic which is able to bring all the historical, literary, philosophical and theological strands into play, giving a special prominence not only to Catholicism but to Orkney, which in his perceptions are inseparable. This dialectic is seminal and serene. Mackay Brown, like Newman, was constantly struggling to express exactly his meaning, which has the capacity to 'bend and sway' within a highly disciplined use of language. This dialectic is also able to inject into the Orcadian repertoire and lexicon a distinctive Orcadian poetics. The introspective world of poetry for Mackay Brown reacquaints Orcadian poetics with the contemplative spirit of Christianity. Poetry is just as valid, and Mackay Brown argues even more so, than the enquiry of science. Orkney poetics is a canvas always bigger than its dimensions and the individual personalities involved, but Mackay Brown holds a special place, which, so far, has not been overtaken or deconstructed.

Edwin Muir: The Other Place

A 'living mind' which Mackay Brown entered into and was embraced by was that of his mentor and friend, Edwin Muir. Muir sets the scene for the Orcadian movement towards an Orcadian 'orthodoxy', crystallising at its centre the many-splendoured facets and features that lie at the heart of understanding Orkney. This understanding is a shared consciousness of a metaphysical Orkney, the 'heart-bread' given expression by means of a 'swarm of symbols'. Muir's *Fable* is a perception of Orkney's natural configurations that lay claim to a higher reality and a metaphysical interpretation.[31] The beauty of the *Fable* was the means by which time, childhood and animals were understood through a biblical religious experience, acting as a prism for Muir and Mackay Brown with their reverent minds. These minds were deeply scarred by a stark Calvinism, which was not a good match for their sensibilities.

The Calvinist Orkney they grew up in was a world that from a Catholic point of view was one where

> a Calvinist is a Catholic obsessed with the Catholic idea of the sovereignty of God. But when he makes it that God wishes particular people to be damned, we may say with all restraint that he has become a rather morbid Catholic. In point of fact he is a diseased Catholic and the disease left to itself would be death or madness.[32]

Muir and Mackay Brown shared as children a terrible fear and guilt which manifested themselves in irrational behaviours. Muir's biblical experience of the Genesis Fall account, the 'forbidden fruit' episode, casts him into a pit of personal condemnation which he never recovered from. His deeply felt remorse sought a reconstructed personal and world order with its obsessively compulsive hand-washing ritual at one extreme to his exquisite perceptions of beauty on the other end of the spectrum. He did find a middle way through marriage that gave him a fruitful stability. Mackay Brown did not have the benefits of Muir's middle-way. The depressive forces of the 'worm' and the 'rag' formed the daily backdrop of a personal struggle, a vivid recollection of which is recorded in his autobiography: 'I will just say I yearned back towards my childhood, and dreaded what was to come. One symptom was that whenever my mother left the house to go shopping, I was convinced every time that she would never come home again. I would shadow her along the street, and dodge into doorways if she chanced to look back. I can't remember how long this state of affairs went on, but it's certain that part of my mind was unhinged.'[33] The fear, dread and guilt can be blamed on many factors both in nature and nurture, but the psychological influences of Calvinism with its theological determinism based on a literal and fundamentalist reading of Scripture were never going to silence a Muir or a Mackay Brown. Their artistic temperaments with their metaphysical aspirations found openings into 'the other place' in the natural configurations of Orkney and the poignant awakening of this 'place' interspersed with pre-Reformation architecture. For Muir, St Magnus Kirk on Egilsay and for Mackay Brown St Magnus Cathedral in Kirkwall pointed the way to the realisation that earlier civilisations could generate other interpretations of society in this life that gesture towards 'the other place'.

It has been suggested that Muir's stature as a writer was compromised by a 'technique of condensing thought into symbol' that 'has not yet been properly understood'.[34] In fact Muir lays the methodological groundwork for an Orkney poetics with the process that catalogues, sorts, classifies, distributes and harmonises, as symbols convey to others an intense consciousness of the reality of the spiritual world. This consciousness for Muir found its rationale through Jungian analysis, whereas for Mackay Brown Catholicism takes hold of his sensibilities and interpretative powers. Muir's journey was towards an unknown destination. This generalised journey became a specific path for Mackay Brown with clear literary and spiritual directions. The process is a diligent patient working out of the many materials where faint shadows and tracings emerge in a shared Orcadian consciousness. This Orcadian context gives a pre-eminent form and ballast, a realism that finds a gentle and joyous resonance in a growing readership that can find consolation and direction in a growing Orcadian 'orthodoxy' wherein universal categories also take hold. There is a clear metaphysical marker between Muir and Mackay Brown and other Orcadian writers who pursue a more inferential literary experimentation on the fringes of their times.

Simon Hall in *The History of Orkney Literature* (2010) gives special emphasis to Muir's childhood experience of Wyre as 'one of the richest descriptions of Orkney anywhere in literature', and he is right to do so.[35] The Wyre chapter has a seminal status. It is foundational of an Orkney poetics. Hall's appreciation of the realism inherent in Muir's texts, especially the Wyre chapter, configure Orkney with the farm and its seasons and rituals as crucial to an encoding that unleashes the 'swarm of symbols'. But is Hall right to champion Muir's assertion that 'the farm at the centre of the universe is a distinctly Orcadian understanding'?[36] This is a very challenging question for our times. Mackay Brown drinks at this 'fountain' with its configurations of barn and byre, seasons and their rituals that command high status in the Orcadian 'living minds'. Muir writes: 'A child has to believe things before he can prove them, often before he can understand them; it is his way of learning about the world, and the only way.'[37] This is such a Newman idea, that now holds a central place in the Catholic interpretation of how we come to faith.

Muir refines his Orcadian sensibilities with a retrospective articulation of childhood according to his particular literary investigations and Jungian analysis. Mackay Brown, however, not only brings his Catholicism to bear to further develop these themes but equally inserts into Orkney literature and lexicon the configurations of the sea, with Stromness holding a pre-eminence, that equally is taken hold of by notions of the universal. An Orkney poetics is to emerge which can hold the forces of nature to account in a metaphysical paradigm. To do justice to God also means being true to nature. Muir's Wyre texts, saturated with childhood memories, open out insights that are biblical and prophetic, and confrontationally so. Mackay Brown's Stromness texts, similarly saturated with like memories, follow the same Muir model but diverge to integrate the curiosities that arise in the day-to-day doings of the sea village, the 'haven in the bay', Hamnavoe.

Orcadian 'living' minds seek in its antiquities rich, spiritual sources and their interpretations are matured by historical forces at play. They do not work in isolation, spurred on by private inferences. Muir and Mackay Brown recognise the reality of divided sensibilities so marked by history as shaping the language they use. Mackay Brown, unlike Muir, does not confront his readers with prophetical statement. His power lies in harnessing the swarm of symbols in tapestry form, seamlessly working the Muir threads. An authentic Orcadian realism that they share emerges to form a creative orthodoxy.

Certain recurring motifs unite the two writers in Orkney matters. The description of new-born lambs makes for an interesting comparison. Muir writes:

> Everything looked soft and new—the sky, the sea, the grass, the two lambs, which seemed to have been cast up on the turf; their eyes still had a bruised look, and their hooves were freshly lacquered. They paid no attention to me when I went up to pat them, but kept turning their heads with sudden gentle movements which belonged to some other place.[38]

This observation, which is memory real and fresh, matches experience, as I know from a rural New Zealand background and familiarity with sheep, until one gets to the phrase 'which belonged to some other place'. The natural and seamless movement from the material reality to metaphysical presence is powerfully effected. Here is the 'technique of condensing thought into symbol' that 'has not yet been properly understood'.[39] The Jungian symbol is at play here for Muir, but Mackay

Brown does not walk this path. His Orcadian 'living mind' links with a more patristic approach set out by the Church Fathers so prized and understood by Newman. An Orcadian 'living mind' is absorbed by an 'ecclesial living mind'. The contemplative imperative and attitude is able to weave together the many-layered experience of Orkney both in its natural configurations and in its history.

Mackay Brown writes about lambs: 'Two of my lambs had been born dead that morning. They lay, red bits of rag, under the wall. I would bury them afterwards.'[40] The context is a short story in which Muir's suggestive Christian meaning is heralded in 'some other place', whereas Mackay Brown is not so much observational as symbolic, and explicitly so, in order to capture the Good Friday metaphor of the Crucifixion and its embedded doctrine of atonement. The 'red bits of rag' are the Lamb of God, Christ, born to die, be buried and to rise again. I would suggest the Mackay Brown text cannot be read without the Muir text. To me they are inseparable. Muir's formative Wyre experiences give profound insight into a wonderful innocence that we are all designed to share in. Mackay Brown also is able to 'stand in the shoes' of this experience. Yet for both writers their metaphysical insights are spurred on by the thorns of personal suffering. Is Mackay Brown himself the 'rag' with the autobiographical voice of Mazarin in the unpublished 'Commonplace Book'? 'He felt that he was three parts dead already—a rather disgusting rag blown about on the window of life.'[41] In addition to the Muir text quoted above later on in the Wyre chapter he writes, 'with my first sight of the two lambs that foreign, dirty-red, rag-like stuff is associated like a stain.'[42]

Orkney 'living minds' converge on 'the old wals of Churches and Monasteries, the defaced ruines of altars, images, and crosses [that] do cry with a loud voice, that the Romain Catholique faith of Jesus Christ did tread this way'. This snippet of local gossip in 1654 holds good for Orkney as it does for its place of origin in England.[43] Mackay Brown writes, 'Was this Magnus a Catholic or not? In Western Europe in the twelfth century there were only Catholics. And the Cathedral in Kirkwall had been built by Catholic masons, for the offering of the Catholic Mass. It seemed to me a thing of utmost simplicity and wonderment.'[44] Muir is the forerunner of such a perception or psychological shock when he writes of St Magnus's Kirk on Egilsay: 'It was the most beautiful thing in sight, and it rose against the sky until it seemed to become a sign in the fable of our lives'.[45] The embeddedness of the *Fable* in Orkney literature is foundational, thanks to Muir's explicit articulation of a metaphysical interpretation of Orkney. Mackay Brown himself says of Muir:

> Muir adventures deep and far into the racial memory, and the treasures of image and symbols he brings back are steeped in the purity and light and tranquillity of the beginning. My poems have a much narrower range in time—a thousand years maybe—and they celebrate as best they can 'whatever is begotten, born, or dies', generation by generation, until they stop with memories of my father and his letters and tailor's shears.[46]

Robert Rendall: The Secret Door

Robert Rendall is another Orkney writer who participates in the 'living mind'. He also gestures towards a metaphysical interpretation and understanding of Orkney that is also enduringly perceptive of 'the other place'. The symbolism of Muir's *Fable* with the 'the byre, the barn, and the midden' being 'at the heart of human civilisation'[47] upon which Mackay Brown too would find and feast on 'the swarm of symbols' is also common to Rendall. The Orcadian sensibilities immersed in Orkney's natural configurations also reach out for traditional and classical literary interpretation. The metaphysical sources common to these sensibilities lend an individuality and a rich creativity to each writer. A commonality is sought in order to find a way of expressing the inexpressible, the beauty privy to each in his enlightenment. The Orkney sensorium reveals the form that is the glory of creation. Muir, Mackay Brown and Rendall each holds a passion for the beauty that has become an Orkney theophany, a 'burning bush' of biblical proportions. In each writer the commonality is also experienced in a growing readership who can through the writers' 'reverent minds' find the joy of their intense consciousness of the reality of the spiritual world.

In *An Orkney Tapestry* Mackay Brown writes: 'Birsay was a sacred place for him [Rendall], not in any solemn sense; but these shores and hills were the source of his purest intuitions; they carried him back to his own childhood to the childhood of the world'.[48] Rendall 'tiptoes' in the 'cosmic dance' of his 'purest intuitions' in 'the childhood of the world'. In Orkney poetical subjective interiors emerge to convey to a readership through 'the swarm of symbols' the perception of 'the other place'.

> But I have seen, like treasure long concealed,
> A sudden radiance break from evening skies,
> And everything on sea and shore and field
> In flawless essence move, without disguise;
> And watched with awe, beside the old sea wall,
> In the hushed silence of a summer night,
> O'er land and sea an innocent beauty fall.[49]

Rendall embraces enlightenment and is well able to articulate it. Yet this embrace also from contemplative attitude and a lectio divina of Orkney emerges with a certain mysticism. The literal approach in biblical matters for Rendall restricts his immersion yet he has to dig and delve to a limited extent in the literary technique and lexicon that others have used before him in order to give voice to this 'seeing'. Orkney's 'secret door'[50] has to be opened in order to see 'the other place' where 'the glory of the Lord' resides. To open that door requires talent and a discipline that first and foremost is spiritual. For Rendall, 'The ocean to itself repeats/ The password given long ago,/ And wave to wave as it retreats,/ Whispers what I can never know'.[51] Rendall's 'heartbread' is a creationist one and the 'password' for him is 'The infinite pattern keeps of logarithmic form/ In wave and shell and storm'.[52] For Mackay Brown this literal view is narrow and one-dimensional.

Paradoxically Rendall is flying in the face of his convictions with his deep appreciation of the Church Fathers. His poems 'Gregory of Nazianzus Bids Farewell to His Bishopric' and 'St Athanasius' (Newman's great hero) shows the intellectual and spiritual depths he has trodden and are woven into his 'Orkney living mind' with its quest for 'solitude, my country life,/ My quiet meditation, and my God'.[53] Equally Rendall understands how to stand alone in religious matters and clearly sees in Athanasius and his stand against the heresy of the Arians[54] one who marks out that biblical road and affirms an orthodox understanding of the Trinity.

Athanasius for Newman heralded a turning point in his embrace of Catholicism in his stand against the consequences of the Reformation principle of 'private inferences'. Mackay Brown too would see Catholicism as his path, wherein the glory of the Lord is a shared consciousness that must embrace a sacramental discipline and a reading of Scripture which although literal also follows other principles of interpretation that do not contradict the literal. Exegesis is a critical factor that would separate Mackay Brown, who knew that his commonality with Rendall only went so far; 'he [Rendall] knew that in these matters we were very far apart; and so a delicate silence was observed'.[55] Rendall for his part wrote to Mackay Brown in 1948:

> You will appreciate all the more when I say that I do not share your leanings to a Catholic approach to religious experience, though I do have a great admiration for certain of the early Fathers, and also have genuine personal friendships with individual Catholics.[56]

As sympathetic as Rendall was to Mackay Brown, he mistrusted him:

> You have a mind that takes imaginative flights … but I have found that to take such flights in fantasies out of one's own mind often results in indeterminate wanderings. I have proved this too often in my own experience. It is a paradox that if we could soar to the clouds we must … keep one foot firmly on the earth. Or is this a bad heresy?[57]

But they were 'yamils [contemporaries], this memorial stane',[58] fishers of symbols. Their 'Orkney living minds' feasted together on the 'tullimentan [glittering] stars'[59] of the Orkney 'fable', a many-splendoured thing. From dialect to English linguistics a pre-theology is set in place to advance the articulation of Muir's 'other place' in which they all share an important enduring affinity.

Ernest Marwick: The Granary

The inclination to catalogue, sort, classify, distribute and harmonise the Orkney reading of sources receives a powerful catalyst from Ernest Marwick. He situated himself as a scholar, compiler, commentator and note-taker in order to bring together what Mackay Brown calls the 'granary'.[60] Mackay Brown writes, 'I am thankful I saw those everlasting things with a child's eye, and the vivid people who lived among them, and their ancient benign rituals and celebration of such things.'[61] From Marwick's 'granary' the everlasting things were ripe for Mackay

Brown's selective imaginative powers, upon which he could perfect his technique, driven to articulate as closely as humanly possible 'the swarm of symbols'. This quest led to the embrace of a religious language, a pre-theological engagement that, although never presented as a dogmatic set of Catholic doctrines by Mackay Brown, emerges in the form of presuppositions and foundations with a clear understanding that the antiquity of Catholicism is an impetus which like sun and water quenches the thirst and refreshes us. This quest is a step too far for Marwick and indeed Rendall, but there is a mutual agreement and recognition of the pre-eminence of the Orkney 'reading' of its sources; 'The stuff of poetry is lying thick all around'.[62]

Marwick, more than mentor, along with his wife Jeanette not only acted as the 'granary' but also as ballast and foil, finely honing Mackay Brown's consciousness of his Orkney audience and acting as perhaps uncertain receptacles of his religious aspirations. Letters to the Marwicks document such assertions:[63]

> 24 October 1946. GMB to EWM ... I am also enclosing some of my own work ... Strange how sickness and the death-wish make such potent symbols in modern literature ... whether you approve of this form of literary expression ... I get great depression from the certain thought that if I printed it for the delight of Orkney people it is primarily meant for, it wouldn't mean nearly as much as a flowery article ... God help us all! ... I hope to see you in Kirkwall ... It's always a keen pleasure to sit over your most hospitable hearth ...

> Saturday, 15 February 1947. EWM to GMB ... I should like you to substitute 'Christ' for 'Our Lord', as it is very possible that the audience will not be a devout one, and might regard the latter as a piece of insupportable presumption. I will risk letting them think that the whole thing is a religious tract ...

> 26 April 1947. GMB to EWM ... Have you ever read John Henry Newman's 'Apologia pro Vita Sua'? I have just finished it and, as always, it has shaken me to the core. There is a magnificent devastating logic in it. Tell Mrs Marwick that she might see me a priest some day yet ...

> 11 May 1947. GMB to EWM ... I am reading 'The Acts of the Apostles'. Saint Paul rather gets up my back, though he was a brave little soul.

Sunday, 25 February 1954. GMB to EWM ... Dear Ernest ... but here is a difficulty. You know that poem (in the Orcadian impromptus) called 'Saint' about the orra-man who was 'saved;'? Well, RR [Robert Rendall] shies away from it like a frightened horse. More than once he earnestly entreated me to modify it, or better omit it altogether: neither of which things I am prepared to do ... originally it read like this: When Peter, orraman at Quoys Joined the Pentecostals They dipped him in the sea ... RR objects to the second line. On reflection I do too, but for quite a different reason, and I changed it to this: Was 'saved' by hell-fire evangelists. Up came RR, from the Herald office waving a proof sheet in the air, and saying it would never do; if anything, it was worse than before. I suppose the whole thing is trivial and amusing. I don't want to hurt Robert's feelings, but someone must make a stand somewhere, and I don't feel disposed to weaken the structure of my poem merely to save the feelings of a group of life-denying schismatics. What will I do? I should welcome your views on this matter ...

23 October 1956. GMB to EWM ... old Scottish extremism in operation—forget about sweetness and light, work till you sprout grey hairs ...

8 August 1957. GMB to JM ... Jeanette my kindest regards ... I see there's another Disruption looming for the Presbyterians. Those wicked Anglicans are behind all the trouble. Behind everything the great Whale of Rome is wanting to swallow them all quick. That it should come soon!

15 November 1959. GMB to EWM ... the true victory is to sit alone and apart with the miracles of words, like Chaucer's adoration of the Virgin within the cloister blissful of thy sydis Took mannes shap the eternal love and pees ...

8 December 1960. GMB to EWM ... I saw Father Cairns for half an hour yesterday. He was passing through on his way to Glasgow ... Last week I did a short story with an Orkney setting for the fourth centenary of the Reformation, in which the whole sordid conspiracy is shown up in repellent detail. I hope to get an X certificate for it— maybe a trial at the Old Bailey.

13 January 1961. GMB to EWM ... postscript ... where would I find something about the Reformation in Orkney?

12 October 1962. GMB to EWM … do not look for monumental tomes on Hopkins … If he infects me with some of his sweet clear spirit, that is all I ask …

1 September 1965. GMB to EWM … You're right about the Celtic element too. I never saw any resemblance, not the faintest between Edwin's poetry and my own, tho' some reviewers of Loaves and Fishes purported to do so.

8 March 1966. GMB to EWM … It struck me that this year (or perhaps next, if 1117 is the true date) is the 850th anniversary of Saint Magnus. Would it be possible to do something about that?

12 March 1966. GMB to EWM … I've been trying to round off the play about Earl Rognvald's crusade and the other day (like yourself) I set out to write some things about my childhood. Lots of things came to the surface, things I had almost forgotten about—it is an intriguing exercise.

30 October 1966. GMB to EWM … Fr Bamber is away for about a month.

1 March 1967. GMB to EWM … I hear the Calendar of L [Love] got severely criticised in TLS [*Times Literary Supplement*]. When garlands come in from one side you must expect a cannonball from the other.

13 October 1967. GMB to EWM … I was just saying to Father Bamber … I hadn't seen you.

24 December 1973 … I am glad Orkney has of recent years attracted new Orcadians from other cities in the south. They have—most of them—come in search of light and a meaning. I think this peaceful invasion will go on, and is to be encouraged; regular transfusions of new blood have kept us a healthy and alert community.[64]

The 'granary store' bound Marwick to Mackay Brown but the selectivity of specific grains as source materials by Mackay Brown spurred him on to go as far as these sources could truthfully take him. The contemplative attitude feasting on the swarm of symbols was the fountain and well and chalice for Mackay Brown that enabled him to spread his spiritual and literary wings. Not this road for Marwick or Rendall. Their 'stations', equally important, fell short by comparison. Yet their commonality forged a strong enduring legacy.

Orkney Poetics

The authority of an 'Orkney poetics' is well-established, at least in Orkney. It has a metaphysical basis, and Mackay Brown sets out its credentials for this in *An Orkney Tapestry*. These credentials are a configuration that weaves together a heraldry driven by mystery and secrets that come from an Orkney 'lore'. One must be very still to enter upon its silence. Images rise up in an illumination from the pageant of history. An Orkney grace and courtesy finds its voice in religion. There are other voices but they are subsumed into a Christian, and for Mackay Brown, Catholic Christian, interpretation severely breached by the Reformation. The articulation of this distinctive interpretation takes language into the metaphysical world of religious language and pre-theologics where Mackay Brown works to weave back together the 'particularity' of disconnected and discordant sources .

Muir laid down the crucible by which Orkney finds its unique identity. The universality of his literary achievements rests on an enlightenment that is biblical and Christian. Specifically Muir's crucible consists of *The Story and the Fable* with its overarching themes of time, childhood, Bible, animals, the Fall and beauty, and of course one cannot omit the Calvinism against which Muir reacts and gives a liberating licence to others, especially Mackay Brown, to react against. Muir's 'fable' resonates with Neoplatonism and gives Orkney its rightful place with its metaphysical interpretation, as did Plato's myth of the cave and his theory of forms, that the appearances in this world of shadows conceal a higher reality. The phenomena of a many-layered Orkney are appearances of a higher reality. Muir has marked out 'the other place' which Marwick, Rendall and Mackay Brown would make their own workspace. The Muir 'fable' underpins an Orkney poetics they each surrender to in a loving literary embrace.

Mackay Brown takes up the Muir 'fable' and injects into it 'figures in an eternal landscape' from the Hamnavoe seascapes. The Hamnavoe microcosm is elevated to universality by his interiority that through personal suffering is purified through a depressive consciousness of 'the red rag'[65] that could go out of the self and in the Orkney 'fable' find truth and beauty. It was enough. For Mackay Brown, Muir was a 'wise gentle benign presence who has looked into the life of things.'[66] There is a level of trust here that is empowering and from which emerges a Mackay Brown who writes:

> The mind and the imagination must be stretched, frequently; must welcome difficulties and dare seeming impossibilities. Once they are tackled and overcome, new exciting vistas open up[67] ... It is possible for an artist or writer, preparing for the day's work, to go into a quiet trance, that need not last beyond five or seven minutes. A word, or a phrase, or an image, or even a rhythm, enters the silence. Other words and images gather about it, a rhythm begins to pulse through the ordered cluster of images—it is the beginning of a new story or poem. It doesn't always work, of course, but it has worked for me, often enough: then the complete consort dances together.'[68]

Rendall too, holds the 'contemplative attitude'. With scientific method and powers of observation his writings show a thoughtful mind grappling with the power of childhood memories and the perceptions of a life lived at the shore:

> Landscapes familiar in childhood ... some link between these subconscious impressions and our emotional mood at the time retains its power in the mind ... The long familiar curve of the far horizon seen from the Birsay cliff-top, the green links of the north banks of Westray, stitched with yellow trefoil, a solitary man hoeing turnips in a field, a black reef of rocks sticking up out of the sea, a mere patch of seapinks—nothing is too ordinary to evoke these instinctive motions of the mind.
>
> I missed a task which had become part of my life, and though marine creatures still fascinated me I slackened off serious study and returned to the contemplative relaxed attitude I had beside the shore in early life ... without losing interest in natural science I came to make it part of a wider enrichment. Over those who haunt our island shores there often comes an indefinable sense of well-being that lifts them up on a crest of inward happiness.
>
> Such magic moments kindle delight in the mind, and in some inexplicable way become significant. Fugitive as they are they awaken sudden recognition. But of what invisible world? That we cannot tell. Yet we feel them to be intuitions of ultimate truth. To capture such a moment in verse is like netting a butterfly.[69]

As Wyre was for Muir, Birsay was for Rendall and Hamnavoe and Hoy for Mackay Brown, these memories are etched into their subjective interiors and configure a stable Orkney poetics. Their subjectivity finds voice in their writings and for the audience, whether Orcadian or not, the objectivity of the land and sea and sky scapes complemented by settlements across the ages and their various civilisations raises the question—is it the objective reality of a natural Orkney or is it the subjective perceptions that endow its naturalness as a natural 'beauty', which is pre-theological? The answer for Muir, Rendall and Mackay Brown is a religious and Christian faith-filled one. God is Creator and worthy of praise. The aesthetic pleasingness of Orkney is pre-theological and Orkney poetics gives a natural freshness and simplicity that wells up and is well suited to the Christian interpretation.

For Muir the 'swarm of symbols' set in motion found a certain serenity in Jungian psycho-dynamics. For Rendall the fundamental simplicity of his Christian Brethren faith took precedence with its literal creationist stance over classical education and powers of contemplation. No 'swarm of symbols' for Rendall. It was enough to embrace a way of life:

> plain-living people, who without giving heed to the why and how of it live lives of ordered simplicity in surroundings of natural beauty, content with their daily lot. Not all, but some. For of this I become more and more certain that here are more folks that some may think who, not consciously 'poetical' or 'artistic', nevertheless have that sensitivity and imaginative vision which make the world such a treasure-house to live in ... they for the most part live and work within sight of the shore. They are familiar with tides and seasons. They work out-of-doors under an open sky—plough, do fencing, feed hens, repair outhouses, walk among their fields, attend the cattle. Work is the salt of country living: without it everything becomes insipid.[70]

The 'swarm of symbols' was everything to Mackay Brown and his mastery of it was never going to find its articulation in a Protestant world view with its utilitarian understanding of language. The pre-Reformation heritage in Orkney and beyond gave him ground and purpose, and spiritual and intellectual depths that matched his own interiority and within which he sought an understanding of his nature and nurture. As he wrote to Ernest Marwick in a long, unpublished letter-poem, that is both a rage against the 'storm' and an embrace of it as his destiny, on 19 January 1954 from Eastbank Sanatorium:[71]

Ernest, today our sky is lowering.
The storm fiends are up and roaring
From Birsay's Brough to the Moul Head
Yelling like to rouse the dead.
Saint Magnus is a ghostly kirk
And Hoy lost in the flying mirk.
Our horse seeks the lee-dyke for shelter.
The rooks ranging helter-skelter
About the sky, and like a flail
Comes hissing down the cruel hail.

Well, I rejoice in such a day.
Lusty winter at his play
Can lure my heart, hunched mean and tight
To tread a measure of delight.
Say what they like, Lear loved his storm,
And rather than be mild and warm
Beside the castle fire, his spirit
Wild realms of grandeur did inherit
That might upon the heath, and he
Raging fulfilled his destiny.

We are a fallen people, our heart
Has shuffled off the hero's part.
On security's queasy lap
We take our slops of sugar-and-pap.
What Welfare State did the Rhymer know?
On roads of legend his feet did go,
And where by market cross and hearth
He moved the folk to tears and mirth,
Drank his ale and ate his crust;
Then lay beneath the singing dust
When his long minstrel day was done
And might had swallowed up his sun.

Lord, send a tempest on us all
Wall batter down the plaster wall,
That stands between us and thy glory
And thunder out thy ancient story.
Put claw and tooth back into life.
Lord, in thy good time send us strife.

Pre-theologics

What has become of poetry now,
Child of the tavern and the plough?
In a London office Eliot sits,
Prince of intellectual wits,
Writing his few lines every year
Between a wry grin and a tear,
Wearing his bowler and his spats,
Sampling cheese and petting cats.
And after him a whole host swarms
Of purblind ineffectual worms,
Weaving not from hearts but tails
A labyrinth of silvery trails.

Dylan is dead, who might have grown
Worthy Thomas the 'Rhymer's' throne.
Boldly he rode and richly earned
His poet's cloak that sang and burned.
Among Welsh chapels and Welsh corn,
He blessed the great earth's teeming horn.
O singing wine and singing bread,
Dylan, your Celtic priest, is dead!
Stale stands the bread, sour the wine
Since Dylan died at thirty-nine,
Ending his song where it began
In praise of God and love of men.

I see now, in this dance of verse,
Our dear islands bear a curse,
And bore it from John Knox's days –
Lack of tongues to leap with praise.
What's the use of laden barn,
What's the good of teeming horn,
If our mouths are touched with lust
And our harps are red with rust?
The poor air of the Hebrides
Vibrates with strings of praise;
There the weaver at his loom
Questions love and life and doom.
And the fisher at his nets
Most melodiously regrets
Vanished cod and vanished glory,

On every grass-blade tap a story,
The barren acres of that sea
Vivid with myth and poetry.

Orkney feeds from a different breast.
Here the enquiring minds blest
Teach your son geometry,
Bid him beware of poetry.
Ancestral myth and modern song
With dead and rotten things belong,
And Saint Magnus' healing bones
Lie mouldering now, as dull as stones;
Enchantment gone from knowe and well
Where every man's a Peter Bell.

Cold and prosperous your smiles,
O barren mathematic isles!
But I would have you dance and sing,
A ragged mild-eyed lonesome thing;
Drinking your ale, coupling in ditches,
Passing your days with rogues and bitches
Wayward as water, swift to flee
The bawd Respectability.

This is mere talk. You, Ernest, know
How poverty can make men grow
Hollow, mean, emasculate
And crop a land with bitter hate.
From a shallow furrow no songs come;
Break the plough, and the harp is dumb.
Robert Rendall's verse was born
On a Scapa hill-side green with corn
Though the mysterious seed was sown
By Orkneymen long dead and gone,
Enduring in the frozen earth
Till our spring-time gave it birth.
And Edwin, that old Father Time
I dream that every beat and rhyme
He hymns, was planted long ago
The ancestors no man can know,
In the bright morning of the world;
Till the long sun and sloping rain

Pre-theologics

Sweetly lured them out again.
Now our good reapers with his scythe
Gives them death to give us life.

Great-bellied plenty, mother of verse,
I lift from you my former curse
(Though bankers I will never greet
With lifted hat upon the street;
The usurious pillars of the state
I dower with several kinds of hate;
And greasy grocers cutting ham,
At you I hurl a fervent damn.)

Edwin and Robert weave their rhymes
Into the fabric of our times.
They too are pillars of the state,
By all men reckon[ed] good and great,
On them Caesar casts honours
And purple pageants when they are gonners.

Poets there are, not of that ilk
Who all their days clad, instead of silk
Go clad in rags, eat meagre bread
And fill a pauper's hole when dead.
Like scarecrows black against the west,
Every fluttering rag is blest
Fixed by fate in a bitter maze
They clap their hands and shout their praise
Knowing their songs, by hook and crook
(Though never printed in any book)
Will blow about the countryside
Wherever lover seeks a bride,
When the crossed foe goes out to fight,
And widows weep alone at night.
The makars, by whose arduous trade
The lilting languages were made,
Who against the journalists
Tilt for beauty in the lists,
And save her, when men call her whore,
Lovely and bright for evermore.

Before my mind knew her intent,
Out in the happy storm I went,

Knowing they were not for me,
The blueprints of prosperity;
I would never own a house,
A wall, a wainscot, or a mouse;
Never merit real or rank,
Or on the counter of a bank
Slap a pile of fivers down;
Or be made provost of the town.

Not for me. For me the gale
That keeps my spirit blithe and hale.
About my ribs the flailing rain
Scourges with salutary pain.
On this blind road I take and bless
The night's star-piercing bitterness.

The Tavern of the Risen Sun
Will fold me, when my journey's done.
Where long-dead poets drank their all
I'll make my pipe and spin my tale.
Meantime the storm, I am content
It is my chosen element.'

Mackay Brown writes with passion and a suffering vehemence. His pure conviction is that the 'blueprints of prosperity are not for me'. Nothing bourgeois about this 'makar'. Mackay Brown did take this 'blind' path, his Catholic faith marking out his 'new springtime' just as the Oxford Movement had for Newman. But it was a rough ride that went against the private judgements and inferences of an Orkney so steeped in the suppressions of the Reformation. He kept his Orkney life intact. It was his joyous cell and monastery from which his *lectio divina*, his Orkney reading, emerged. In matters spiritual Mackay Brown was a 'pious laic', able to plough furrows in an earth that had become intractable to re-open ancient well-springs that others were, and will be, nurtured by in the years ahead. There is no doubt that Orkney was his truth and beauty to which he must be faithful. As he fought for his health both physically and mentally he found in Catholicism powerful testimony to his experience of the glory of the Lord, reading the sweetness of the old religion and Orkney as one and the same. He was only too aware of suppressive sectarianism but remaining true to 'the simple graces and courtesies of daily living'[72] he was free to explore his inner world and give it expression most fully in his writing. This is where he is most truly to be found. Catholicism was tolerated by his friends and family but not shared and understood. It just was not 'respectable'. Newman himself suffered the same social ignominy upon his conversion in England. But there was much Catholic nurture and formation as Mackay Brown struck out on his own and made the most of the local parish connections as far as his quest for privacy would allow. His correspondence and Catholic visitors were important to him and he valued their support and fraternity as far as his quest for privacy would allow. His great capacity for friendship took him far and wide but his preoccupation with a deep reality was an inner matter with literary outcomes. The 'mere talk' tinged with 'bitter hate' he confided to Ernest Marwick in 1954 was tempered over the years to become a marked serenity as he dared to give his 'dear islands' respite from the 'curse' 'from John Knox's days' and once again restore the right for 'tongues to leap with praise'.

Notes

¹   Mackay Brown, *An Orkney Tapestry*, p. 19.

²   *Lectio divina* is Latin for 'divine reading'. It is a traditional Benedictine (monastic) practice of scriptural reading, meditation and prayer intended to promote communion with God and to increase the knowledge of God's Word. It does not treat Scripture as texts to be studied, but as the Word. Traditionally *lectio divina* has four separate steps: *read, meditate, pray* and *contemplate*.

³   von Balthasar, *The Glory of the Lord II*, p. 15.

⁴   Mackay Brown, *An Orkney Tapestry*, pp. 1–2.

⁵   In the early twentieth century there was a rediscovery of the authentic thought of Thomas Aquinas which brought profound renewal and reform throughout academia and the Catholic Church itself. The current shape of Catholic theology, spirituality and ecclesial perspective is by and large a direct product of the *ressourcement* movement.

⁶   Fergus Kerr, *Twentieth-Century Catholic Theologians. From Neoscholasticism to Nuptial Mysticism.* Oxford: Blackwell Publishing, 2007, p. 119.

[7] von Balthasar, *The Glory of the Lord I*, p. 127.

[8] George Mackay Brown, *For the Islands I Sing. An Autobiography*. London: John Murray, 1997, p. 121.

[9] von Balthasar, *The Glory of the Lord II*, p. 15.

[10] *Ibid.*, p. 29.

[11] Kerr, *Twentieth-Century Catholic Theologians*, p. 132.

[12] *Ibid.*, p. 14.

[13] *Ibid.*, p. 19.

[14] Mackay Brown, *An Orkney Tapestry*, p. 19.

[15] von Balthasar, *The Glory of the Lord II*, p. 22.

[16] *Ibid.*

[17] Mackay Brown, *For the Islands I Sing*, pp. 80, 50.

[18] John Henry Newman, *Apologia pro Vita Sua*. London: Penguin, 1994, p. 119 (orig. London: Green, Longman, Roberts & Green, 1864).

[19] Mackay Brown, *For the Islands I Sing*, p. 50.

[20] *Ibid.*, p. 51.

[21] *Ibid.*

[22] *Ibid.*

[23] George Mackay Brown, letter to Ernest Marwick, 1947. Orkney Archive, Ernest Walker Marwick Collection, D31/30/4.

[24] George Mackay Brown, letter to the author, 15 March 1992. See Appendix.

[25] George Mackay Brown, letter to the author, 2 September 1983. See Appendix.

[26] Long-standing friend of George who drove him to Mass until 1985. See Appendix.

[27] See Appendix.

[28] George Mackay Brown, letter to author, 15 November 1991. See Appendix.

[29] In conversation with the author in 1995. Mackay Brown was always intensely interested in what was said at the group (which I attended) and the psychology of certain responses that were at variance with Church teaching.

[30] George Mackay Brown, letter to the author, 15 March 1992. See Appendix.

[31] Edwin Muir, *The Story and the Fable: An Autobiography*. London: Harrap, 1940.

[32] G. K. Chesterton, 'The Catholic Church and Conversion', in *The Wisdom of Catholicism*, compiled and annotated by Anton C. Pegis. London: Michael Joseph, 1950, p. 795. This Chesterton extract comes from a much-loved book by Mackay Brown. He presented a copy as a gift to a fellow parishioner in the 1960s.

[33] Mackay Brown, *For the Islands I Sing*, p. 46.

[34] Ritchie Robertson, 'Edwin Muir', in *The History of Scottish Literature*, ed. Craig Cairns, 4 vols, 1987–8. Aberdeen: Aberdeen University Press, vol. 4, p. 144.

[35] Simon W. Hall, *The History of Orkney Literature*. Edinburgh: John Donald, 2010, p. 69.

[36] *Ibid.*

[37] Edwin Muir, *An Autobiography*. London: Hogarth Press, 1954, p. 35.

[38] *Ibid.*, p. 31. Also cited in Hall *The History of Orkney Literature*, p. 71.

[39] Robertson, 'Edwin Muir', vol. 4, p. 144.

[40] George Mackay Brown, *A Time to Keep and Other Stories*. Edinburgh: Polygon, 2006, p. 41.

[41] George Mackay Brown, 'The Commonplace Book 1946–1948'. Unpublished and cited in Murray, *Interrogation of Silence*, p. 20.

[42] Muir, *An Autobiography*, p. 36.

[43] Eyston, *A cleer looking glass for all wandering sinners*, cited in Shell, 'Abbey Ruins', p. 23.

[44] Mackay Brown, *For the Islands I Sing*, pp. 52–3.

[45] Muir, *An Autobiography*, pp. 15–16.

[46] Mackay Brown, *For the Islands I Sing*, p. 165.

[47] *Ibid.*, p. 36.

[48] Mackay Brown, *An Orkney Tapestry*, p. 182.

[49] Robert Rendall, 'The Masque', in *Collected Poems*. Edinburgh: Steve Savage, 2012, p. 149.

[50] Robert Rendall, 'The Riddle', in *Collected Poems*, p. 226.

[51] *Ibid.*

[52] Robert Rendall, 'Fossils and Fish', in *Collected Poems*, p. 125.

[53] Robert Rendall, 'St Gregory of Nazianzus Bids Farewell to His Bishopric', in *Collected Poems*, p. 53.

[54] Arianism is defined as those teachings attributed to Arius, which are in opposition to orthodox teachings on the nature of the Trinity and the nature of Christ.

[55] Mackay Brown, *An Orkney Tapestry*, p. 186.

[56] Robert Rendall, letter to George Mackay Brown, 8 April 1948. National Library of Scotland, George Mackay Brown Manuscripts, Acc. 4864/15–30.

[57] *Ibid.*

[58] Robert Rendall, 'The Fisherman', in *Collected Poems*, p. 68.

[59] Robert Rendall, 'Celestial Kinsmen', in *Collected Poems*, p. 89.

[60] Mackay Brown, *For the Islands I Sing*, p. 77.

[61] George Mackay Brown, 'Enchantment of the Islands. A Poet's Sources', in *Flightpath*, a Loganair magazine, 1993. Edinburgh University Library, Special Collections, George Mackay Brown MS 3118.16.

[62] George Mackay Brown, 'Rooted in One Dear Familiar Place', in 'Letters' section, Royal Society of Literature quarterly, 15 September 1994. Held in Edinburgh University Library, Special Collections, George Mackay Brown MS 3118.16.

[63] Letters from George Mackay Brown to Ernest Walker Marwick, 1946–. Orkney Archive, Ernest Walker Marwick Collection, D31/30/4.

[64] Handwritten note by George Mackay Brown: a preparatory comment for a recording with Marwick for a programme, *Good Morning Scotland* (1 January 1974).

[65] Mackay Brown, 'The Commonplace Book 1946–1948', cited in Murray, *Interrogation of Silence*, p. 20.

[66] George Mackay Brown, 'Thoughts of an Old Age Pensioner', August 1986. Orkney Archive, Ernest Walker Marwick Collection, D124/2/2/5, p. 9.

[67] *Ibid.*, p. 12.

[68] *Ibid.*, p. 17.

[69] Robert Rendall, 'An Orkney Shore', in Neil Dickson, *An Island Shore. The Life and Work of Robert Rendall*. Kirkwall: Orkney Press, 1990, pp. 172–4.

[70] *Ibid.*

[71] Letter-poem from George Mackay Brown to Ernest Marwick, 19 January 1954. Orkney Archive, Ernest Walker Marwick Collection, D31/30/4.

[72] Mackay Brown, *An Orkney Tapestry*, p. 19.

Orkney is the Glory of the Lord

Only that which has form can snatch one up into a state of rapture. Only through form can the lightning-bolt of eternal beauty flash. There is a moment in which the bursting light of spirit as it makes its appearance completely drenches external form in its rays. From the manner and the measure in which this happens we know whether we are in the presence of 'sensual' or of 'spiritual' beauty, in the graceful charm of interior grandeur. But without form, in any event, a person will not be captivated and transported. To be transported, moreover, belongs to the very origin of Christianity.[1]

Mackay Brown's stability and muse was Orkney. This was his exterior and interior world, from which his *lectio divina*, his Orkney reading, emerged. His personal existential struggles as 'worm', 'rag' and 'scarecrow' only served to act as spurs and thorns to a literary resilience that is marked by a religious enlightenment. The poem 'Summer Day' from 1947 is testimony to a powerful religious experience which is rooted in Christianity. This poem (the first draft of what became later the tribute to his father, 'Hamnavoe') is a classic mystical insight into 'the other place' (Edwin Muir first used this phrase, and it was also alluded to by Robert Rendall) and it has many features which concur with a biblical and ecclesial theophany. Mackay Brown is able to find his place in the 'scheme of things'. His microcosm is specifically a Stromness against the backdrop of Hoy. Orkney expands these first horizons into the powerful realism that is the natural world which is a thread of God's creation. The seamless transition from the natural to the supernatural which is a special feature of a distinctive Orkney poetics is worked by Mackay Brown to great effect. He experienced at first hand the eternalising of time within which he found a great freedom in his use of set forms.

Ernest Marwick understood this and wrote in 1965:

Although he has succeeded at last in giving his work a universal significance, it was Orkney, and especially his native town of Stromness, which formed his mind and attitudes (although the priceless gift of imagination may be in part a legacy of his Highland mother). He was born into a close, ending in a pier where fishermen congregated. He listened to earthy tales, and often to bold, magnificent myths, in Peter Esson's tailor shop. He scrambled up the hill through stepped or cobbled lanes and looked on the beauty of the harbor and the hills of Hoy. He discovered in the quiet countryside behind the town the wonder of grass and green corn almost as if it was a sacrament. All this has gone into his verse and stories, together with an innocent bacchanalian exuberance, and has become entwined with an almost mystical interpretation of Orkney's past which sometimes confuses the hard-headed Orkneymen of today.[2]

Later in this same collection Marwick writes that Mackay Brown had an 'instinctive recognition to the faith of the Catholic Church'.[3] Marwick's mentoring allowed Mackay Brown to be who he was, but as much as Mackay Brown shared his enthusiasms with Ernest and Jeanette and they supported him as far as they could, ultimately, and rightly so, Mackay Brown had to go on alone with his keen sense of conscience and duty. Mackay Brown, poet and artist, engages with Primary Form (God): 'gladly I put my hand into the fire of images' to make accessible for others through secondary form—through words, concepts, images, patterns. But the secondary form must be able to make the Primary Form present as a source of the inner radiance that is original and can break forth anew from its centre into a specific historical context. To admire secondary form in its literary detail is not enough on its own to guarantee one's adherence to faith. Mackay Brown's mind is a reverent one that through the 'contemplative attitude' interprets on a daily basis a many-layered Orkney, spurred on by his own personal sufferings. It was due to this personal enlightenment that he never compromised or confused his writings with a bourgeois art divorced from the worship of Primal Beauty.

Mackay Brown had enough inner asceticism to give his sufferings and torments a discipline that did suit his nature and by which he could manage to come through the temptations (and there were many). It gave him the means by which he could immerse his nature seen here in 'Summer Day', wherein 'There is a moment in which the bursting light of spirit as it makes its appearance completely drenches external form in its rays'.[4]

Summer Day 1947

Anchorite of God, I raised eyes
One golden summer morning from my script
And saw beneath me
The small town's heart pulse

The sunlit hours away. Fishing boats
Raised anchor, offering red sails
To the west wind, drifting
In the tide-dark sound

Under the dark eagle-capped pillars of Hoy.
The coach with sweating horses
From Kirkwall drew up
At the white Custom House,

And towards noon the wealthier merchants
Strolled in blackcloth across the square
Consulting watches, talking
In deep grave tones.

The town lay all afternoon, tranced
With sapphire. Dogs sought the shadowed doors.
A child's bare feet
Fluttered across the cobbles.

At evening the dark sails returned. The harbour
Spun with life. Gaelic fisher girls
Made melancholy croon
Over stinking stalls,

And ragged boys ran home, with bunches
Of burnished herring. From the dance loft
Cups rattling, the screech
Of a cracked violin.

Hoy gloomed the Sound. One lyrical star
Prologued night's pageantry. The shawled harlot
Crossed the wet field to
The bailie's granite house.

Vanity of vanities! By taper light
I read now, thrilled in Time, men walk blind
The cloud-dappled alleys of God's eternal city.

Tranced

This early poem is given prominence here in order to witness to the authenticity of Mackay Brown's religious experiences, the fruits of which were an array of religious language inserted into a specific Orkney poetics and lexicon. His mastery of literary technique may be in its infancy here but the religious experience is one that stays the test of time in theme and lexicon, in its biblical and ecclesial stance. 'Tranced' is the crucible of the Orkney *lectio divina*. This is a recurring word in Mackay Brown's poetry. The 'contemplative attitude' is much in evidence in this poem.

Mackay Brown structured and wove his own version of textual allegory in order to bear witness to a profound ever-absorbing meditation and contemplation, centred as it was on the numinous sources of Orkney.[5] The numinous sources of patterns of settlement, land, sky and sea, architecture and the place of man, woman and child, took anchor within the vocation of the poet, who esteemed the role of the story-teller but as poets do, has a more essential message for the reader because of a transcendent voice-over. This voice-over of God in Mackay Brown is at its height, crystallised in the key religious experience that came early. Its textual form is realised in 'Summer Day'.

Here is found the sense of the holy that attracts or repels; Mackay Brown was attracted. Calvinism repelled him. The Catholic sensibility, with its easy integration of faith and reason, reassured him, as it had Newman. Calvinism detaches faith from reason and left Mackay Brown at the mercy of his emotions, unbalanced and unable to find an inner psychological security. This 'splitting' of faith and reason had come from the Reformation, where the *fides quae*, the religious facts about God, were separated from *fides qua*, the way these facts are lived; the cognitive is separated from the non-cognitive, the propositional is separated from the non-propositional, and this ultimately leads to the separation of faith and reason that are inseparable in Catholicism. It is in 'Summer Day' that a classic religious experience is revealed. It is classic because it fits the criteria set by a number of scholars and religious practitioners—from the medieval English mystics[6] who distilled their religious experience into writing to the more modern philosopher, William James.[7]

The mystic way was described as having three stages by St Bonaventure (1221–74), the teacher of St Thomas Aquinas. Firstly, there is a *purgative* stage where the mystic is prepared and purified by prayer and discipline or asceticism. Mackay Brown underwent levels of the purgative in his Orcadian beginnings in Stromness, that were marked by illness, pain and suffering. He was led to the Cross, where his endurance was able to find a personal loving confirmation from which came illumination. The second, *illuminative*, stage is where the mystic enjoys an experience which is emotionally and spiritually illuminating. Finally, the *unitive* stage is where the mystic enjoys a sense of oneness with God. Aquinas continued the classification of Bonaventura. He defined mystic experience as not *about* God, but as experience *of* God.

It was in the medieval distillation of Christianity that Mackay Brown was schooled in the pre-Reformation world of sensation, its sensorium. Mackay Brown clearly found how to 'read' the numinous sources of Orkney. Land, sea and sky stimulated the perceptions of heavenly rhythms and patterns and the way of literature specifically reinforced the authenticity of these perceptions that took the word-smith in Mackay Brown to new levels of awe and wonder and complexity. Yet it is not necessary to contain Mackay Brown within the definitive mystic experiences of the medieval past. Even William James's classic pluralistic and psychological study describes mystic experience as being more similar to music than conceptual speech, with frequent use of paradoxes, for example, whispering silence, dazzling obscurity. Mystical states are like windows into a more inclusive world. James found four characteristics that converged in these mystic states. Firstly, there is an *ineffability* where words are unable to describe their contents, hence the poetical use of language where language is suffused with its primary source. Secondly there is a *noeticism* where states of knowledge, not just emotional experiences, bring new insights beyond what the intellect can grasp. Thirdly, there is a *transience* where these experiences cannot be sustained for long. Fourthly, there is a *passivity* where the subject is overwhelmed by the experience.

In my discussions with Mackay Brown in 1995–6 about the mystic nature of his work, he always firmly denied he was a mystic. He was not comfortable with being seen as such, always maintaining he was very earth-bound. He was deeply wary of raw emotional states. That is why Newman, who also was extremely wary of the evangelical emotional fervour of his day, was such a spiritual master for him. Newman's classic conversion account, the *Apologia pro Vita Sua*, remained a pillar for Mackay Brown, and gave him a way to manage his emotional instabilities and temptations through the various phases of his life. Faith and reason in unison brought the poet in Mackay Brown through ineffability to noeticism, transcience, passivity and much more.

Mackay Brown through original patterns of Catholicism creatively innovated a lifelong 'allegory-in-the-making' in order to accommodate the experience of God in his life. In a twentieth-century Orcadian adaptation of the medieval tradition of the literary anchorite,[8] he withdrew increasingly from secular society, for what appeared to the world as literary reasons, but in reality became religious reasons, so as to be able to lead an intensely literary, prayer-oriented and ascetical life, wherein he was able to craft his penetrating realisation of St Magnus, his literary high-point. This was no dry historical study or romantic fantasy of emotional adventurism. It was an anchoring in faith and reason that enabled his literary powers to develop, as well as his psychological dilemmas to be managed. Faith and reason took hold within, and, as far as circumstances allowed, he led a Eucharist-focused life. He imposed upon himself what amounted to a vow of stability of place, and ideologically he could be considered dead to the world. The anchoritic life is one of the earliest forms of Christian monastic living. Bede and Julian of Norwich in particular appealed to him immensely. My understanding of him is that this style of life was where he was able to be most truly himself. There were many threads to his stability of place in Stromness, where his love of set forms was literary and personal. The daily routines of writing, reading, listening to music, socialising with family and friends, correspondence and getting to Mass when circumstances permitted meant he could reach far and wide and deep from this foundation.

Mackay Brown's spirituality was always going to be larger than that of those around him, and over and above the set forms and routines of his day-to-day existence. He lived through a time of transition, the twentieth century, with its deconstructive tendencies towards nihilism. Textually, Mackay Brown found a way to allegorically explore the layers and facets of time by means of an ancient religious faith expressed anew, its vitality and vigour finding new ways of being lived and loved. Where other writers on Mackay Brown have pieced together the biographical and historical continuity of published texts, their insights are, to me, at an awkward tangent to the man-author. An emphasis needs to be given to his religious experience so evident in the 1947 'Summer Day'. It is in this key text that the Mackay Brown allegory is crystallised and his existence takes on an enduring resilience in the form of his clear choice of Christianity in its pre-Reformation perceptions and teachings. This is not to say that Mackay Brown took no account of Catholicism, post-Reformation or post-modern, but his 'holy ground' is to be found in the 1947 text and it is from this text that all other texts can be seen to derive and be fulfilled, given the spiritual energies that it contains.

In order to establish 'Summer Day' experimentally and experientially as a text within which a profound religious experience is found, it is examined in detail. Contextually, it is similar to texts found in the pre-Reformation genre of the medieval dream poem, for example William Langland's work *Piers Plowman*.[9] Mackay Brown was subject to many influences, ancient and modern, as he worked in a deep, shared reality, but the release he found in his early days of literary formation was in a medieval richness, a liberation in a pre-Reformation world that relished the naturalness of nature in all its sensual perceptions. Nature does not lie. His own sense of order and light, dark and dread was framed in a medieval cosmic portrayal not yet penetrated by the existential reconfiguration of the Reformation.

The allegory begins. Mackay Brown is already on the restless search that marks the poetic transition from the natural to the supernatural. Mackay Brown experiments with the medieval dream device, steeping it in his own formative religious experience. This is his 'way' of literature, where each of his literary works becomes a dream within the dream that is prophetically foundational in 'Summer Day'. The season of summer is explicitly in agreement, from which the mellow numinous enlightenment draws the narrator as 'anchorite' and 'hermit'. While Mackay

Brown would not himself journey on physical roads and paths he is the pilgrim nevertheless, who will journey by means of the text that exteriorises the world within. The interior life of the anchorite and mystic creates space for Mackay Brown to find self and God in the process of writing. A place to exercise the spiritual eye that 'sees … beneath … the small town's pulse'. The act of 'seeing' is with the inner eye that does not separate the social, moral and religious dimensions. They are the 'seamless garment' by which God is encountered and known.[10] The metaphor of 'beneath' separates Mackay Brown, 'the anchorite writer', from the town (Stromness). This separation is irrevocable; there is no going back. The religious experience has taken hold and saturated Mackay Brown's existence with the 'absolute' that is God. This separation is 'I am more than the small town's heart pulse'. I am from this and I am still here and understand it for what it is historically and socially but now I understand and know there is something more. Given that Mackay Brown has a sense of place that is Orkney and specifically, in the case of this poem, Stromness and Hoy, there is no doubt the 'beneath' also refers to visually looking down on the small town from the height of Brinkie's Brae, a place where Mackay Brown walked and mused often. In 1951 he writes, 'from the point of view of worship it was almost as good as having been in church'.[11]

The poet sketches out his place of 'rest', his 'tidedark Sound' splashed with the colour of 'red sails' and the human activity of 'fishing boats raising anchor'. They are 'offerings' to the command of nature with its 'west wind' to which the 'drifting' boats are subject. The literal meaning is a micro-cosmic beauty, a thumbnail sketch from which other meanings can be drawn. Mackay Brown is always more than the literal and he stretches forward to penetrate the layers of existence by means of what will become 'the Mackay Brown allegory', a sort of 'Picasso-blue-room'. The thumbnail sketch is in place with water never far away; 'they sounded so sweetly'. The senses of sight and sound, the presence of time attest to a higher reality, 'the other place'. Mackay Brown's 'drift' of mysticism releases author and reader into a private state to which degrees of assent are asked of the reader. There is also a saturation here of biblical resonance: the turmoil of Genesis rested in Galilee and Psalm 23 (He makes me lie down in green pastures; he leads me beside still waters; he restores my soul …).

'Under' continues Mackay Brown's spatial relationships with the 'beneath' of Stromness. The contrast of high and low, above and beneath expands the literal to take the poet and reader to the allegory-in-the-making. The mystic mountains of Hoy steep the text with the mystery that nature commands upon its subjects, who make up their 'offerings', hoping in some way to bring a measure of control as their lives contend, with what is perceived, to be an unseen world. This world is shafted with a strong sense of judgement. The 'eagle-capped pillars' that are Hoy peer down at the endless repetitions of human activity. The natural harmonies of the world-of-birds is other-faced with what may seem an unpredictable ferocity that could bear down on human life at any moment. It is not altogether a comfortable use of imagery. Being human projects in a contentious way against the inscrutable ways of a powerful God. This also is a resonance of Mackay Brown's invocation of the Nordic 'corridor'[12] that brought fate to Orkney. At the Reformation a Nordic fate would blend with a Calvinistic predestination that harked back to this more primitive dialogue with warrior gods, who 'ruled from abodes of ice and tempest … They uttered dark inscrutable decrees … the wisdom of Odin and Thor appeared as fate'.[13]

Meanwhile the Kirkwall commercial world penetrates the twenty miles or so to Stromness—with its 'coach with sweating horses' bringing kindred spirits to the 'custom house'. The 'wealthier merchants' draw up the tensions of a class struggle as they emanate economic and social power with 'blackcloth' and 'watches', and 'deep grave tones'. These surely must be the Calvinist burghers that for Mackay Brown contradict a simpler way of life. The lower classes are shown to be living closer to the world that God made and instructed. The overbearing foreboding is prophetic and apocalyptic. The 'blackcloth' is exterior clothing but also the blackness of the inner life. The theme of time marching on to the grave 'in deep grave tones' has the sense of a funeral procession.

Mackay Brown's religious experience saturates the text. He raises the religious temperature with the mystic blue 'sapphire trance'. The sea and sky merge into an 'inscape' that Mackay Brown recognises (and rejoices in) in the work of Gerard Manley Hopkins. This holy light engulfs Mackay Brown and the town with its comings and goings. The 'dogs sought shadowed doors' suggests the dark deeds that seek concealment.

They do not have the power to deny the 'child's bare feet fluttered across the cobbles'. Evil does not engulf innocence. It is the other way round. The holy light of redemption suffuses all. These words, 'child's bare feet fluttered across the cobble', have a natural infusion of grace that strikes its echoes into the reader, taking the sense to rare levels of meaning. The holiness of work is gathered up 'spun with life' in the 'harbour', the place of safety and sanctuary.

The Celtic 'corridor' is invoked with 'Gaelic fisher girls' and their 'melancholy croon'. Mackay Brown is weaving the allegorical threads of 'the old harp of the Gaelic'[14] of his ancestral line (through his mother) and the insights he has into the loss of 'laughter and poetry and Celtic legend' that came at the Reformation with 'a kind of racial mutilation'.[15] Mackay Brown writes: 'In my own writing, a strong Celtic element is discernible, a mingling of mysticism and intricate image'.[16] But patterns of migrant work and settlement kept the ancient Gaelic threads alive against the 'harsh saga-uttering harp of the Vikings'[17] and the 'bleak gloomy faith'[18] of Calvinism.

'Ragged boys ran home with bunches of burnished herring' does not deny the other 'dance' but readers are left to place themselves here—the dance of the rattling cups and screech of a cracked violin are feeble re-configurations of the class struggle. The happy poverty of food on the table, the sea harvest of polished, shiny resplendent herring (burnished) draws a 'line in the sand', with social commentary laying bare the reality of a time past in Stromness. It also serves to prophesy an unnatural separation in cultural development. Mackay Brown always brings the reader back to the natural, for nature, the wild beauty of Orkney, does not lie. The lie is the 'dance of the rattling teacups'. The 'melancholy croon' of the Gaelic fisher girls equally speaks to a special humility. The plight of the migrant worker contextualises the patterns of work with the poignant sadness drawn from the harshness of suffering and struggle at the bottom end of the economic scale.

Mackay Brown's 'tranced' lyric holds its sombre elements in 'the bursting light of spirit' which 'completely drenches external form in its rays'.[19] This enlightenment, personal to Mackay Brown, invites the reader towards a biblical resolution. His allegory-in-the-making always gently tends towards its cosmic proportions. Hoy is no longer 'eagle-capped', 'gloomed the sound'. And Hoy does have that configuration, its ice-age majesty proportionally oblique against its surrounds, standing for all time in a heraldic stillness. The 'one lyrical star' is enough to redeem the oblique 'gloom' as it prologues the pageant of the night. This pageant is selectively focused on 'the shawled harlot', who 'crossed the wet field to the Bailies' granite house'. Visually the reader is tantalised into the embrace of a fallen and still-falling humanity. But redemption is at hand in more than 'not-knowing'—it is an 'unknowing'—this is a 'blackcloth' deed, this seemingly incongruous sin seen on the night-dark streets and alleys of cobbled Stromness. The 'buying and selling' of the sexual act concealed from the light of day is known to God.'Vanity of vanities!' The biblical discourse of the Hebrew sage Ecclesiastes with its sceptical irony is more in the way of Mackay Brown's *via negativa*. His pre-theology is one that does not deny the reality of how people live and does not reside in simplistic statements of beliefs, ethics and retribution. The 'one lyrical star' has the power to redeem, as does 'the child's bare feet fluttering over the cobbles'. Like the Hebrew sage, he squares the meaning of human experience with the transitory nature and vanity of all things.

It is by 'taper light' that the anchorite (Mackay Brown) will now 'read' (and be read). 'Time' is understood as a many-layered thing for Mackay Brown:

> The Orkney imagination is haunted by time; it is Edwin Muir's great theme, and in thus matter he speaks for all of us ... what fed Edwin Muir's heart and mind with such archaic pellucid imagery? ...I think it is more the look of the islands that suggests heraldic stillness and a hoarded symbolism—quarterings on the hill, pasture and meadow and cornfield, a slow change through the year; and older still, the great shield of sky swarming with azure and gules, and clouds like fabulous beasts rampant.[20]

These will find experimental space in the proportions of allegory in future texts.'Thrilled' in 'Time' holds an exaltation, a state of knowing and understanding that stands as the 'Messianic Secret' while those 'beneath' and 'below' walk 'blind' in 'the cloud-dappled alleys of God's eternal city'. This exaltation is not a Zen experience of empty detachment but a committed Christian act of faith and reason. There is a great love here for Stromness. This act of love is the supreme ordering of Mackay Brown's exterior and interior life. The Mackay Brown soul is brought to know God in the eminently fruitful primal sources of the Stromness microcosm. The 'secrecy' of this religious experience that imbues the text with the mystery of God is Mackay Brown's 'burning bush' experience, his 'theophany'. It is marked by the Jamesonian characterics of ineffability (words are unable to describe their contents), noetic (they are states of knowledge not just emotional experiences and bring new insights beyond what the intellect can grasp), transient (these experiences cannot be sustained for a long time) and passive (the subject is overwhelmed by the experience).

The moral blindness has not come from a theology that denies the reality of how people live. It has not come from simplistic statements of beliefs, or an ethical system enforced from an 'eagle-capped' retribution. Mackay Brown's understanding, his 'knowing' about redemption, is more subtle. These insights are themed into the Mackay Brown allegory-in-the-making. He is not 'blind' any more. He sees and knows. He penetrates what lies beyond appearance, never forsaking the realism of appearances in their material sense. The peaceful and serene gaze of the Catholic-poet-philosopher takes root. It will never be uprooted even though what lies ahead is a constant test of allegiance. There is a truth here in this 'Summer Day' text that cannot be contained in words, only hinted at with the religious language that cannot (and is not intended to) force an explicitness: 'this is a religious experience'.

Seeing the Form: God

This text holds within it a 'peculiar dignity', 'a special power to open up depths'.[21] The experience upon which it is based witnesses to a 'state of rapture', 'the lightning-bolt of eternal beauty flash', a moment in which the bursting light of spirit as it makes its appearance completely 'drenches external form in its rays'.[22] Ernest Marwick himself in 1965 concedes the sacramental and mystical interpretation of Orkney's past. Does this hold for the present and future? Does the 'likeness' drawn here by Mackay Brown correspond to the original natural reality of Orcadian configurations of Stromness and its horizons? Is his vision a private one enclosed in a contemplative subjectivity that is personal to him and him alone? Or is his experience one of 'seeing the Form' of the glory of the Lord?

Von Balthasar argues that 'Only that which has form can snatch one up'. Mackay Brown would not have this experience and the consequent interpretation of it unless there was a reality to which it is attached. Is he the only one to have such an experience? Certainly Muir and Rendall gave their voices to an Orkney poetics which is similar. Furthermore, in August 1951 Mackay Brown in his evocative style captures 'From Brinkie's Brae'[23] a form: 'It was a rich and dramatic landscape as anyone can conceive'. Like Muir's Wyre text, Mackay Brown inserts into Orkney poetics and lexicon a spiritual beauty and an aesthetic measure: 'The form of the beautiful appeared to us to be so transcendent in itself that it glided with perfect continuity from the natural into supernatural world'.[24] Mackay Brown's cradle of Calvinism had no scope to work with an aesthetic measure. The Reformation mindset is one that does not accept the beautiful as a theological category. The Protestant one-dimensional view of the beautiful focuses on the question of the relationship between revelation and this worldly beauty. This is a good question but not a sufficient one. Mackay Brown finds liberation in the pre-Reformation sensorium to be allowed to immerse himself in a sunset with reefs of crimson and gold, the silver gleams of the distant lochs, the vacant wine-red moor, the sounds of the sea, the Kestrel's graph of flight; the sight, sound, touch, smell, in unison 'remind men of the vastness of eternity'.[25] Calvinism with it puritanical 'eagle-capped' eye marks such sensual experience as sinfulness. This was a lifelong struggle for Mackay Brown (and Muir) and I would suggest was a causal feature of his depression. He 'knows' he is in the presence of a spiritual beauty forged by the pre-Reformation sensorium. Its grandeur is an interior and external reality where there is no separation. 'We climbed into the silent town, all four of us, and thought that, from the point of view of worship, it was almost as good as having been in church'.[26]

This is the forecourt of theology, 'having been in church' where there is a greater beauty in the sacrament of the Eucharist. From an 'adequate theological culture and with a more powerful vision and deeper creative insight'[27] the layman Mackay Brown, poet, with his *lectio divina* of Orkney and its ' gale of life' gives way to an emergent heraldry, 'a swarm of symbols' seamlessly moving from the natural to the supernatural with a technique that argues for 'no separation'. Seeing the Form, God, is a pre-theological project that immerses Mackay Brown in the Trinity.

'Hamnavoe', which emerged as a revision of 'Summer Day', presents an acceptable and accessible encounter with God that existentially underpins the purposeful energies of Mackay Brown's writings. It can be used as an 'emblem' of the Mackay Brown interior space or psyche, the power house of his literature from beginning to end. Here is his sense of religion, of history, of society and of truth. Here is his sense of the century he lives and dies in and his sense of the future. It memorialises a time and a place and the man. The tranced light, the portentous darkness, are suffused in all tenderness here in this 'narrow' little unpublished poem, contained and enclosed. But it is not claustrophobic, it is an interior to which we too can belong. There is intimacy and infinity which the reader can assent to and belong to because it rings true. It is a touchstone that Mackay Brown textually sets on paper about being in Stromness, being in Orkney, being in the world. The hiddenness, the insignificance, the vulnerability, the smallness, the awkwardness, the sanctity, later to undergo revisions, never quite disappears from view as one reads through Mackay Brown literature because this is Mackay Brown's soul. He says himself (in comparison to Edwin Muir):

> My poems have a much narrower range in time—a thousand years maybe—and they celebrate as best they can (whatever is begotten, born, or dies, generation by generation, until they stop with memories of my father and his letters and tailor's shears.[28]

Narrowness is emblematic, less is more, and as such is inserted by Mackay Brown into a distinctive Orkney poetics.

Attunement

Mackay Brown's reverent mind attached itself here on Brinkie's Brae to the 'Form' and the consequent pliancy 'attuned' through a natural aesthetics became what Rendall would call the 'secret password' that opens up the beautiful that arises from an inspiration that is from above and within. There is no separation, only the seamless transition from the natural to the supernatural. Attunement is a concept used by von Balthasar and prefigured in Newman's concept of 'realisation'. The process of artistic creativity that is shared by artist and audience tracks the artist not consciously pushing his own idea but rather allowing, through attunement, to paradoxically be grasped by what is ungraspable, to be a receptacle for its rays. The artist Mackay Brown skilfully translates the vision into sensual form and in so doing is not obstructing the illumination of the action of ideas. This is a dynamic process navigated by the artist and made present and accessible to the audience. Artists' external behaviours can mask an interior humble receptivity in silence, 'only if he knows how to be quiet will the anima[29] sing to him'.[30]

Attunement is a dynamic process that contains the elements of aesthetics and theology and as such is pre-theological. This is the perfect work space for the artist and an emergent 'swarm of symbols'. Von Balthasar explains the existence and life of the artist as like an instrument that is tuned by the Spirit, the breath of which rings out as an Aeolian harp in tune, in concordance with the rhythm of God himself. This is not a mysticism that is constantly striving upwards to attain an immediate experience of God. Mackay Brown is the 'wire that conducts the current'.[31] As he writes in his autobiography on Francis Thompson's 'Hound of Heaven':

> I think, looking back after forty-five years, that the poem had many flaws in its pure gem-like flame; but I could not have enough of that wonderful discovery. I read it over and over, until I had it by heart. And I knew that the man reeling from delight to vain earthly delight was a Catholic—a very sad and weak and fallible one—and that the Hound in relentless pursuit of him was Christ, or the Church. And for some reason, these facts gave to the poem an extra relish.[32]

There is a demand here that the Christian be attuned to God and equally to Christ and to the Church. Mackay Brown is attuned in just such a way, and it is a struggle fought and persevered with on a daily basis, while others fell away. But Mackay Brown recognised a 'peaceful invasion'[33] in patterns of migration to Orkney, many migrants who came to Orkney looking for the consolation and ballast of the aesthetic, and also a pre-Reformation sensorium still able to rise up in a contemporary Catholicism as well as in artistic endeavours.

> I am glad Orkney has of recent years attracted new Orcadians from other cities in the south. They have—most of them—come in search of light and a meaning. I think this peaceful invasion will go on, and is to be encouraged; regular transfusions of new blood have kept us a healthy and alert community.[34]

Seeing the Form: The Bible

The 'Summer Day' experience is genuinely biblical and consistent with covenant theology of both Old and New Testaments. Mackay Brown is enthused and inspired by Scripture from the creation accounts in Genesis and the wisdom literature of Ecclesiastes in particular to the Passion of Christ, His Crucifixion, Resurrection and Parousia. Hence his marked devotion to the Stations of the Cross as encapsulating everything he ever did and wanted to say. The New Testament was a completion of the Old and his exegesis was a Catholic one.

What follows are excerpts where Mackay Brown speaks for himself with his insights on Scripture and how he interprets it as poet and writer. These excerpts are not exhaustive but are selected to give prominent support to his Catholic exegesis and formation:

Vocation

> I don't feel I have any mission at all. I mean, I don't feel poetry's a mission either, it's just the only thing I can do, you see. I have a sort of gift with words, and I indulge this gift. Whether it is a mission or not, I wouldn't claim, but I just try to do what I can with them. This is something that troubles me all the time, and I'll have to do it so long as I am the way I am.[35]

The Muir Vision

> Like most Scottish children of his generation, he knew the Bible intimately; his father, like Burns's, read 'the chapter' regularly, to the family circle. It is a Scottish tradition, now broken, that ought to be mourned over. The Bible was the only literature many Scottish people knew, for generations and even centuries; and it is great literature, and had a profound effect on the imagination and the outlook of the whole nation.[36]

> What he has bequeathed to us is a symbol: spring, well, fountain-head—the purity at the heart of creation. His greatest poem is 'The Transfiguration'. During the time that the actual transfiguration of Christ lasted—if we can use the word 'time' at all in such an occurrence—the whole earth was drenched and irradiated in utmost purity of light, and evil was no more,

So from the ground we felt that virtue branch
Through all our veins till we were whole, our writs
As fresh and pure as water from the well,
Our hands made new to handle holy things,
The source of all our seeing rinsed and cleansed
Till earth and light and water entering here
Gave back to us the clear unfallen world ...

It is a vision as splendid and marvelous as Dante or Blake. The poem I like to think, may have had this beginning: a small boy in a green island stands beside a woman who is filling a bucket with bright water from a burn; water for farm animals and farm folk to drink, water to wash hands that have been ploughing or fishing, water for the flagstone floor and the wash-tub; the sun shaken all day from the water-bucket in a niche on a farmhouse wall. Then by lamp-light and fire-light, the old farmer opens the Word and begins: After six days Jesus took with him Peter, James and John ... and led them up a high mountain by themselves. There he was transfigured before them. His face shone like the sun, and his clothes became white as light' ... Simple events of a simple day. And yet, to the child who was there, they are treasures beyond price: the 'things beautiful and good' that makes worthwhile all the pains and disasters of life—and that may, in the end help to save the sum of things.[37]

No Separation between Old and New Testaments

I only rarely turned the pages of Scripture. That great poem Ecclesiastes meant much to me. But this, 'Unless a seed fall into the ground and die, it remains alone. But if it dies, it brings forth fruit, a hundred-fold'—the words sank deep, and seemed to illuminate a huge tract of darkness.[38]

No Separation between the Seasons Natural and Spiritual

I happened to meet the oldest monk one day at the shore. He said, in Irish Gaelic, that summer and winter are but a prefiguration of the soul's light and darkness. At winter solstice, the sun seems to be on its death-bed. In the spring the stone of death is rolled away, and the resurrected sun walks across the earth bringing plants and animals and fishes and birds and folk in its wake. And now in high summer, there is no doubt of the supreme victory of light: all creation flourishes in its abundance. So, in the spiritual domain, was it with Christ and his kingdom.[39]

Genesis Creation Accounts

… that wonderful word that took six days to utter …

the islands an echo of that first harmony … your souls are going to die of starvation among the tinsel of Vanity Fair.[40]

Getting the Balance between Faith and Reason Right

It is overweighted with religion—I mean, the emphasis on religious motifs is too strong,—and it misses out on a lot of sweetness and light.[41]

Ideas and Beliefs about Faith and Reason and Disruption at the Reformation

In a letter to Stewart Conn (16 July 1967) Mackay Brown gives deep and taut insights into his ideas and beliefs as well as into his play *A Spell for Green Corn*:

… it's a *religious play* (not moral, of course, anything but) but religious—the relationship between man and nature and supernatural powers …

Episode 1 (the Miracle) is set in the Age of Faith, when people were poor, illiterate, believing (superstitious the rationalists wd. Say, but I'm not a rationalist and so I say 'believing').

Crude simple people fisherman (hunters) … farming … Age of the Saints—therefore of miracles—in western hagiography and in the gospels of course the provision of miraculous food is commonplace. Yet even these primitive people have difficulty in swallowing the fish-from-stones. All except the tinker, whose faith is deepest of all (tho' he is an immoral vagabond.)

Transition from fishing to agriculture … man has to plough, sow, harrow, be patient all summer, reap, thresh, winnow, grind, bake-and-brew. The fact that a loaf of bread can come from a seed corn in a hole in the ground is still a great mystery, and the peasants are aware of it. Hence the midsummer fire on the hill (which was one of many rituals carried out communally to ensure growth of crops, a fertility rite.) But now we have come to an age when all ritual, mystery, symbolism were actively discouraged by the church, and they have carried it out half surreptitiously. Sanctity miracles are looked on as the stock-in-trade of papists for keeping people ignorant and poor. What I am suggesting is that the deliberate destruction of rite and symbol murders a most delicate part of the human spirit—the naked WORD of the preacher is not enough—and therefore some of the saint's miraculous powers must be taken over by the artist (and in 17th century Scotland the witch.)

We crave for beauty; and if we don't get it something in us warps and atrophies.

... detestation of Presbyterianism for the folk culture of the time— how in Orkney ... the ministers and elders trampled on the ballads and stripped their kirks of all external beauty—this in contrast to the beautiful churches full of statues and paintings and images, and the free uninhibited culture, of pre-Reformation times.

Now there is no saint to feed the people miraculously—the burden falls on the fiddler and the witch (... to keep open the sources of life by means of secret fertility rites ... witchcraft. I think ... pious girl who clings to enough of the old lingering superstitions to make her a focus of suspicion and ultimately a scapegoat and a sacrifice.) We know that poetry and music do not feed people ... what I am wishful to say ... is that man is one, and that you can't divide body and mind and spirit in him—the hunger part is a hunger of the whole man.

There is another chasm ... we are suddenly in the Age of the Machines ... the blind fiddler as a strange pathetic survival from a past age, an eloquent braggart and perhaps a bit of a fake who feels himself vaguely threatened by the Machine.

Local myths—especially ... —enter into it; and one vivid childhood memory, the blind fiddler who visited Stromness every autumn to play to the Lammas Market crowds, and seemed to me so pathetic, ageless, strange, frightening.

I'm all for restraint, reticence. I distrust all displays of naked emotion.[42]

... man and earth take corruption one from the other, they being inseparable dust, so that the sick field that summer was a figure, a symbol of inordinate cruelty and uncharity, an infamous shameless withershin[43] dance of evil through the island—pride, sloth, greed, anger, envy, lust, gluttony ...

What word? All the whole word, The Utterer with The Uttered, yea and in especial The Uttering, the sweet continual channering of the dove down the blank winds of history, the unfinished God-tiding, the life-bearer, word world without end ... And where found? No-where here found. In bonds lay the word, a prisoner in the kirk pulpit—how should it get free among the ploughs and the nets, that season of famine? ... Maskers ... know that in God's gift lieth a mystery like unto holiness, a shadow of creation, a far sweet whisper. This is it, art—what ye call poem, pattern, dance. One cold act of beauty (in default of sanctity) might yet flush the hill with ripeness. So a young man, one in all lewdness and vanity steeped, a makar, put on him that summer for a brief time the Saint's mask (for well ye know the artist can mime and counterfeit anything whatsoever in hell or earth or heaven for the summoning, by ceremony, of a thing truly desired) ... And on into deeper silence, and into a silence be-yond silence, ... and on still, till at the heart of the hill was this only, *silence silence silence.*

In that last silence the word moved, the word moved, and the bird shrieked it out under the furrows ... Yet the word that the fiddle found was more than BIRTH, it was altogether different, it was the merging of all these words in the complete dance, a new and holy mystery. It was RESURRECTION.[44]

Scripture Speaks to and for All Peoples in All Times and Places

... great stories of the Old Testament ... far more than the legends of a tribe of wandering shepherds; they shed meaning on all human existence.[45]

Theological Aesthetics

'In principio erat Verbum'. Our western form of religion, Christian-ity, thinks of the Word as illuminating all history with beauty, wis-dom and truth. For poetry and the other arts, to be handmaidens of that Supreme Word is a worthy enough calling. Poetry keeps the flame alive.[46]

Faith without Reason

1 February 1955. Scotland waits breathlessly for the advent, out of America, of Billy Graham. We are assured there will be a mighty shaking of dry bones in the Gorbals and the Glens. But I myself mistrust mass emotionalists, whether in politics or religion; especially when it is organized on super big business lines; remembering how the Lord cleansed the temple of super big business men with a cat-o-nine-tails, and praised the humble and the weak.[47]

5 April 1955. I heard Mr Billy Graham on Sunday morning over the radio. Even without seeing him, you could tell he was sincere—passionately sincere even. And he had a great gift for preaching—no doubt about that— ... His great strength is the utter simplicity of his beliefs. There is no room for honest doubt there ... And the great authority is the Bible. Billy's refrain is 'the Bible says ...' but while you are reaching for your weapons of intellect and imagination to demolish Billy, he is safe inside his fortress of 'the Bible says.'[48]

3 May 1955. Transformation. What of religion in Orkney now? ... The big tide of Billy Graham flowed and ebbed again. Has it scattered any marvellous jetsam on our shores? It is too early to say yet. But if the campaign was successful in the next twelve months or so we should notice a considerable increase in generosity, tolerance and compassion, wherever we go in Orkney. We should notice that the crude improvised masks of sin and time have been torn from scores of faces, and gladness shining everywhere.[49]

Scripture and Tradition

No harm in studying the Scriptures, so long as one knows what one is about. It is such a richly poetic-symbolical body of work, some people read into it (especially a book like Revelation) all kinds of meaning. The Reformation happened because people were making private inferences. The Church is there to prevent such strayings. 'This is what scripture means', the church is never tired of saying, 'this and nothing else, unless the Holy Spirit unfolds some new meaning ... It shouldn't be forgotten that the scripture we have is only a translation of translations—and meaning alters subtly with each translation.[50]

Reflections on the Jewish People

> 25 September 1956. Go down Moses. Anti-Semitism will never be popular in Orkney because it has nothing to bite on ... In pre-war days a lonely figure could very often be seen on Orkney roads. Every croft and farmhouse was a station in his endless pilgrimage ... His name was Louis and he was a Polish Jew. There was nothing in that mild little pedlar to rouse the faintest animosity in anyone. If all Jews are like him, we thought, they must be a good and gentle race ... Its only about Lammas Market times nowadays that we have a chance of seeing some of the chosen people.[51]

Seeing the Glory of the Lord

> John the Baptist. He was not the light, but was sent to bear witness to the Light, The Glory behind the Light, Creator of stars and moon and the sun of midsummer. The glittering of the fish scale the bronze ear of barley the ice crystals the tree white with frost and the tree laden with leaves and apples and laughter And the men and women and children whose mouths shine with praise in the holy places ... A marvelous boy came from the north had sat on the temple steps with the doctors of theology, discussing first and last things with a grave urgent sweetness And John said, breaking bread with his parents, 'The cousin was there, The first raindrops have fallen of the great waters that will purify the world I am to stand next to him in the next surge, the river of the dove.[52]

> Transfiguration, 6 August 1993. There's a man burning on the side of the hill. A blaze like crystal! A star on the mountain side![53]

Seeing the Form: Orkney Landscapes

The sensual perceptions rise up time and time again and these are Orcadian perceptions, formative of an Orkney poetics. Orcadian society is set through various timeshifts as a one-dimensional caricature against the wild beauty of Orkney and patterns of human settlement that come and go, leaving their marks of a hoarded heraldic symbolism, according to the Mackay Brown allegory. His coherence is always 'the other place', the Primal Form, the glory of the Lord, that tends towards literary device but is never able to contain the Mackay Brown vision. His sense of place, Orkney as a whole, Orkney in its patterns of settlements, is never portrayed with brushstrokes of the simple rustic life of pastoral ballad or Arcadian happiness. The oblique characters that live and breathe and work within these settlement patterns are tormented and haunted with impending death and decay. The usurpations of lower social orders by the rich and powerful, an enforced emigration, have a wider voice of pilgrimage and diaspora, never an Orcadian stasis. The literary ground is always shifting as the Mackay Brown coherency is in a deep space 'where gladly he puts his hand into the swarm of images' to save those gone and going days for us.

Hamnavoe

> ... the novel [*Greenvoe*] suggests, faintly and fleetingly that the ancient pattern may have a dark hidden secret endurance. It may assert itself again after centuries of steel and plastic and concrete (as the grass-blades pushing through the broken paving stones of Troy or Babylon). *Greenvoe* is a kind of twentieth-century variation on Oliver Goldsmith's 'The Deserted Village'.[54]

Rackwick

> I think that the most beautiful place in Orkney is a little valley in the island of Hoy called Rackwick. The Atlantic waves beat forever on a wide curving beach of red boulders. Only a thin ribbon of road connects Rackwick with our modern atomic civilization. Otherwise it is completely isolated in a kind of timelessness, by great barriers of red cliff and gloomy hill. You only know you are in the twentieth century by the wooden shop and the patches of oil on the rocks excreted by the motor boats of the fishermen. Smell. Taste, sight, hearing—all the senses are more vivid in this place. Life becomes at once simpler and more significant; you can almost persuade yourself that television and newspapers and the tubercle bacillus are a complete illusion, and never have existed and never will.[55]

Birsay

> Perhaps the most fascinating parish in all Orkney is Birsay. It is a small Orkney in itself, containing everything in its narrow bounds—lochs,

and cliffs, rich tilth, history and poetry, old nameless barrows and monolith and a small happy village by the sea's edge. In addition, one senses here the living presence of ancient communal virtues that are rapidly being lost in some other parts of Orkney. The young and the old have a graciousness of speech and manners that is particularly beautiful to observe nowadays, when it has become so rare. Wherever you turn in this parish, beauty meets the eye in a different guise. Birsay is fortunate that its beauty has been celebrated in picture and song, nowhere so memorably as in the poems of the modern Orkney poet, Robert Rendall. Birsay for this fine writer, is more than a place; it is a symbol of all that is best in the past and the present, of all that is hopeful for the future, of all that is lovely and consoling in sea and sky, in cornfield and barren hill, in man and bird and beast.[56]

The three above examples let Mackay Brown speak for himself with his insight into reading Orkney as a special place within which there is a deep sensual perception suffused with form and beauty in a tranced aesthetics which are resplendent in a joyous glory as they rise up out of the insidious turmoil of change and decay and the moral drama of the oblique caricature of human behaviour. Orkney, storehouse of the sacred and the profane, 'where God and man work out together a plan of utter necessity and of unimaginable beauty'.[57]

Notes

[1]   Hans Urs von Balthasar, *The Glory of the Lord. A Theological Aesthetics. I: Seeing the Form*. San Francisco: Ignatius Press, 1982, pp. 32–3.

[2]   Ernest W. Marwick, 'Profile of George Mackay Brown', 1965. Orkney Archive, Ernest Walker Marwick Collection, D31/30/4, p. 2.

[3]   *Ibid.*

[4]   von Balthasar, *The Glory of the Lord I*, pp. 32–3.

[5]   'Numinous' is a term used to describe that which is perceived to be mysterious. It is associated with the work of Rudolf Otto (1869–1937) a Lutheran theologian influenced by Kant and Schleiermacher. The inner sense of the holy lies according to Otto at the heart of all the great religions.

[6]   Richard Rolle, Julian of Norwich, Walter Hilton, Margery Kempe, William Langland.

[7]   William James, *The Varieties of Religious Experience*. New York: Penguin, 1985.

[8]   The literary recluses of mediaeval England include Simon Stock, the hymn-writer; Thomas Scrope, the historian; Geoffrey, the grammarian; George Ripley, the alchemist; Margery Kempe and Julian, the mystics; Richard Rolle, composer of poetry and prose; and Symon, compiler of a manual of meditations.

[9]   William Langland, *Piers Plowman with Sir Gawain and the Green Knight, Pearl, Sir Orfeo* (Anon). The Millennium Library. London: Everyman, 2001, p. 3.

[10]   John 19:23–4: 'His undergarment was seamless, woven in one piece from neck to hem'. The soldiers who crucified Jesus did not divide his tunic after crucifying him, but cast lots to determine who would keep it because it was woven in one piece, without seam. There is the possible allusion to the high-priestly robe which is without seam.

[11]   George Mackay Brown, *Northern Lights. A Poet's Sources*. London: John Murray, 1999, pp. 103–4.

[12]   Mackay Brown, *An Orkney Tapestry*, p. 20.

[13]   *Ibid.*, p. 44, p. 56.

[14]   George Mackay Brown, 'Mary Jane Mackay 1891–1967 (A Memoir)', in Mackay Brown, *Northern Lights*, pp. 124–5.

[15]   *Ibid.*

[16]   *Ibid.*, p. 132.

[17]   *Ibid.*, pp. 124–5.

[18]   *Ibid.*

[19]   von Balthasar, *The Glory of the Lord I*, pp. 32–3.

[20]   Mackay Brown, *An Orkney Tapestry*, p. 19.

[21] von Balthasar, *The Glory of the Lord I*, p. 65.

[22] *Ibid.*, pp. 32–3.

[23] Mackay Brown, *Northern Lights*, pp. 102–3.

[24] von Balthasar, *The Glory of the Lord I*, p. 34.

[25] Mackay Brown, *Northern Lights*, pp. 102–3.

[26] *Ibid.*, p. 103.

[27] von Balthasar, *The Glory of the Lord II*, p. 15.

[28] Mackay Brown, *For the Islands I Sing*, p. 165.

[29] soul.

[30] von Balthasar, *The Glory of the Lord II*, p. 251.

[31] *Ibid.*

[32] Mackay Brown, *For the Islands I Sing*, p. 50.

[33] Marwick, 'Profile of George Mackay Brown', p. 2.

[34] *Ibid.*

[35] George Mackay Brown, 'The Poet Speaks', typescript, 3 May 1965, of interview by Peter Orr of the British Council, 14 October 1964 (National Sound Archive). National Library of Scotland, George Mackay Brown Archive, Acc. 1020/6.

[36] George Mackay Brown, 'The Story of Scotland. Edwin Muir', 21 November 1988. Orkney Archive, George Mackay Brown Collection, D124/2/2/12, p. 2.

[37] *Ibid.*, pp. 6–8.

[38] George Mackay Brown, 'Thoughts of an Old-Age Pensioner', August 1986. Orkney Archive, George Mackay Brown Collection, D124/2/2/5, p. 8. John 12:24.

[39] George Mackay Brown, 'The Architect. A Story', October 1993. Edinburgh University Library, Special Collections, George Mackay Brown MS 3118.27.

[40] George Mackay Brown, 'The Resurrection'. National Library of Scotland, George Mackay Brown Archive, Acc. 4864/15.

[41] George Mackay Brown, comment on Paul Butter's book *Edwin Muir* (Oliver & Boyd: London and Edinburgh, 1962), in a letter to Willa Muir, 17 November 1966. National Library of Scotland, George Mackay Brown Archive, Acc. 51/5.

[42] George Mackay Brown, letter to Stewart Conn concerning the play *Spell for Green Corn*, 16 July 1967. National Library of Scotland, George Mackay Brown Archive, Acc. 4864/19.

[43] In a direction contrary to the sun's course, considered as unlucky; anticlockwise (Scots).

[44] Mackay Brown, letter to Conn concerning the play *Spell for Green Corn*.

[45] George Mackay Brown, typescript, November 1988, for *Glasgow Herald*. Orkney Archive, George Mackay Brown Collection, D124/2/1/2.

[46] George Mackay Brown, 'Poetry Keeping the Flame Alive', *Spotlight* (1988), p. 49. Held in Orkney Archive, George Mackay Brown Collection, D124/2/4/27.

[47] George Mackay Brown, 'Billy Graham', Island Diary, *The Orkney Herald*, 1 Feb. 1955. Held in Orkney Archive, Ernest Walker Marwick Collection, D31/30/1.

[48] George Mackay Brown, 'The Voice', Island Diary, *Orkney Herald*, 5 April 1955.

[49] George Mackay Brown, 'Transformation', Island Diary, *Orkney Herald*, 3 May 1955.

[50] George Mackay Brown, correspondence with author, 15 November 1991. See Appendix.

[51] George Mackay Brown, 'Go Down Moses', Island Diary, *The Orkney Herald*, 25 Sept. 1956. Held in Orkney Archive, Ernest Walker Marwick Collection, D31/30/1.

[52] St John's Kirk 750th anniversary 1991 booklet. Edinburgh University Library, Special Collections, George Mackay Brown MS 3119, 1986–94.

[53] *Ibid.*

[54] George Mackay Brown, from a 200-word summary of *Greenvoe* for the publisher, Harcourt Brace, March 22 1973. National Library of Scotland. George Mackay Brown Archive, Acc. 10209/8.

[55] George Mackay Brown, *Landscapes from Memory*. Typescript signed 'Hjal', p. 11. Orkney Archive, George Mackay Brown Collection, D1/296/1.

[56] *Ibid.*

[57] Mackay Brown, *Magnus*, p. 65.

✝ 3 ✝

Passion Partner

Grant that I may carry within me the death of Christ, make me a
partner in his Passion, let me relive his wounds.[1]

George Mackay Brown's piety is, on its literary evidence, a medieval one,
and there is no doubt that he staked his sanity and well-being on it. It
is an ancient piety that re-opened an earlier period of Orkney history
that had been convincingly suppressed at the Reformation. Delving
into his various archival papers there is much unpublished writing
that reveals the manner in which he struggled and battled within his
inner world. In so doing he becomes absorbed in the Cross, gradually
finding his way as a partner in the Passion of Christ. The medieval
liturgical fragment from the 'Stabat Mater' quoted above, with a con-
centrated meditation on the Passion of Christ that was so popular
in the primers of the late medieval period (used by the laity), can be
used to examine the formations of the Mackay Brown piety. It could
be argued that Mackay Brown's writings are a literary litany in which
his particular form of allegory is able to bring a re-opened world view
into the twentieth century with an unabated freshness. As a Passion
partner Mackay Brown experiments with Anglo-Saxon and medieval
literary devices, displacing his own torments into a deep reality where
he learns how to forge images and symbols. He is the dreamer, the
Oak Tree, and Everyman. He is a Passion partner, but not with a lush
romanticism or devotional sentimentality. He is a faith-and-reason
poet conversant in many genres, reclaiming the medieval Everyman
stripped of individuality in order to create a universal moral message
for the twentieth century and beyond.

A Prose Poem

In an unpublished manuscript entitled 'Man into Oak', typed in 1946,[2] Mackay Brown uses the literary device of the dream vision. In these formative early beginnings of his literary career his religious experience, as documented in 'Summer Day' (1947), shows a natural disposition that expresses itself allegorically in the medieval tradition. His readers are not in their turn going to naturally take up his complex use of allegory but this prose poem (of which there are a number of examples in the unpublished materials of the Orkney Archive) stands testament to a formative spiritual and philosophical stance at the core of Mackay Brown. This stance enables a contemplative ability to stand in oneself at the deepest level and simultaneously stand outside oneself through the mediation of symbols. Marwick worked hard to mentor Mackay Brown to refine his texts for an audience able to access his materials. Mackay Brown's interior space of 'Summer Day' has a natural affinity with a pre-Reformation sensorium and from those thousand or so years ago he proceeds forward to the twentieth century. What is natural for Mackay Brown is not necessarily natural and accessible to his audience. An Orkney audience, a Scottish audience, did not necessarily have the appetite for his swarm of symbols, unleashed from the opening up of a world view that had been closed off at an earlier time.

'Man into Oak' recounts a revealed knowledge or a truth not indicative of a normal waking state. Mackay Brown's use of the prose-poem genre began to flourish suddenly, forged through the decade 1940–50, a period of illness and death—the possibility of his own as well as the actual death of his father in 1940. For all the possible reasons that underpin his physical and mental health, his coping strategies become well entrenched as his cognitive and emotional needs are funnelled through his writing and growing religious practice. This too is responsively characteristic of medieval Europeans with their pre-Reformation sensorium, by which we may make sense of what Mackay Brown calls 'the gale of life' of which death is very much a part. Whether or not the dream vision is of divine origin here as he comes to terms with, or does not, tuberculosis and the prospect of death, the prose-poem genre is used as a creative gateway to imaginative possibilities that transcend the here and now. He innovates with his own distinctive theo-logic displayed in the prose poems. This theo-logic is firmly pre-theologic; Mackay Brown is never a theologian.

In May 1946 he wrote to Marwick:

> I somehow have the feeling that a good prose poem exists by reason of the continuous waves of suggestion it throws out. Every word and line must, of course, have significance. I have tried to make my prose poems distilled short stories, with all the power of the lyric to surprise and strike with wonder. The prose poem is, I assure, you, a most exciting medium, and English poets have not explored it nearly enough.[3]

And again, in October 1946, he had 'been experimenting with a form of composition which I call "prose poem" for lack of a better word. It is more akin to musical form than to poetry'.[4]

He typically innovates by following a structure whereby he is the narrator, allegorically recounting his experience of falling asleep, dreaming, and waking, modelled on the medieval 'Dream of the Rood'. This dream, which forms the subject of the poem, existentially processes events in waking life. The 'vision' addresses these waking concerns through the possibilities of the imaginative landscapes offered by the dream-state. In the course of the dream, the narrator, often with the aid of a guide (here it is the Oak Tree), offers perspectives that provide potential resolutions to his waking concerns. These 'waking concerns' are documented throughout this period, especially 1944–7. The poems are: 'Christ Poem' (July 1944), 'The House of Death' (March 1945), 'Dream of Winter' (March 1946), 'The Prisoner' (August 1947), and the prose poems: 'Swan's Way' (February 1946), 'Journey to Avalon' (June 1946) and 'Man into Oak' (June 1946). These early poems and prose poems maybe dim lanterns of their finely honed descendants but they are not 'dim' in their existential battles from which emerge a strong and enduring faith having squared up to disease, suffering and death.

Marwick wrote: 'some important things had happened. His tuberculosis took a more acute form, necessitating a stay of several months in a local sanatorium. This may have been a blessing in disguise, for modern drugs halted the progress of the disease and he was eventually to take a more active part in life and to think of a career.'[5] This is the sanitised version of what was clearly not only a life and death struggle but also a desperate psychological and spiritual battle that saw Mackay Brown's existential formation win through. The company of other writers and the power of education gave him a way forward. Marwick gives a trustworthy and balanced witness to 'his distaste for Calvinism and its fruits, have been replaced by a positive philosophy. The receptive attitude of mind, the instinctive identification with the old faith, had long been there ... After his submission to the Church, which followed prolonged and agonising thought, he began to look more deeply into the spiritual realities that give meaning and potential to the life of man.'[6]

The early and raw poems reproduced below witness to Mackay Brown's struggle, which has much in common with that of Gerard Manley Hopkins; Hopkins was to become the greatest of his literary mentors. This affinity was a powerful life-long sustaining force. Mackay Brown could be his distinctive self in an ancient well-spring, a deep shared reality, well-fortified not only by 'the other place' but also by 'literary others' who had to face their own demons, to great literary effect.

Man into Oak

This prose poem is a pure distillation worked out deep within himself, as he was forced to grapple with inner forces of body and soul to make sense of an existence that hovers between life and death during the years 1940–6. Psychology is not enough to work out the processes he is going through. It is on the level of body and soul that the great themes of dark and light, life and death, had to overcome a sharp dualism, which is an easy temptation to submit to. 'Man into Oak' (for which in a letter to Ernest Marwick in 1946 he says: 'I make no claims ...') documents the inner torments and experience of a reconfiguring that enabled him to find a sort of repose and inner 'oak' from which he could hold the swarm of symbols at bay, weaving them into a seamless tapestry. Here is Mackay Brown's 'forge', his 'threshing floor' where he works out with God 'his plan of utter necessity', his trade and craft. Mackay Brown is in control at a very deep level of the symbols as poet but not otherwise. The inner discipline of the poet is overlaid with an external appearance of being weak, sick, vulnerable, always needy, passively manipulative, and he was very conscious of it.

I am a man who could not suffer man's nature, so I passed through the gate of death and was changed to a tree. A tree has no emotions, no ambitions, is not required to be respectable.

Mackay Brown separates 'himself' in a willed detachment that shifts his 'core' to a psychological state that becomes remote, static, unaffected by 'the gale of life' and can withstand intolerable levels of pressure. Mentally this is a better interior space.

A tree is perfect and fixed in the amber of nature, and cannot be said to live, unless mere growing and drinking is life. A tree has no knowledge of time and chance, though time and chance afflict it, in rhythms slower but no less certain than the seasons which clothe it and strip it.

The resin 'amber' is hard, durable, beautiful in its colour and translucency, restorative in its capacity to preserve as it undergoes the natural processes. Mackay Brown at maximal distance between himself and his torment, finds a way forward:

I became a tree, stepping down in nature, and so suffered defeat though many men would say now that my being as a tree is more noble and more beautiful than my being as a man. So nobility and beauty may mean something after all, but only in men and not in a tree.

His identity does battle with an ultimate lowering into the negativity of self-loathing to the point of complete mental collapse as an incisive dualism catapults him to a separation between body and soul. The soul is struggling towards an 'out-of-body' experience because his body is experienced as a negative state. He is saved by the good, beautiful and the true but the body will not detach, deliberate as the forces of dualism are.

This I saw at the moment of death, and it was the peak of my life's wisdom. It is a privilege to be a man and exult. Beggar and duke, to endure is to conquer. To conquer is to live, to become involved with God. I, a man, sinned in wishing for death. I did not wish to endure, and there is no breaking point in endurance. A man can endure till endurance becomes oblivion and conquest. Conquest is oblivion, but not self-oblivion. Conquest is oblivion imposed by fate, the oblivion of the fallen leaf. Death is self-oblivion, is defeat.

This is not psychological, it is a spiritual battle and the 'self-oblivion' so sought after, by becoming a tree, is perceived to be an act of sin.

> Oblivion and death are opposed, as conquest and defeat are opposed. I, a man, convinced myself that I was unable to act and suffer the part of man. I cringed from the shape of the spear and the shape of the trowel.

Is this a foreshadowing of Magnus the Martyr facing his own sacrificial death? The deep all-encompassing psychological penetration is in contact with the Christ-hero and his purposefulness for his adherents. Mackay Brown facing his own death is now a devotional interface of Magnus, always more than a literary device. He is a Passion partner of Christ, specifically in the Magnus persona. Beauty and nobility brought an engagement, an involvement with God. This is a powerful religious experience and is classically and biblically so. A repentance in upward movement, still saturated in suffering, shows a willed acceptance because it is God who gives the consciousness of 'disease'. Is this Mackay Brown's tuberculosis or original sin (he was not baptised at this point in 1946) or both, inseparably entwined? The seed of the acorn has to die.

> I imagined a disease shape with such passionate intensity that the disease germ came like a lover and leeched to my man's fibres … My buried body curled round an acorn, which fed on its decay like the germ of a dream, time and chance and the law of growth happened to flesh and acorn, but they knew neither time nor chance, only the unutterable law of growth, twining into the root, and branch and foliage of the oak tree.

> I, a dryad, these things to you on a summer evening when the wind stirs my foliage and the sun is warm on my trunk of great antiquity. I neither hear nor see, but I act and suffer, though I have no knowledge of action and suffering. Man's mind is a quick brilliant thing, like this stream that murmurs and glitters in the evening sunlight. A thousand years ago when the man died out of me, had I been the great oak I am today, men had toppled me with great crash and destruction to the earth, and to make winter logs of me. Three hundred years ago, so short a time, men had built me bodily into the side of a great echoing warship.

Mackay Brown has the power now to time-shift and holistically give his own mortal body, fragile as it is, enduring value.

> All ways I am the servant of men. On this golden evening, this very evening, a man who is a bad poet, and an insignificant philosopher stands looking at the inscrutable mystery of me, and compares some organisation of which he is a proud member to an oak tree which sprang vividly towards heaven from an insignificant acorn. Always I am a servant of man's body and mind. So perhaps I am still a part of mankind, as mankind is involved in me and in all nature. Man's mind is a quick brilliant thing, which may soon reach the ocean of all knowledge. In him perhaps only have I life, and all nature. So I, dying, a young minstrel among a savage sylvan people, in the age of the bronze. Defeated and afraid, ignorant and acquiescent, and one in imagination with the dryad in the oak tree that whispers and laughs as the summer wind sets golden spangles dancing among the leaves.

This prose poem is undoubtedly as deeply Mackay Brown as it is is possible to be. He shares himself and his torments here with the reader, who may or may not assent to the descent and ascent of body and soul in its classical and biblical proportions and rhythms in a 'sequence of controlled pulsing images'. He is learning his craft. It is an enduring feature of his highest achievements in literature. He has descended into the interior suffering formations of his subjectivity to re-emerge with an ascending joyous exultation. But there is no separation between the descent and the ascent; they need each other. There are too healthy shades of doubt (where have I just been? Is it real?) steeped in a delicate humility which was very much a mark of the man as I knew him, accompanied by a constant innocent kneeling on his part before God, only too aware of how he fell short. Mackay Brown found place and purpose where many would not be able to perceive and endure. His 'acquiescence', a word specific to his state of mind and will that means a reluctant acceptance of something without protest, is evidence of his silent consent or assent, his blessing elicited but not without a sense of reluctance as his ego (always fragile and vulnerable) gives way to this place of quiet rest, this 'other place'.

Some Pre-theological Experimentations

As Mackay Brown found himself in a seething cauldron of physical and mental illness he clearly found in writing a way through. What Marwick identified as 'callow' writings illustrate the incisive themes of darkness, torment and suffering. What they lack in technique they make up for as evidence of an intensely bitter passion that gives a deep insight into Mackay Brown's inner world. Marwick tempered and restrained certain themes that were never going to strike resonance with a local audience. 'Kirk Elder' (reproduced below) is a damning attack on Mackay Brown's cradle Calvinism.[7] He brings to his observations a fierce judgement and hostility towards Calvinism which remained through his life and was deeply felt. Positively, this is an acknowledgement of the fissure created at the Reformation. Sham religious behaviours are nothing new and tarnish all the great religions and they are to be exposed for what they are. The savagery of the phrase: 'Whose shrunken soul is mean with hate' raises questions—who is the kirk elder or does he stand for all kirk elders? Is Mackay Brown savaging the Presbyterianism of his day or a theological determinism driven by the Protestant work ethic and a painfully felt judgement upon himself as 'rag' and 'scarecrow' and 'worm'? I think it is worth noting that locally he presented as the paradox that he was, his vulnerabilities not squaring with the notions of bourgeois respectability. These early writings evidence the private torments of what he perceived as 'the shouting gates of hell' on his own doorstep. These are his honest perceptions and they are not a stereotype or a psychosis. They are his experiences of the Orkney of his times.

Kirk Elder. March 1943

Observe him on his way to church—
The pious plainness of his dress;
A haloed bowler on his head;
His face alive with holiness.

He worships at the shrine of love,
Whose shrunken soul is mean with hate:
Opens his wallet with an air
And slaps a pound note in the plate.

O demons of the judgement day
Hedge him and guard him well,
This puissant prince, and flag him through
The shouting gates of hell.

Mackay Brown had to face death early, and the prospect of judgement and the afterlife was a constant companion. 'Called' and 'summoned' he must go alone to that 'cosmic place' described almost as an empty void where time gradually loses it grasp as its 'echoes' and 'dust' give way to the 'flowering tree', 'bloody' and 'immortal'. But it was not his time, the 'golden door' did not open and he found a feminine guide who 'brought me home'.

The House of Death. March 1945

At the door of the house called death I knocked
Seeking admittance, but no one answered.
The sound of my knocking
Echoed in the lonely halls.

The windows all were broken, barred across
With dingy wood, and spun around with desolate
Spider's webs, and heaped with
Dust of a million suns.

Inside, I knew, was a flowering tree
Of plenty, nourished with fallen blood.
There hung ripe fruit, whose taste
Was immortality.

No one answered at my knock. Within the wall
A mouse scuttled, suddenly afraid.
Fiercely I beat the door of gold, of adamant.

'Summoner, at your imperious call
I crossed the snow mountains. It seems in vain
I left the fields of dawn
And my happy comrades.'

On the way back there were flurries of snow.
Rain fell plenteously. The rivers were swollen.
Then one evening the moon,
A shepherdess, brought me home.

'Home' was a ' wintered place' where he could 'dream' his 'body pinned against the night with burning stars' and the 'ten pale pen-grooved fingers' could pen their way to give meaning to his passion forged in 'The red spreading/ Wound in the breast where I had torn myself/ And gorged my throat with blood'. A bloody tuberculosis is interchanging with the bloody sacrifice of the 'bleeding sun-priest mounting the altar of heaven' and an exultation in the new springtime where 'Birds flocking home/ Over the singing waters'. Mackay Brown is Passion partner and presiding poet.

Dream of Winter. March 1946

These are the sounds that dinned upon my ear—
The spider's fatal purring, and the lowing
Gigantic of vast mammoths held in ice.
No human sound there was: only the evil
Shriek of the violin sound of human woe
And conquest and defeat, and the round drums
Sobbed as they beat.

I saw my body pinned against the night
With burning stars. There was no glory now
In that thin hairy head gone soft with dreams.
No joy of flashing claws: only ten pale
And pen-grooved fingers. The red spreading
Wound in the breast where I had torn myself
And gorged my throat with blood.

Then the dream broke, and I awoke from evil
—the flame of evil that consumed my brain
In sleep and darkness—and saw that it was Spring,
Great strands of light woven across the world,
The bleeding sun-priest mounting the altar of heaven,
And green laughter of children.—Birds flocking home
Over the singing waters.

The 'death door' was one Mackay Brown knew well and his power to dream and free-write whilst being serene about it was hard but the bitterness and hostility subsides gradually as he learns how to craft symbols in 'the fire of images'.

Is God to blame for all this suffering? What an empty question! Look at the agony on this crucifix I have round my neck. This crucifix is the forge, and the threshing-floor, and the shed of net-makers, where God and man work out together a plan a plan of utter necessity and of unimaginable beauty.[8]

An imposed and enforced life became the prison against which he learnt the stretch of the creative, how to accept stillness and silence as the only place where he could truly be 'tranced in a round of deep/ Enduring darkness'. Perceptions of light glowing and fading according to the season, the sounds of birdsong, mercy, sweet Christ, freedom, were enough to breathe purposefulness into the Mackay Brown propensity to dream. Whether his psychological states were drug-induced or a feverish symptom of tuberculosis, or evidence of the personal Mackay Brown passion where he learns to make the crucifix his own forge and threshing floor, he still hesitates, 'Breathing towards death'. He sees himself, the displaced, in an out-of-body experience 'It was I, and yet not I.—And then the Ford drove up. I saw myself get out— And yet it was another—anxious, reluctant'. It was not his time to die, it was the time to write. 'But the love was lost in a maze of hesitating.' But he did not hesitate in his writing vocation. He may have lost the love at the adamant golden death door and later in life on the verge of relationships which inevitably ended in disaster because his true love was his writing:

> I don't feel I have any mission at all. I mean, I don't feel poetry's a mission either, it's just the only thing I can do, you see. I have a sort of gift with words, and I indulge this gift. Whether it is a mission or not, I wouldn't claim, but I just try to do what I can with them. This is something that troubles me all the time, and I'll have to do it so long as I am the way I am.[9]

He had sensed out the glory of the Lord, and it was compelling to the point of acquiescence, where he could feign resistance in a 'maze of hesitating' no longer.

> *The Prisoner*. August 1947
> In my prison cell the long days glow and fade
> In summer, birdsong and sapphire light

And cool star clusters. Winter noons shed
An icy whiteness, tranced in a round of deep
Enduring darkness. The days and years revolve
But bring no change or hope. Only the prison walls
More solid grow, and the square barred widow
—That precious trap of light—contracts in the wall.

There are other prisoners in this craggy fortress.
Sometimes at night the iron corridors
Are thick with flying messages, tapped out
On hollow walls … 'Halcro was hanged tonight'
'Mercy, sweet Christ' … 'The warders are on strike' …
'these walls are safe: what do we know of freedom?'

I have long forgot my crime … Once, in
A dream
I saw a traveller sprawled in deep ditch water,
Primrose and flies covering his broken ribs
Breathing towards death.—It was I, and yet not I.—
And then the Ford drove up. I saw myself get out—
And yet it was another—anxious, reluctant
But the love was lost in a maze of hesitating
As the seconds ticked away. The car drove off.
I cannot tell what deserts lie between
That dream and this reality. The love was lost,
And now the days spin webs round my lost
Freedom.

If the gray governor were to come tonight
And say 'The doors are open'—I should stand
Shaken with dread, that curse burned on my brow.

From learning the craft of sign and symbols in 'callow' verse and 'dim lanterns' Mackay Brown is able to firm up his inner complexities into more compelling writing, always experimental, but 'infected' and 'infused' by a spirituality that readers will relish and be nurtured by in a singular Orkney poetics woven into a sweet medieval Catholicism. Passion partners are readers too, in a communal reading from within 'a great company of minds and hearts … set on a quest for the ultimate meaning of things'.[10]

Stations of the Cross: Variations on a Theme

Mackay Brown, impelled by his curious form of passivity, was never content with achieving celebratory representations of the Orkney countryside or nostalgic lamentations of its disruption. He had a powerful perception of nature, which he was able to capture with his 'pen-grooved fingers' but 'the red spreading/ Wound in the breast' never allowed itself to rest in English literary pastorals. He wrote in the English language but did not bow completely to its literary conventions. His sea village childhood, from which he was never alienated, allowed his unstable self to be seasoned and matured and to compress his 'heartbread' into expansive and fitting genres shaped by liturgical forms which gave purpose and meaning to his inner life, and that of others. He found a place, a set form, in the 'fire of images' that had at its centrepiece the Cross, from which a serene outpouring took him and his readers far and wide, and able to go deep because he himself was in a shared deep reality, ancient and ever made new.

The concepts of house, gate, door, station, calendar appealed to him enormously. Therein he could stabilise the rush of emotions, the many strands of history, the time shifts and their lush thrusting phenomena, the tensions and tragedies of life, the flickers of hope and light in what Cardinal Newman would immortalise for many in his 'Lead Kindly Light'. And of course the Bible and the sacraments were easy pickings for him. He did have a bitter lament about the Reformation from which he never stepped back, but what was a personal crown of thorns matured into an all-encompassing serenity. It was the Stations of the Cross that ultimately gave a stable and enduring level of resolution to his life and literature when he surrendered to a pre-theological deep reality evidenced in the unpublished early writings. It was here that he learned his poetic craft.

Newman's *Apologia* had shown him how to surrender from a 'maze of hesitating', how to attune, realise and contemplate and find a marked serenity through an inseparable faith and reason. But Mackay Brown had to go on in a different century with all its tragic tensions. Literature was his 'Way' and the Mackay Brown soul, it seems to me, is finding for himself, what von Balthasar calls a *katalogical* perspective[11] in the primal source of the Trinity, the defining touchstone for every Christian. Mackay Brown is shown in his prose and early poems (the 'callow' verse) as being caught up in a raw emotional state: he is going in all directions, but reason is at work, and he is drawn into the workings of the Trinity, Father, Son and Holy Spirit, and how theology understands and writes about it, or artists paint it. Mackay Brown gave visual prominence to Andrei Rublev's icon of the Trinity at his home in Mayburn Court, and he was a great fan of the 1966 Tarkovsky Russian film on the life of Rublev. The katalogical perspective is a lesser known and a controversial Catholic theologic perpective. Aquinas's analogical perspective is the Catholic orthodox mainstay, wherein there is an upwards understanding of the relationship between Father, Son and Holy Spirit from creation to Creator. The katalogical perspective works downwards from revealed archetype to the image. Von Balthasar would hold the position that these perspectives do not contradict each other. The insights he gained from the mystic Adrienne von Speyr would describe them as *bi-directional* holding *tensions* in the concepts of *difference-in-unity* and *unity-in-difference*— these concepts are very much at the forefront of contemporary Catholic trinitarian theology and anthropology.[12]

Balthasarian concepts can be seen at work in Mackay Brown and his literary 'Way' as he experiments with various genres—always variations on the theme of 'Stations of the Cross'. These literary variations seek to hold the flux of tensions in a bi-directional use of sign and symbol. He works in accord with the philosophical method of Duns Scotus and Gerard Manley Hopkins that inseparably gives full justice to God and nature. This method sees no separation between Duns Scotus's particularity and universality and Hopkins's inscape and instress. Mackay Brown uses this method to great effect. Von Balthasar's katalogical perspective is seen in Mackay Brown, who unknowingly is doing what comes so naturally to him, pursuing difference-in-unity and unity-in-difference in his mastery of set forms, all the time doing full justice to God and nature. This is such a Catholic response, and clearly Mackay Brown does as Newman articulated: 'he treats all subjects of literature as how a Catholic would treat them, and only could treat them'.[13]

The Stations of the Cross is a Catholic sacramental practice that has its origins in fourth-century Jerusalem. Pilgrims flocked to the Holy

Land and the Church of the Holy Sepulchre (built in 335). Egeria, a woman from Gaul, kept a diary as she joined Christians from all parts of the Roman world walking westward on Holy Thursday from the Garden of Gethsemane to the Church of the Holy Sepulchre, where they celebrated Jesus' death and resurrection. Christian pilgrims brought back to Europe (and Orkney) their memories of the liturgies, devotions and shrines they experienced. Soon churches and shrines were being built throughout Europe (and Orkney[14]) modelled on the pilgrim sites, and Jerusalem's devotions and liturgies permeated the liturgical and religious life of Christians throughout Christendom. The fourteen stations of the *Via Crucis* in Jerusalem line the walls of every Catholic Church, as seen in Kirkwall's Church of Our Lady and St Joseph and the Italian Chapel, both regular places of worship for parishioner Mackay Brown. Each station is a halting place that follows a key event in the life of Christ in an ordered array of images. Each station is accompanied by a meditation and set prayers.

Reproduced below from *An Orkney Tapestry* is Mackay Brown's Jerusalem Stations, where he writes his own meditations so incisively. The influence on his writing of Catholic liturgy and especially the set form of litany is powerfully distinctive. He is very comfortable working in this genre. Mackay Brown is not a liturgist creating a form of the Stations to be used as a private devotion. Ian Ker, biographer of Newman, makes the point that 'the quality of brevity ... its abrupt, rapid heavy monosyllabic rhythm' created a 'vehicle of prayer that was totally accessible' and 'could express the devotion of a community engaged in a common act of worship', free of social distinctions.[15] Furthermore, Ker makes the point that G. K. Chesterton had observed that English Catholicism had since the suppression of the Reformation, when the English language was 'at the moment when our modern language was being finally made', had to find means of expression in foreign languages.[16] Mackay Brown works in the Stations to bring back into the English language, that he has chosen to write in, set form and a restoration of the lexicon, a hybrid of Latin, Orcadian, Norse and Scottish vocabulary. In doing so his reading of history and spirituality is a contemplative one. All the tensions of history and language are woven into the set form, holding together unity-in-difference and difference-in-unity.

The Jerusalem Stations of the Cross

Earl and Bishop and captains rode on hired horses to Jerusalem. In the Church of the Holy Sepulchre they went slowly along the fourteen painted Stations of the Cross, following Christ—the one painful broken death-going that redeems the multitudinous trespasses of mankind, lost in the huge waste between Eden and Paradise.

They were sailors. They saw the Via Crucis in terms of a ship on the sea. The whole world was a vessel voyaging through space and time, both free and fated, and Christ the Hero a captain-captive.

I JESUS IS CONDEMNED   The young Hero steps on board the ship. The death voyage begins. Soldiers stand all about him, a steel vigil.

(The Norsemen knelt. They said the Pater Noster. They said the Ave Maria. They said the Gloria. They rose to their feet.)

II JESUS IS MADE TO BEAR HIS CROSS   A sail goes up with a cross on it (as if this ship were to be stroked out, cancelled). Beyond the headland, a wind strikes the death ship. The Hero stands at the helm.

(Pater Noster. Ave Maria. Gloria.)

III JESUS FALLS FOR THE FIRST TIME   Darkness. The gale tears the helm from the Hero's fist. The death ship rolls among the waves. The soldiers drag the Hero to his feet.

(Pater Noster. Ave Maria. Gloria.)

IV JESUS MEETS HIS MOTHER   The darkness is riven. A planet, Star of the Sea, lights the Hero's path for an hour, an illumination piercing and pure.

(Pater Noster. Ave Maria. Gloria.)

V SIMON HELPS JESUS TO CARRY HIS CROSS   A man from the rowing benches, with thick shoulders, takes the helm from the storm-broached Hero, at behest of the soldiers.

(Pater Noster. Ave Maria. Gloria.)

VI VERONICA WIPES THE FACE OF JESUS   They shelter in a bay. The Hero steps ashore. A croft girl wipes sweat and salt and blood—a mask of carnage—from the Hero's face, most tenderly, with a new cloth from the loom.

(Pater Noster. Ave Maria. Gloria.)

VII JESUS FALLS FOR THE SECOND TIME   The ship clears the headland. The Hero navigates. Terrible the storm about the helm—about faltering Hero and fallen Hero and Hero flung to his feet once more.

(Pater Noster. Ave Maria. Gloria.)

VIII JESUS SPEAKS TO THE DAUGHTERS OF JERUSALEM At the shore of the Island of Women, much lamentation (and ever will be) for fisherman and sailor, for sea loss and stark shapes in the sand, and especially for this death-bound skipper, the Hero (it had been promised them) that would rescue their island from the Dragon of hunger and loss.

(Pater Noster. Ave Maria. Gloria.)

IX JESUS FALLS FOR THE THIRD TIME   The Hero has fallen on deck a third time. No hero rises. Blood-and-Salt-and-Thorns is dragged to its feet by the soldiers.

(Pater Noster. Ave Maria. Gloria.)

X JESUS IS STRIPPED OF HIS GARMENTS   And Nakedness is thrust at the helm. There is no shame or mockery they will not put on him, the soldiers. They have made him, in that Dragon-wake, barer than beast. Red from lash and seaweed, the Hero flings from a sudden rasp of rock!

(Pater Noster. Ave Maria. Gloria.)

XI JESUS IS NAILED TO THE CROSS   The ship is broken under the Hero. The waters of the end are all about him.

(Pater Noster. Ave Maria. Gloria.)

XII JESUS DIES ON THE CROSS   The waters come in even unto his soul. Salt blocks the throat.

(Pater Noster. Ave Maria. Gloria.)

XIII JESUS IS TAKEN DOWN FROM THE CROSS   The Hero is cast ashore on the Island of women. Three dark shawls at the rock, after sunset. A heavy shadow lifted from a wash and glim of surf. A loud gull cry. And the face of the woman who holds the Hero bright as a star.

(Pater Noster. Ave Maria. Gloria.)

XIV JESUS IS PLACED IN THE SEPULCHRE   Fishermen lower the

Hero into his shore grave. From shore to shore of the world the Dragon walks. The voyage is over.

(Pater Noster. Ave Maria. Gloria.)

Fourteen pictures along three walls; but for their genuflections, one might think they were visitors in a gallery looking at art. They are not looking at anything; they are looking into the fourteen mirrors that show God's love of men, and men's answer to God—not static pictures, but a moving glimmer and brilliance and darkness; time and space reflected infinitely in every direction; the very Face that brooded on chaos among, now, their own proud lascivious cruel greedy faces. In those fourteen mirrors they glimpse themselves. The image changes from water to fire. Rognvald, Erling, John Peterson, Aslak, Solmund, Audun strut, a moving hedge of steel, under the torment of sun, along the Jerusalem—Golgotha road. They are bearers of the lash, the parchment, the dice, the thorns, the nails, the hammer, the lance. On they clash. In the forge of his passion The Word will transform these terrible instruments into a chalice, and, of his endless courtesy, give it back to them. On they clash, and on, into the red-dappled smithy.

The pain of the mirror has flung the pilgrims down fourteen times. They are long in rising from the Station of the Tomb. They have repented a sin or two, many times, in confessional and bed-closet; now, here, at last, forever, they will passionately that their whole cruel history—its symbol the dragon-headed Viking longship—might be drowned and buried with the dead Christ. They cross themselves. They rise with difficulty from the fourteenth station. They turn. The open door of the church is before them, a silver murmuring arch: the unresolved fifteenth station. They leave the church, they are gathered into the life of the streets and the seafront; all the viciousness, vanity, lust, that have been and will be again. But on behalf of a whole people they have confessed, they have been shriven, they have done their penance, a dove out of the storm has fallen on them. They move through the door—the fifteenth mirror, where all is glimpsed darkly—into (for however long) the light of grace; towards another keel, new masts, a more perfect voyage.[17]

The Rackwick Stations of the Cross: From Stone to Thorn[18]

In 1983 Mackay Brown wrote: 'Those fourteen couplets condense everything I wanted or want, or will ever conceivably want to say'.[19]

The mason made stations of the Cross for the chapel, putting blue and red clay and egg-yolk among the shallow scratchings of fourteen stones, so the passion of Christ along the three walls of the church was like the year-long labour of a crofter from furrow to loaf-and-ale. The cross a ploughshare; Veronica a croft girl risen in pity from her spinning wheel; lance and sword the harvest sickles; the flagellating flails, the grinding millstones and black oxen of execution; the last stone, tabernacle of birth and death and resurrection—from it issues for ever the Bread of Heaven.[20]

At first glance this liturgical poem follows the Catholic sacramental ceremony of the Stations but with an Orkney twist of symbols. Yet the ideas of the farmer with his croft and plough and cornstalk ritualised into a Catholic vision[21] depend for their success on more than 'mystery, beauty and the supernatural'.[22] Such a condensation by Mackay Brown is first and foremost doctrinal. The symbols and ideas are mysterious and beautiful as they transcend domestic detail and contrivance and hold within themselves faith-and-reasoned doctrines axiomatic to Catholicism. But Mackay Brown is not a theologian. As poet he is in a pre-theological space, holding all the tensions symbolically in his taut liturgical set form to enrapture the reader in the interpenetration of Rackwick and the life of Christ.

> *Condemnation*
> The winter jar of honey and grain
> Is a Lenten urn

Condemnation is personal and communal in the seasoned 'winter jar' and 'Lenten urn'. The forgoing of 'honey and grain' is the Lenten fast directed towards the 'urn' of ashes and death. The turning away from self to acknowledge one's death in the death of Christ forsakes the simple and primal pleasures of ale. There is a richness in the paradox of the 'kenning': in nothing is everything, in emptiness is fullness, in pain is pleasure.

> *Cross*
> Lord, its time. Take our yoke
> And sunwards turn.

To take the Cross as the yoke and turn to the sun is the discipleship of the parable of the sower. The yoke for the Kingdom is the biblical bonding that is the active participation in the great truths of Christianity. The suffusion of suffering is the labour of love that sets up the sacrifice. The 'time' is now with its sense of urgent immediacy. The servitude of the farmer at his plough is the servitude of the disciple with the Cross. The working together bonds the disciple to his master in a Kingdom bond, an intimate communion, a spiritual marriage. The 'turn''sunwards' elicits the new life and hope as the imagery of mill and grindstones crush and turn towards the Light. This is the Lord's call to his disciples as in Matthew 11:25–30: 'Come to me all who are weary and carrying heavy burdens, and I will give you rest. Take my yoke upon you, and learn from me; for I am gentle and humble in heart, and you will find rest for your souls.' This is the historical embryo of all later Christianity.

> *First Fall*
> To drudge in furrows till you drop
> Is to be born.

The 'First Fall' of Adam and Eve and their original sin (which is ours too) captures the biblical toil and trouble: 'to drudge in furrows till you drop'. The furrows are where the Sower will cast his seeds, his Word. The unrelenting pressure of suffering in life and especially work 'till you drop' brings us to our falling. These falls, this is the First, are necessary for the Kingdom and the final fall will be our death 'Is to be born'. Eternity is the outcome, the reason of all reasons, the love of all loves. Suffering and punishment will never have the last word.

> *Mother of God*
> Out of the mild mothering hill
> And the chaste burn.

In a subtle and significant alternation of man/woman, Mackay Brown works his couplets to encompass the feminine in the divine plan in keeping with the original patterns of Catholic teaching about Mary, Mother of God. Mary emerges from 'the mothering hill' to make human trials fruitful. Her 'mildness' invokes her mediation on our behalf. The strong sense of work equals difficulty equals discipleship-in-the making 'mothers' us forward out of the 'hill' of 'furrows' and the 'burn' purifies with its waters of baptism for the Kingdom. To be chaste is to be full of faith. Redemption is well underway, mediated by Mary, Mother of God. The mediation of 'mothering' is a creative midwifery and birthing. The 'hill' of 'furrows' is earthy, prominent, stable and a foundation that redemptively slopes towards the start and finish of salvation. To say 'Mary' is really saying 'Jesus'.

> *Simon*
> God-begun, the barley rack
> By man is borne.

The couplet alternation continues with Simon (of Cyrene) taking up the 'barley-rack', the Cross in the kenning and sprung rhythm of 'God-begun'. The assertive initiative taken by Simon in helping Jesus to carry the Cross is a free choice to take up the Cross all must carry to be 'begun in God'. The 'barley rack' works on a number of levels: the harvest mechanism to stretch and shake violently to separate the grain from the chaff for the new life to begin, to be begun in God. The barley grains will become whiskey and ale, distilled stage by stage. The Cross as instrument of torture encompasses the suffering of all and distilling stage by stage 'is borne' for the Kingdom.

> *Veronica*
> Foldings of women. Your harrow sweat
> Darkens her yarn.

From assertive to passive, Veronica, woman, moves pliant, bent, kneeling, able to be plied. 'Foldings of women', speak to an embrace, a hidden gentleness and deeply embedded humility upon which the 'harrow sweat' of the Messiah stains and textures the 'yarn' or veil.[23] The 'harrow' works the imagery of the parable of sower as the heavy frame with iron teeth is dragged over ploughed land to break up the clods of earth, to remove the weeds that cover the seeds. This is the 'work' of discipleship for the Kingdom. Veronica is all women and her 'yarn' the spinning thread of the narrative which is the Christian discourse.

Veronica emerges from the oral tradition of Catholicism, wherein are found various legends derived from early memories of the sixth station on the Via Dolorosa in Jerusalem, marking the site of her home, from where she came forward with a linen cloth in her hands to wipe the dust and blood off Jesus's face. Tradition has it that she was the nameless woman who had a bleeding disease for twelve years and who had been cured by touching the fringe of Jesus's garment while he was being thronged by the multitudes at Capernaum. In gratitude, she followed Jesus afterwards, wherever he went. As she wiped Jesus's forehead, the image of his face became imprinted upon the cloth. News of this phenomenon allegedly spread all the way to Rome, where the emperor Tiberias summoned her. Legend has it that just by looking at the image of Jesus's face upon the linen cloth, Tiberias was cured of his affliction. Thereafter, the handkerchief acquired the name, the 'Veronica', i.e. the true image (*vera icona*). Mackay Brown had many 'Veronicas' in his life.

> *Second Fall*
> Sower-and-Seed, one flesh, you fling
> From stone to thorn.

The 'Second Fall' captures the repetitiveness of capacity of human falls from grace, we keep falling and falling. The 'Sower-and Seed' gives us redemptive hope, always falling but enabled to find the new Kingdom life in the 'one flesh' and 'fling' the wild whirling dance full of vigour and energy and the force of divine intentions. 'One flesh' pulls the Genesis Yahwist Creation narrative and its intense nuptial communion of man and woman into the frame of the parable, twisted and reconfigured into the Orkney microcosm. 'Stone' and 'thorn' are at work to constantly break down and promote the new growth for the Kingdom. Stones will grind the grain and thorns will be woven into the Crown.

> *Women of Jerusalem*
> You are bound for the Kingdom of Death. The enfolded
> Women mourn.

The 'one flesh' union moves ceremoniously on to the 'Women of Jerusalem' as they accompany Jesus to His death; they are bound (bonded and directed) to their own deaths. 'Enfolded' by God, their journey is one of prayer, as they mourn. The sense here is steeped in biblical and psalmist resonances: 'I will conceal you with his wings' (Psalm 90 (91)). The depth of sorrow here is palpable; it is intensely personal but rises through the universality of experience. Mackay Brown moves prismatically to assert and claim the spiritual Kingdom, the other face of Jesus's parable.

Third Fall
Scythes are sharpened to bring you down,
King Barleycorn.

The 'Third Fall' intensifies the malevolence of the world depicted as the long curved blades of 'Scythes' swinging over the ground for the reaping. As the barley falls, so do we, the sharp blades working the death ceremony with a well-defined and clean-cut severity. There is no ambiguity here. The King of all grains, Barleycorn, Christ, is down. This consistent imagery is threaded with the symbolism of whisky. As Jesus turned water into wine, barley becomes whisky, a golden liquid holding the secrets of the earth. Mackay Brown's love affair with alcohol has an esoteric dimension, a ritualistic imbibing with religious overtones.

The Stripping
Flails creak. Golden coat
From kernel is torn.

King Barleycorn is stripped of clothing, 'the flails creak', a whipping becomes a stripping of barley and body and soul. The 'golden coat', the seamless garment, 'from kernel is torn'. The threshing of the stalk and grain beats and brings in the barley harvest. The 'kernel', the softer part within the whole grain, the nucleus, the essential part is pulled violently and forcefully. All the reader's senses are engaged. The touch, taste, sound, smell and sight working the imagery towards the symbol of Catholicism, the seamless garment.

Crucifixion
The fruitful stones thunder around,
Quern on quern.

From the Crucifixion climactically steps out the Atonement. From the grinding 'stones' comes the 'fruit' for the nourishment of others, the disciples. Christ's body is broken, ground on the Cross. Grain becomes flour becomes bread becomes Body. The 'thunder' of the millstones circling death 'quern on quern' are against the silence of existence. Crushed, clashing, grinding, round and round. Reconciliation of God and humankind is being accomplished through the passion of Christ. Making amends, atoning for is contained in the sacrificial death of Christ. This Christ-Station is cosmic as Christ reconciles the world to himself. Anthropological and cosmic dimensions work inseparably towards the Resurrection.

> *Death*
> The last black hunger rages through you
> With hook and horn.

At last death comes: 'the last black hunger rages through you'. The externalisation of the imagery takes an inward turn of pain in the last impulse of life, the tension between soul and body. Prodded and poked, pushed and trampled, gored in an overwhelming consciousness of pain. The starkness is complete that encompasses the sacrifice that atones for sin.

> *Pieta*
> Mother, fold him from these furrows,
> Your broken bairn.

Then this furrowed pain embraced in the foldings of the Pieta, Our Lady of Pity, Mother. Mary receives 'her broken bairn'. Mary is Mother of God but also all mothers as asserted for the women of Jerusalem. The child, all children. From those furrows, the ploughed trenches of death, the foldings draw new life in their press of pliant creases, the enfolding of prayer.

> *Sepulchre*
> Shepherd, angel, king are kneeling, look,
> In the door of the barn.

The Sepulchre, the tomb cut in rock, the burial cave and the reader is back to the tenderness and hope of the Incarnation. It is 'Always Christmas' for Mackay Brown with shepherd, angel and king kneeling, looking in the door of the barn. The Church of the Holy Sepulchre in Jerusalem, which Mackay Brown only visited in his dreams, is the Holy Barn, where the seed is stored. The Church is such a Barn. The reader is complicit and a partner in this Passion with all its dramatic tragedy but the tenderness and hope of the Incarnation (the Word made flesh) bears the distinctively Orcadian Mackay Brown signature.

These two sets of 'Stations of the Cross', as intensely contemplative as they are poetic, evidence the robustness of Mackay Brown's craft and situate him in 'Grant that I may carry within me the death of Christ, make me a partner in his Passion, let me relive his wounds.'[24] The medieval mind-set is enough to give him the confidence and literary drive to go into the novel genre, to expand into a comprehensive reading of Orkney in which *Magnus* and then *Vinland* takes him into 'a great company of minds and hearts … set on a quest for the ultimate meaning of things.'[25] Or is Mackay Brown taking an Orkney poetics into this great company, this deep reality below and above the mere appearances of a many-layered Orkney? He is adept at a bi-directional katalogical perspective that holds all the tensions within its grasp.

Notes

[1]   Stabat Mater. Cited in Eamon Duffy, *The Stripping of the Altars*. London: Yale University Press, 1992, p. 259 (a liturgical fragment from *Analecta Hymnica Medii Aevi*).

[2]   George Mackay Brown, 'Man into Oak. A Prose Poem', June 1946. Orkney Archive, Ernest Walker Marwick Collection, D31/30/2.

[3]   George Mackay Brown, letters to Ernest Marwick, May, October 1946. Orkney Archive, Ernest Walker Marwick Collection, D31/30/4.

[4]   *Ibid.*

[5]   Marwick, 'Profile of George Mackay Brown', 1965, p. 6. Orkney Archive, Ernest Walker Marwick Collection, D31/30/4.

[6]   *Ibid.*

[7]   George Mackay Brown, June 1946. Orkney Archive, George Mackay Brown Collection, D31/30/2.

[8]   Mackay Brown, *Magnus*, p. 65.

[9]   Mackay Brown, 'The Poet Speaks'.

[10]   George Mackay Brown, *Vinland*. Edinburgh: Polygon, 2005, p. 254.

[11]   Hans Urs von Balthasar, *Theo-Logic. II: Truth of God*. San Francisco: Ignatius Press, 2004, p 169, 173–218.

[12]   Michelle M. Schumacher, *A Trinitarian Anthropology. Adrienne von Speyr and Hans Urs von Balthasar in Dialogue with Thomas Aquinas*. Washington, DC: Catholic University of America Press, 2014, pp. 30–1.

[13]   Newman, 'English Catholic Literature', p. 179.

[14] Orphir round church was built in the late eleventh or early twelfth century, reputedly by Earl Hakon. Dedicated to St Nicholas, its design was inspired by the Church of the Holy Sepulchre in Jerusalem.

[15] Ian Ker, *The Catholic Revival in English Literature, 1845–1961*. Leominster: Gracewing, 2003, p. 38.

[16] *Ibid.*

[17] Mackay Brown, *An Orkney Tapestry*, pp. 118–21.

[18] *Ibid.*, pp. 31–3, also in Mackay Brown, *The Collected Poems*, pp. 178–9.

[19] Held in Edinburgh University Library, Special Collections, George Mackay Brown, MS 2846.1.

[20] Mackay Brown, *An Orkney Tapestry*, p. 30.

[21] Sabine Schmid, *Keeping the Sources Pure. The Making of George Mackay Brown*. Bern: Peter Lang, 2003, p. 99.

[22] *Ibid.*

[23] A Dégert, 'St. Veronica', in *The Catholic Encyclopedia*. New York: Robert Appleton Company. from New Advent: http://www.newadvent.org/cathen/15362a.htm.

[24] Stabat Mater, cited in Duffy, *The Stripping of the Altars*.

[25] Mackay Brown, *Vinland*, p. 211.

✙ 4 ✙

The Eucharistic Jesus

Is God to blame for all this suffering? What an empty question! Look at the agony on this crucifix I have round my neck. This crucifix is the forge, and the threshing-floor, and the shed of net-makers, where God and man work out together a plan of utter necessity and of unimaginable beauty.[1]

Magnus

St Magnus was a defining influence on Mackay Brown. His life was framed by St Magnus. Daily it gave him strength and purpose. Not only did the historical strata of the martyrdom of St Magnus resolve the political complexities of an Orkney power struggle it also resolved the emotional turmoil and psychological struggle of Mackay Brown's inner world. His subjectivities twisted and turned in the early prose poems, found sanity in the set forms and orthodoxy of Catholicism and emerged to explore questions of identity. As the identity of Orkney, Magnus led Mackay Brown to the truth of himself:

> At first William, Bishop of Orkney, disapproved of such vulgar credu-
> lity, but later his eyes were opened—literally and metaphorically—to
> the presence of something rare and strange and new in the life of the
> islands; a sweetness and light unknown before'.[2]

How could the murder of one man bring peace and stability to his-
torical tensions? On the face of it how could this medieval saint bring Mackay Brown to such literary and spiritual maturity? The 'presence of something rare and strange and new in the life of the islands' was more than enough for the Mackay Brown soul to find himself in.

The fragilities of his personality found the demands of worldly relationships impossible to deal with, other than passively, and not always

to his benefit. On one level his passivity was very vulnerable, on another that same passivity was drawn to go through a narrow door, to the 'sweetness and light unknown before'. Initially, the figure of Christ was his direct target but it was Magnus that interceded on his behalf (as saints do) and spirit-guided the way for his soul and its growth in medieval eucharistic piety.

'Without the violent beauty of those happenings eight and a half centuries ago, my writing would have been quite different. (I was almost going to say, it would not have existed.)'[3] He may well have 'latched on to other themes'[4] but not been able to penetrate the depths and breadths of the Magnus face of Christ. This was the true Mackay Brown path that was able to weave together all the discordances of existence—then, now, and to come—into the 'seamless garment'. *Magnus* was able to give full power to the 'eucharistic' novel in the style and manner von Balthasar had asserted. There is no theological commentary here by Mackay Brown but an authentic quest to express the glory of revelation, of the Lord, passed on to the laity. As poets and artists, these laymen have perceptions that 'the run-of-the-mill clergy'[5] do not.

Mackay Brown definitively accords to Magnus, especially after his death and through the power of his relics, an authentic religious power. Medieval Christianity understood a basic assumption of the pagan world that the sacred breaks through the profanity of the mundane. Mackay Brown, nurtured in the Orkney of pagan and Christian phenomena, came, through Magnus, to understand the saint's particular manifestation of sacred power as a convincing proof of the triumph of Christ over the demonic. Bede records in his *Ecclesiastical History of the English People* that Pope Gregory the Great instructed the missionary Mellitus to build Christian shrines over pagan temples as an apologetic tool to show the pagans of Britain that the relics of the saints overcome the power of the pagan deities.[6] This was a common assumption of the Church. The conflation of the sacred and the profane was not an antiquarian curiosity for Mackay Brown, well versed in Bede and the influence of the Northumbrian Church on early Christianity in Orkney. The Gospel fidelity of Magnus in his age and time was re-opened by Mackay Brown, who achieved what the historian and hagiographers could not and cannot do and imaginatively reinstated his authenticity into the collective memory and tradition of Orkney. The novel *Magnus* draws out Catholicism from the suppressive stereotypes imposed at the Reformation, as Mackay Brown contemplatively enters into an intimacy with the saint himself.

Pre-theology, through symbols, maps out clear directions in *Magnus*. At its centre is the Eucharist, not as doctrine or dogma, but as the eucharistic Jesus. The charism of unity, the Eucharist, is the strong anchor that 'makes' the Church. To the spirituality of communion Mackay Brown gives full allegiance, and it is centred here on the eucharistic Jesus and its realisation in his Passion, death and Resurrection. The beheading, the blood-soaked sacrifice of Magnus, is the core of the Mackay Brown's writings; without this it would have become reduced to mere human, psychological and sociological threads in an imaginative interpretation of history. Magnus was a symbol, the 'jewel' who was spiritual guide to Mackay Brown, who found such liberation in him:

> …a jewel enduring and flaming throughout history. Therefore all our little journeys and fights and suppers that seem so futile once they are over, are drenched with the symbol, and retain a richness they never had while they were being experienced. Men handle the jewel and know themselves enriched. But the symbol remains an abstraction. The sacrament deals with the actual sensuous world—it uses earth, air, water, fire for its celebrations, and it invests the creatures who move about these elements with an incalculable worth and dignity.[7]

Herein is the eucharistic Jesus, embraced in an Orkney Eucharist that has all the hallmarks of the Eucharist of the medieval period. This is a time of transition as the thought forms of the ancient world give way to the rising influences of the Middle Ages. Platonic thought forms gradually gave way to Aristotelian ones and the sacramental synthesis of the Fathers. This period had continued the Gospel fidelity, using sign and symbols as Jesus had done. Symbolism is realist and ontological. Signs signify what they symbolise by participating in the reality itself. Medieval piety moved towards an emphasis on the historical Christ and away from the emphasis of the patristic heavenly Christ. Mackay Brown, 'drenched' in the 'jewel' Magnus, explores the human emphasis of both Magnus and Christ. Mackay Brown is a silent spectator and is very comfortable as such. Yet there is so much going on in the inner life of his devotion, so marked by a medieval style of piety. He relives the Magnus events and, in so doing, the Christ events. This existential penetration of Magnus is not as a series of Stations, but in the cosmic drama of the Eucharist. The eucharistic Jesus is bringing Mackay Brown into the medieval world, re-opened by his intercessor Magnus, and into a contemplation and mysticism that was natural to him.

In *Magnus* Mackay Brown writes at length (thirteen pages) on the Catholic Mass and its classic medieval eucharistic theology. In the heart of the novel, in the chapter 'The Killing', he does not preach at his readers (Mackay Brown is never the preacher). He is well able to put all the theology and philosophy into these pages in his literary and pre-theological arrangement of sign and symbols. The 'sun touched the hills of Rousay in the west ... the kirkyard's stones ... caught in a net of shadows ... the little crofts begot black bulwarks of darkness'.[8] These images participate in their actual reality. This is an iconic Orkney scene. It is no fantasy. The kirk, priest and the threads of liturgy of the Word in the Tridentine Latin Mass move directly to the messianic banquet, the 'marriage feast' and the 'wedding garment'. The 'Everyman' emphasis on the human Magnus is interchangeable with the human Jesus in a Gethsemane abandonment. Medieval thought forms are to the fore, and Mackay Brown works originally from the garment to 'the slow cold formal dance' of the Latin liturgy at the altar, the exchange of gifts bringing man and God, the human and the divine together, and the world of human work to a cosmic harvest time. The Eucharist is 'giving thanks' for the Body and the Blood; 'the divine essences, and the mouths that will taste it will shine for a moment with the knowledge of God'. The Word will still stand 'before the fires of creation ... inviolate among the ashes of the world's end'. The Mass, 'time's purest essence', both in and outside time concentrates 'complex events into ritual words and movement of a half-hour'.

Mackay Brown's craft of the symbolic narrative is steeped in the biblical world with its transition from the ancient world's thought forms through Catholicism. His heraldry in *Magnus* depicts the Church as the seamless garment gathered up from the body of Jesus (John 19:23: 'they also took his tunic; Now that tunic was seamless, woven in one piece from the top'), taken down from the Cross, its weave 'eternal, seamless, incorrupt'.[9] The Church is a 'heraldic garment'.[10] The 'very ancient rune-scrawled heraldry of Scandinavia'[11] is woven into the seamless garment, reinterpreting the fate of the 'fate-ridden tribes of the north', documented as they are in the sagas. Sacrificial altars are now those of Christ, where a priesthood stands and history is seen across a broken tomb, the Easter mysteries alpha and omega, beginning and end and within which is found renewal.[12] These may be the words of Bishop William and axiomatic to the novel and to Catholicism, but they are also axiomatic to Mackay Brown's interpretation of St Magnus and to his personal faith. The Mackay Brown signature, his easy interchange from the material to the spiritual, from the earthy reality and its higher transcendent reality is put to the reader in a dream-like allegory. This easy interchange is between this world and the next to the point where there are no seams or boundaries.

It can be confusing for readers if they are not able to 'shift' within the philosophy of the narrative. A Platonic thought form giving emphasis to the transcendent spiritual reality of an unseen world conflates with an Aristotelian emphasis on the material concreteness of the seen world. Mackay Brown writes according to medieval thought forms and rejects 'The body–spirit dichotomy, or the body–intellect dichotomy, ... a bitter prideful cleaving of the wholeness of man's nature. Earth and man and sun and bread are one substance; they are made out of the original breath-smitten dust.'[13] Dualistic separations are faithfully rewoven into his study of Magnus, surrounded by the 'keeper of the loom',[14] his weaving imagery consistently turning our defiant perceptions toward the unseen world where 'prayers ... right actions, blessings, holy observances, penances, pilgrimages ... will be woven into the immaculate garment'.[15] This is the Christian paradox modelled for us by Jesus, parable by parable, miracle by miracle, patiently teaching the opposite of what we have been led to believe is the norm. Jesus patiently teaches us to look at things differently, how they really are. Jesus through Magnus through Mackay Brown is raising reasoned questions about what is real. What things have existence? What is a thing and can we sort them into categories? What does it mean to have being? And much more. It is the mystery of the eucharistic Jesus that holds the key to existence.

Magnus makes the case for a sanctified world, mantled in his heraldic garment, his Joseph coat, with worldly tensions held in the 'force' of the crucifix forge wherein he finds his coat of peace, and his virginity is his 'hard immortal diamond'.[16] Mackay Brown is in keeping with a nuptial appreciation of the body in its maleness and femaleness, and he explores their unity-in-difference, difference-in-unity. He is in tune and harmony with twentieth-century theological understandings as they too went deep to revisit the primal sources. But this is not theology, it is the pre-theological Mackay Brown, giving voice to the purposefulness of procreative sexual acts or choices not to act, so contentious and unfashionable in the contemporary world. Mackay Brown's precise choice to use Gerard Manley Hopkins's 'immortal diamond' where 'Flesh fade, and mortal trash / Fall to the residuary worm;'[17] to attribute to Magnus's virginal body that it will be 'at one what Christ is'.[18] Mackay Brown deeply sensed the truth of the virginal body, the ensouled-Magnus-body is Christ-bodied, as martyr, is over and above his own sexual dilemmas. He knew that his writing demanded his all and any syphoning off of energies in sexual relationships seriously depleted his inner resources to accomplish what he had discovered as his path and Way. He has been accused of being obsessively puritanical about sexual matters especially in later life when he redrafted texts to take out what some would interpret as giving an emphasis to a lusty salaciousness.[19] I think this is wide of the mark. From my earliest conversations with him (from 1976) he was very conscious of how easy it was to write according to the appetites of the audience. This was very much a conscience issue. He felt morally bound to separate himself from such literary tastes. He was not that kind of writer and I would say he definitely thought such practise on his part would be deeply sinful. His conscience was sharp and incisive in such matters.

The ultimate body is the Resurrection Body which for now is the eucharistic Body. It is the Eucharist in a 'Ritual half-hour' that brings the eucharistic Jesus from the 'Whole web of time' where the 'Whole web of history trembled' with its distinctive 'Recurrence of pattern-within-flux'. The Messianic Banquet takes to its heart the 'Actions of Everyman, once the bread of divine wisdom is in his body' and is able to 'Direct his purified will into the future'. In the 'Weaver's workshop' we are clothed in a 'New coat' in 'Round of time'[20] and its 'Subtle weave of imagery'.[21] This Everyman body is the medieval thought form giving emphasis to its humanity and an anthropology that is deeply sensual, marked by original sin, with great capacity for faith and reason within the community enwrapped in a symbolical coat that 'In a mystical way it gives warmth and dignity'.[22] This 'storied garment' is a free will narrative, wherein every aspect of life has place and purpose as 'a creative stitch is put upon the mystical garment'.[23] Axiomatically, the Word stands 'inviolate'[24] 'the end and the beginning'.[25]

> Events are never the same, but they have enough similarity for one to say tentatively that there are constants in human nature, and constants in the human situation, and that men in similar circumstances will behave roughly in the same fashion'.[26]

Mackay Brown is speaking with great clarity about the poet, the artist, the musician, and their relationship to these 'constants'. 'They gather into themselves a huge scattered diversity of experience and reduce them to patterns'. This is the creativity of a reasoned mind working persuasively towards the crafting of symbols: all voyages become The Voyage, all battles The Battle, and all feasts The Feast.[27] These radiant 'jewels', abstract as they are as the reasoning mind abstracts their essence from the actual sensuous world, operate in a sacramental and consecrated world, according to Mackay Brown, because of faith. This is his stance. He has chosen it and explained it. In the Mass, he himself again and again enters into, predominantly in Orkney in the modest little Kirkwall Church and the various locations (including his own house, at the Italian chapel, Mayburn Court, St Mary's in Stromness, Braemar on the outskirts of Stromness, St Magnus Cathedral, the Scout Hall in Kirkwall when the parish Church was being reconfigured). Mackay Brown's inner life is powerfully driven by the Mass and a place where social and class distinctions are shed in the *koinonia* of the Eucharist. This is the sacrament of communion with one another in the One Body of Christ. This is the full meaning of eucharistic *koinonia* in the Catholic Church and was so from the outset. St Thomas Aquinas wrote, 'the Eucharist is the sacrament of the unity of the Church, which results from the fact that many are one in Christ.[28]

The 'Priest raised the Bread of Heaven', 'By the utterance of five words is drenched, interwoven, imbued, possessed, informed with divinity', 'The chalice was elevated', 'The priest mingled the broken bread with the wine, figuring forth Christ's resurrection', 'The priest consumed the Host', 'He set the Precious Blood to his lips', 'Sanctus: the word pulsed like a star in the murk of the nave', 'Laid aside his patched filthy coat of sins', 'Corpus Christi- shone between his lips for a moment. He was part of the feat. He felt secure then, like a guest in a lamp-splashed jubilant castle. Go now and carry the peace of Christ into the world'. Mackay Brown puts into words what every Catholic experiences in the Mass. This is how a Catholic reacts and responds to, 'The cup of blessing which we bless, is it not the communion of the blood of Christ? The bread which we break, is it not the communion of the Body of Christ?' (1 Corinthians 10:16).

The Magnus-martyr narrative and it's understanding of the eucharistic Jesus, textures the ecclesial, seamless garment woven by Mackay Brown from Norse and Christian ideas of Necessity, Fate and God's Will so distinctively and with great spiritual and philosophical confidence. Their threads would be static archaisms if it were not for Mackay Brown's commitment to a Newmanesque release of continuities from a suppressed past. What the Oxford Movement did for Newman's conversion, an Orkney Poetics is empowering Mackay Brown to assimilate the Reformation appetites for Calvinism that he was nurtured in and reinterpret them in a pre-Christian configuration of Fate. Mackay Brown's originality is found in his perceptions of symbols, mystical and ephemeral, never static, always delicately poised stretched across a fulcrum of tension. His time-shifts and discordances only seem so if the reader is enclosed in a one-dimensional world and experience.

Catholic Philosophy

Mackay Brown has a passion for Catholic philosophy and he takes up the big philosophical questions. God's nature, the Trinity, with simultaneous procession of being, from an Eternal Present which such a Divine Being, God, would possess, has a foreknowledge that in no way influences or determines human free will. God 'sees' from an Eternal Present. Mackay Brown explores in *Magnus* how this is so: what do we mean by divine foreknowledge, what is the meaning of Eternity, how can moving in and out of time convince of human free will, that we have free choices in the face of 'Fate', and is this Christian God one who rewards and punishes justly?

His exploration and experimentation is a pre-theological one that makes no doctrinal demands upon the reader, suffused and tranced in the Hopkinsesque inscapes and instresses that 'read' Orkney, its history, its natural world in keeping with the realism inherent in the old religion. This re-opening of an Orcadian medieval Catholicism is refined and threaded with the questions and disputations and proofs of the great philosophers: Boethius, Aquinas, Anselm, Duns Scotus all working and reasoning from the faith position founded on revelation first and foremost.

The Catholic passion for philosophy was no less present in medieval Orkney, as one examines the monastic settlements that have intensively left their archaeological and documental, liturgical remains as evidence. The great religious orders made their presence felt in the islands—the Augustinians, the Franciscans, the Benedictines—linked with Aberdeen, the Northumbrian Church and Rome to give Orkney its place in the universal Church. So what exactly was this philosophical worldview, this mind-set that Mackay Brown found so liberating? *The Orkney Tapestry, Magnus* and its later off-shoot *Vinland* move and breathe, in an ideological committing to that world. The vision, a 'tranced' rapture encapsulated in 'Summer Day', is worked out intensively, implicitly, symbolically throughout the Mackay Brown literary corpus, but most fully and specifically in *The Orkney Tapestry, Magnus* and *Vinland*.

The great questions of Creation and our place in it, a realistic anthropological understanding of the human person, the meaning of history, the questions surrounding whether we have free will or not and to what degree, are keenly explored with an intellectual passion in the medieval Church. Catholicism is critiqued for its passion for philosophy but from the first days of Christendom it carried with it not only the Hebrew but also the Graeco-Roman civilisations and their thought-forms. A marked feature of Catholicism, then and now, is its adeptness at understanding and managing 'change' whilst keeping the constants intact. This feature is deeply embedded in Western philosophy specifically because of Greek civilisation. From Plato and Aristotle the parameters are set, and I include here Hopkins's essay 'The Probable Future of Metaphysics'[29] knowing Mackay Brown's deep immersion in his writings, verse and otherwise.[30] Hopkins puts it neatly:

> The tide we may foresee will always run and turn between idealism and materialism: this is clear from history ... there is a particular refinement, pitch, of thought which catches all the most subtle and

true influences the world has to give: this state or period is the orthodoxy of philosophy.[31]

The philosophical spectrum between the idealism of Plato and the
materialism of Aristotle and all the shades between which at 'different
times like a shifted light give prominence by turns to different things'.[32]

Boethius,[33] emerging from the Neoplatonism in the early days of
Christianity, solves by seminal analogy the questions: what do we mean
by divine foreknowledge, what is the meaning of Eternity, how can
moving in and out of time convince of human free will, that we have free
choices in the face of 'Fate', and is this Christian God one who rewards
and punishes justly? By means of analogy he explores the nature of an
infinite and eternal God. Such a nature understands according to its
own nature (infinite and eternal). Such a nature has no past or future
but only an eternal present. The movement of time is transcended by
a single, simple, unified present. Such a nature has one single vision
as if the infinity of things past and present were occurring in a single
instant. God has a knowledge of an unchanging present. To make the
point clearer (as Mackay Brown has worked out for himself) God's
vision is compared to human vision and to achieve this he uses literary
device to open a door into the transcendent. Through this opening
he connects symbolically with an all-seeing, all-knowing God who
sees all things in an eternal present. Humans contrastingly relate by
the difference of seeing things in a non-eternal present. The constant
comparison by using the analogy of an infinite God compared to finite
humanity is a powerful learning tool to grasp the difference between
being free or not free. Mackay Brown asks the reader in the manner of
the Boethian Neoplatonic device to envisage all the phases of Orkney
history and its artefacts in an Eternal present. In this manner the divine
mind looks down on all things and, without intervening and changing
the nature of things it is viewing. Archaeological artefacts evidence the
contingencies of phenomena that come and go as do their successive
civilisations. One cannot overstate how Orkney is so perceptively and
cognitively challenging because of its rich archaeological heritage so
visible throughout the islands.

Mackay Brown in the manner of Boethius[34] is able to distinguish between *providence* and *fate*. God's governing plan for creation, as it exists

in His own mind is called *providence*, whereas *fate* is God's governing plan as it exists within creation. *Providence* considers God's plan from the perspective of the unity of the divine mind, *fate* considers God's plan from the perspective of the diversity of the physical world. *Providence* is general or universal, *fate* is specific or particular. *Providence* is the divine plan, *fate* is the material outworking of that plan. Mackay Brown's mastery of this insight gives him the calm serenity he finds in the Divine Mind, the Divine Intelligence. By this serenity he can hold the tensions of *fate*, as understood by the pagans, Nordic and otherwise, in the Trinitarian God wherein Divine reason itself is seated in the Supreme Being. His literary time-shifts work out the movement of *fate* in their specificity in time and place within the infinity of *providence*. The martyrdom of Magnus, in a specific time and place, is the operation of his *fate* through which *providence* joins it to the proper order.

Is this the analogy Mackay Brown uses in *Magnus* in particular? He puts on record his philosophical readings in his autobiography. Modestly, Mackay Brown writes:

> Somehow I got hold of a commentary by a Jesuit priest, Fr Coplestone, on Kant's book. The commentary dispelled the sense Germanic fogs. I enjoyed Coplestone … But even now the commentary has faded. The Scottish fascination with philosophy—Kant himself had Scottish ancestors -never rubbed off on me. Hume was incomprehensible too, and boring. The fault is in myself; I have known fine minds who have been enthralled life-long by Hume, and by other philosophers, even the difficult modern ones. The minds of writers work in a different way, in pulsing controlled image sequences, which are no less strict than the workings of music or mathematics or philosophy'.[35]

Mackay Brown has an affinity with Jesuits and their intensive formation, Fr Coplestone included. Sympathetically and with rigour, they are working in the living minds of the Church, Catholicism ancient, but ever new.

Mackay Brown struggled first hand with the problem of evil and being free in the face of suffering. He worked these questions out firsthand, in his own life, and by the time he read about them in outline and simple brushstrokes, rather than have an appetite for a precisely argued rationale, he went his 'way' his 'path' of signs and symbols and the pre-theological of poetical inspiration. The act of 'seeing' can give

Orkney history a reading that is able to conflate its pivot points into an eternal present, a simultaneous procession, a stream of consciousness and at its heart is 'holy fire', that Mackay Brown is tranced by, as evidenced in 'Summer Day'. In the constants and set patterns of Catholicism he found a 'quarry of images' where 'gladly I put my hand to save that day for you'. It is from this 'knowledge' that he devises the 'time-shifts' to keep the reader tuned in to a higher and deeper realism that is never dogmatic or doctrinal in its thrust.

At the Reformation in the sixteenth century the Reformers were driven to 'dehellenise' Christianity and purify it of philosophy. Their principle of *sola scriptura*, on the other hand, sought faith in its pure, primordial form, as originally found in the biblical Word. Mackay Brown not only the master of symbols but is philosopher working in the 'living mind' of medieval Catholicism. One cannot overstate how much he is entirely familiar and adept, and original, in reacting and responding to the questions that preoccupied the medieval Church and indeed the Church today. His creative orthodoxy breathed in the matters of the Free Will ethos of Boethius, Augustine, Aquinas, and Duns Scotus. The conflation of Fate and Calvinism is his own fresh working arrived at symbolically to find a stable resolution to the difficulties and tensions of a theological determinism that Mackay Brown clearly repudiates whilst recognising its developmental place in history both in the Nordic pagan religion and Protestant religion.

> Fate had ruled the lives of the first settlers. The predestination that after centuries of catechism and kirk discourse was now a part of their outlook is only a more sophisticated name for that fate, and certainly one reason why they felt at home with Calvinism, in spite of everything.[36]

In matters of fate Mackay Brown is also immersed through the conduit of Gerard Manley Hopkins the philosophy of Blessed John Duns Scotus, an important thinker in Christian thought. His late thirteenth-century life and stance is one that is enshrined on in the epitaph on his tombstone: 'Scotland bore me, England received me, France taught me, Cologne in Germany holds me'.[37] It was Duns Scotus who gifted to Catholicism the interpretation of the Incarnation wherein every creature, in and through Christ, is called to be perfected in grace and to glorify God for ever. This interpretation led to the dogma that asserts that Mary, Our Lady, is *preserved* from original sin as a consequence of her Son's redemptive passion and death.[38] Furthermore, he brought great attention to the issue of human freedom. Scotus brought a great clarity and insight when he articulated the difference between the perfect will of God and the imperfect human will.[39] This distinction is a critical one when we attempt to compare God to ourselves. The basis of our personhood, our freedom, and our dignity lies in our will and freedom itself is not license to see God, or discount the existence of God, through the human will alone. There is a bi-directional relationship, tense and fraught with doubt that was never accomplished so perfectly in a human being as it was accomplished in Mary.

Duns Scotus developed a point to which modernity is very sensitive. He introduced an approach that emphasised freedom as a fundamental quality of the will. At a later period, this line of thinking turned into a voluntarism, in contrast to the Augustinian and Thomist intellectualism. The Scotist vision did not fall into the extreme positions that came later where freedom is detached from truth. A free act is the result of the concourse of intellect and will, where the will always follows the intellect. Such was Mary's free act at the Annunciation. In the face of revelation through the Angel Gabriel, she listened from a position of faith and reason. Here is concourse or confluence of intellect and will that squares up to doubt and finds the freedom to assent. Mary's consent consequentially leads to the Incarnation. Mary, preserved from original sin, exercises the freedom of difference-in-unity and unity-in-difference where God is revealed Word or Logos. The Scotus vision affirms the love that transcends knowledge, modelled by Mary, the human being open to God, making the most of her feminine disposition to listen to the voice of Divine Revelation. She accepted the word of God and shows how this acceptance brings light and hope.

The Scotist vision is a deep examination of that supernatural *sensus fidei*, of the People of God, who already believed about the Blessed Virgin and expressed in acts of devotion, in the arts and in Christian life in general with the specific contribution of their thought. This supernatural sense of faith is that capacity infused by the Holy Spirit that qualifies the laity, to do as Mary did, to embrace the reality of the faith with humility of heart and mind. In this sense, the People of God is the first teacher. The medieval laity had long had faith both in the Immaculate Conception and in the bodily Assumption of the Virgin, while theology had not yet found the key to interpreting it as doctrine. This supernatural *sensus fidei* is at work in Mackay Brown, his free consent so apparent throughout his writings from their 'callow' beginnings to the mature published works. The written testimony of light and hope came increasingly as his intellect followed his will in spite of personal doubts and dilemmas. His personal investigation of fate and freedom is a literary pre-theological one.

Vinland

The Mackay Brown reading of history is made plain in *Vinland*. The eucharistic cosmic vision of *Magnus* is complemented by an investigation of fate and freedom by means of the 'clear directions' of the chapter headings: Vinland, Norway, Orkney, Ireland, Breckness and Tír na nÓg. Like Newman he gives a positive insight in his attempted synthesis of the historical change and development by articulating the continuities of Orkney's various phases of enculturation. Whether this synthesis comes off is ultimately a matter for the reader to decide but in terms of Orkney's identity a turning point has been achieved. The martyrdom of Magnus is at an understated pivotal tangent to *Vinland* but the driving question for *Vinland* is not the *Magnus* 'how does the Christ-faced atonement of the sacrificial death of Magnus win peace for Orkney in the Eucharist' but the very ancient and modern sensitivity to 'what exactly is the relationship between fate and free will, how is the determinism of fate supplanted by Christian freedom'? What started as a children's story expanded to far-reaching philosophical dimensions: the life of Ranald Sigmundson is a pageant of tensions, attentive to the details of a 'realisation' of medieval life in Orkney and its correlate geographical and historical influences. There is a wonderful wisdom about this novel and a most vibrant peace of mind woven into this synthesis of change and development. It is an Ecclesiastical summation complete with Hebrew and Greek reflections. Mackay Brown contemplatively gives a fully rounded final version of his thinking in old-age. Ranald Sigmundson (or is it Mackay Brown?) gives voice to his reading of Orkney history and his own existential quest.

an Irish monk who had stayed for a while with the brothers at Warbeth had told him the marvellous tale of the voyages of Saint Brandon
who had sailed out to find the Island of the Blessed in the western sea;
and of how in this hut by himself, so that he could solve the riddle of
fate and freedom, and so make preparations for his last voyage upon
the waters of the end.[40]

Mackay Brown takes up his customary interchange of genres and
sources and lexicon. Here the stark bleakness of the Anglo Saxon
wanderer and voyager is blended with Irish mythology and folklore
and the Christianised version of St Brendan, searching for the Tír na
nÓg, one of the names for the Otherworld, the metamorphosis of which
is Heaven. The Orcadian version is a Norse one, as Edwin Muir had
laid out the parameters in his poem *The Voyage* with its configurations
of a deeply rooted ancient world and its unchanging constants which
matched the hellish torments that preoccupied a twentieth-century
trajectory, so familiar to the modern poets such as T. S. Eliot and Dylan Thomas. Mackay Brown found in Muir's parameters the 'key': 'In
1946 his book of poems *The Voyage* appeared. The key had been in my
hands all the time—I read *The Voyage* with delight'.[41]

Mackay Brown takes a fresh tack coming to the philosophical questions to work out for himself the concepts, ideas and arguments that
have confronted him as poet and master of symbols. I do not think
his reading of Orkney history is naïve, uncritical and is certainly not
uninformed. His medieval mindset, his Catholic mind, is not asserting doctrines and dogmas. He is not even a 'Catholic writer' as such,
although on his journey he became a Catholic because this was where
he was led. His mind, his heart and soul are deeply connected with an
ancient past deeply sustaining while he is in the process of returning
to primal sources and patterns as he squares up to the medieval world
from a twentieth-century world.

'Ranald and Peter the abbot talked many times about fate, and evil
and good, and free will'.[42] Ranald is definitely the character he is, but
also the voyager Mackay Brown himself, having discourse with the
abbot. Mackay Brown would have dearly loved to have such discourse
with a Catholic priest himself. He expressed to me in 1995 that there
are times when one really needs to have that baring of the soul and
its questions with a priest but although I think he got some aspects

of that with his Jesuit parish priests, Fr Cairns and Fr Bamber, the priestly philosophical and intellectual stature faded quickly after they had gone. As he had witnessed himself as a small child sitting on his doorstep in Stromness the vibrancy of the characters who were in dialogue with their own imagination and their characters (talking to oneself), he also did the same, and I saw him do it myself, meeting him in the street a week before he died. And of course he says in his autobiography he has many a long conversation with Mrs McKee from *Greenvoe*.[43]

The abbot gives him the means of setting the fresh parameters of the discourse on free will and determinism, Providence and Fate, giving articulation to the transition from Nordic paganism to Christianity. The '... shadow of fate that had hung from—it seemed—the beginning of things upon the minds and actions of the northern peoples ...' where 'Individual men and tribes behave as they do because their history was written down for them from before the beginning,' 'It is in the very marrow of our bones, it is carved deep in our hearts' and 'Bestows a kind of wild freedom'.[44]

Birth and life and death are held within the 'Tight fist of fate' until we 'Go down ... into the invisible dust'. There is an inevitability and determinism which narrowly prescribes 'Other ways of living,' 'But fate has cast us in our parts' and there is 'No use trying to tear ourselves from the web that fate has thrown about us'.[45] The abbot gently gives Ranald insight and understanding into the Aristotelian thought-forms demonstrating the relationship between 'Inevitability—causation—determinism', and the nature of the God who has 'Omnipotence and omniscience'. This is the God who is 'Prime Mover' and 'no different from fate itself'. The God who in his nature is 'Mystery' and 'Beyond the power of the minds to understand'.[46]

This is the God who is the primal source where 'There is freedom', and 'the possibility at every moment of our lives to choose either this or that'. Reason may demonstrate a proof but it is faith that leads to an awareness: 'Man is born aware ... of ... a wild sweet freedom when all seems possible'. The Greek thought-forms, 'No matter what mask he wears, this Everyman ... finds himself, mind and spirit and body'[47] give way to medieval ones seamlessly keeping the lines of continuity but expanding to encompass the Christian world view with a suitable anthropology that quests forward to the humanism of the Renaissance and the Reformation.

It is the inseparability of Faith and Reason so distinctive to Mackay Brown's 'originality'. He writes with characteristic signature:

> The whole of man's life is pervaded by sweetnesses that have no physical or mental source, they touch his mind and heart and spirit even in places of stone and thorn. Often he denies them ... further on, the enchantment touches him again.[48]

The contemplative attitude, attunement and realisation learnt so well from Newman:

> For us contemplatives ... a man can summon it at any time by prayer and meditation ... must beseech for the good of humanity and indeed all of creation. 'Here, on this ground, there seems to be a state beyond the dark operatings of fate, a place of light and peace.[49]

This 'sweetness' and one is conscious of the wild rapture from the youthful religious exuberance of 'Summer Day' in 1947. This 'sweetness' is the mature Mackay Brown, the old-age pensioner, the Orkney poet and sage giving his verdict and answer on the 'big questions' that pushed him hard all his life.

Christian Platonism of the early Church and the conventions of the Pastoral genre woven together encompass the set form, 'This is the House of Life ... Obey the rule of the House, and you will learn acceptance and a kind of peace.'[50] The 'Analogy of the House and garden and wall and gate' compare well to Plato's Cave putting across the idea that the Greek world is a world of darkness and shadows, a world of appearances, but there is another world wherein is the true reality. This works well with the Nordic paganism Mackay Brown is squaring up to through Ranald. But 'The answer is silence.'[51] Mackay Brown so 'at home' in silence, the silent medieval spectator with an inner life that has found the true reality. We remember to how Jesus himself models for us the purposeful use of silence. Mackay Brown has learnt to understate the Christian world view and write in a way that the reader can take it or leave it as an optional extra. He does not mention Jesus directly, he alludes to him, his life and his teachings suggestively in the delicate touch of his signs and symbols. He learnt first-hand in Reformation Orkney:

Sometimes as he grows older, the man mentions the garden to this or that one or that that he thinks might be interested. Mostly, they give him cold looks, but now and then a face smiles, transfigured for a moment before the old shadows of getting and spending fall again, the adamantine duties of the House ... Our lives are full to overflowing ... and yet since his visit to the garden man can tell by the deadness in the eye or in the voice ... they are deceiving themselves ... wistfulness in their boasting as if they know that their 'good things' are but a shadow of a more perdurable hoard.[52]

And for himself he knows:

Often the man, all doubts and despondency about the garden after years of sterility, will turn a corner in his daily round, and there, unexpectedly, the unseen fragrances are all about him ... What saves us is the unsullied vision.[53]

The wild beauty of Orkney with its creation story and Gospel narrative is his glory of the Lord as his life matures and makes towards death the 'dark night of the soul' can be hard and unrelenting but when consolation does come and it surely does, all the soul-making-work is more than worth it.

Vinland climaxes with the question that so powerfully turns many away from Christianity: how can such a good God with omnipotence and omniscience allow evil and suffering? The martyrdom of Magnus and its personal and historical tensions makes the argument for the Christian understanding of free will pacing itself between 'Is it possible that such cruelty and ruthlessness can in time to come beget sanctity?'[54] 'With God all things are possible.'[55] The *Vinland* theodicy clearly rejects David Hume's eighteenth-century perspective on the age-old dilemma: Is God willing to prevent evil, but not able? Then God is impotent. Is God able to prevent evil, but is not willing? Then God is malevolent. Is God both willing and able to prevent evil? Then why is their evil in the world?[56]

Mackay Brown is a different kind of philosopher from the Enlightenment kind:

The Scottish fascination with philosophy—Kant himself had Scottish ancestors—never rubbed off on me. Hume was incomprehensible too, and boring. The fault is in myself; I have known fine minds who have been enthralled life-long by Hume, and by other philosophers, even the difficult modern ones. The minds of writers work in a different way, in pulsing controlled image sequences, which are no less strict than the workings of music or mathematics or philosophy'.[57]

Mackay Brown is doing what philosophers do, when clearly he is an original thinker who finds in medieval thought much affinity with Duns Scotus and the Catholic philosophical tradition that flowed through him.

Mackay Brown's 'pulsing controlled image sequences'[58] lead the *Vinland* theodicy through the abbot to explain why God allows evil in the world. Ranald himself through St Magnus follows the classical Catholic trajectory that evil is a privation, evil in itself is not something, it is the absence of good. Evil enters the world when humans and angels sin, when they turn away from the highest good, God. An apparent good, what seems at any given time as a good but is later revealed not to be good, is chosen over a real good which emerges over a longer time period of sacrifice and endurance. Evil is not willed by God. Evil is willed by those who do evil. God permits people to choose evil and permits evil to happen to them. God may even permit people to choose evil ultimately and damn themselves. Freedom and free will are so axiomatic to Christianity and therefore in stark contrast to the exploration of the Nordic paganism of *Vinland*. Ultimately Magnus demonstrates by means of his God-willed martyrdom which is also Magnus-willed. In the face of the social evils in the power struggles in Orkney and further afield at that time with its structures of domination and repression, Magnus brings good from evil just as in Scripture—the Old and New Testaments in unison—evil is not a problem. Evil is seen as part of the divine mysteries and cannot be solved by theodicy or theodicies.

This is the Christian perspective and the resolution of *Vinland*, so deeply personal to Mackay Brown, takes up the Ecclesiastes mantra 'Vanity of vanities, all is vanity ...' The complicity of human society in social evil is repetitive and patterned across history of humanity. The Atonement of Christ in his sacrificial death on the Cross is imitated in the death of Magnus to incarnate Love in the face of the harsh reality of social evil. This atoning sacrificial act reconciles, the price of sin is paid.

The 'Light ... Feeblest of all lights ... The candle that burns all night in a cold cell of this monastery ... But now and then ... a great company of minds and hearts is set on a quest for the ultimate meaning of things, for that goodness and truth and beauty that are at the heart of life ... The world is wrapped in night and sleep. The solitary sits at his candle, and his spirit is abroad on the ocean of God's love.'[59]

Mackay Brown signs off, his conscience having made his peace with 'pulsing controlled image sequences'. He could be accused of 'a God of the gaps' fallacy as his reason falters in the quest of Mystery. But it his faith and his reason which make his narrow path so attractive and compelling. His path is a narrow one, his willed choice. Such narrowness brought him from those days of callow beginnings as evidenced in the 'Man into Oak' to the maturity of much loved novels where he is in 'a great company of minds and hearts ... set on a quest for the ultimate meaning of things.'[60] Voyager Ranald-come-Mackay Brown buried as both are at Warbeth, the site of the monastery he had recreated, knows a thing-or-two:

> the voyages of Saint Brandon who had sailed out to find the Island of the Blessed in the western sea; and of how, at last, he had thought it best to come occasionally and live in this hut by himself, so that he could solve the riddle of fate and freedom, and so make preparations for his last voyage upon the waters of the end.[61]

Mackay Brown at home in Mayburn Court in Stromness was in his cell and hut, where a good life was a creedal one, difficult as it was, in search of the true light, the Light behind the light, the Light that can make the sun and moon and stars, the Light of the world.

Notes

1   Mackay Brown, *Magnus*, p. 65.
2   Mackay Brown, *For the Islands I Sing*, p. 9.
3   *Ibid.*
4   *Ibid.*

[5] von Balthasar, *The Glory of the Lord II*, p. 15.

[6] Bede, *Ecclesiastical History of the English People*, ed. and trans. B. Colgrave and R. A. B. Mynors. Oxford: Clarendon Press, 1969.

[7] Mackay Brown, *Magnus*, p. 130.

[8] *Ibid.*, p. 126.

[9] *Ibid.*, p. 29.

[10] *Ibid.*

[11] *Ibid.*, p. 32.

[12] *Ibid.*, p. 33.

[13] *Ibid.*, p. 130.

[14] *Ibid.*, p. 59.

[15] *Ibid.* 60.

[16] *Ibid.*, p. 63.

[17] Gerard Manley Hopkins, 'That Nature is a Heraclitean Fire and of the Comfort of the Resurrection', in his *Poems and Prose*, ed. W. H. Gardner. London: Penguin, 1971, pp. 65–6.

[18] Mackay Brown, *Magnus*, p. 63.

[19] Fergusson, *George Mackay Brown. The Life*, pp. 281–2.

[20] *Ibid.*

[21] *Ibid.*, p. 131.

[22] *Ibid.*, p. 101.

[23] *Ibid.*, p. 102.

[24] *Ibid.*, p. 128.

[25] *Ibid.*, p. 129.

[26] *Ibid.*

[27] *Ibid.*

[28] St Thomas Aquinas, *Summa Theologica*, Question 73, 'The Sacrament of the Eucharist', Article 3.

[29] Gerard Manley Hopkins, *The Journals and Papers of Gerard Manley Hopkins*, ed. Humphrey House and Graham Story. London: Oxford University Press, 1966, pp. 118–21.

[30] Mackay Brown, *For the Islands I Sing*, pp. 149–58.

[31] Hopkins, *The Journals and Papers*, pp. 118–19.

[32] *Ibid.*, p. 119.

[33] Boethius, *The Consolation of Philosophy*, trans. W. V. Cooper. London: Dent, 1902, Book IV, vi.

[34] The evidence for Mackay Brown's reading of Boethius is in his much-loved book by G. K. Chesterton, *The Wisdom of Catholicism* Anton C. Pegis. London: Michael Joseph, 1950, which includes a chapter on Boethius. See Chapter 1, n. 28.

[35] Mackay Brown, *For the Islands I Sing*, 1997, p. 131.

[36] Mackay Brown, *An Orkney Tapestry*, p. 44.

[37] Pope Benedict XVI, *General Audience* , 7 July 2010. http://w2.vatican.va/content/benedict-xvi/en/audiences/2010/documents/hf_ben-xvi_aud_20100707.html

[38] *Ibid.*

[39] Alexander Broadie, *The Shadow of Scotus. Philosophy and Faith in Pre-Reformation Scotland*. Edinburgh: T&T Clarke, 1995, p. 38.

[40] Mackay Brown, *Vinland*, p. 254.

[41] Mackay Brown, *For the Islands I Sing*, p. 64.

[42] Mackay Brown, *Vinland*, p. 205.

[43] Mackay Brown, *For the Islands I Sing*, p. 177.

[44] Mackay Brown, *Vinland*, p. 205.

[45] *Ibid.*, pp. 205–6.

[46] *Ibid.*, p. 206.

[47] *Ibid.*

[48] *Ibid.*

[49] *Ibid.*, p. 207.

[50] *Ibid.*

[51] *Ibid.*, p. 208.

[52] *Ibid.*

[53] *Ibid.*, p. 209.

[54] *Ibid.*

[55] *Ibid.*

[56] David Hume, *Dialogues concerning Natural Religion*, London, 1779.

[57] Mackay Brown, *For the Islands I Sing*, p. 131.

[58] *Ibid.*

[59] Mackay Brown, *Vinland*, p. 211.

[60] *Ibid.*

[61] *Ibid.*, p. 254.

✝ 5 ✝

The Seamless Garment

They ploughed my back like ploughmen drawing long furrows.
  Psalm 128.

It is impossible to say where the natural perception of God in the
world ceases and the supernatural, Christian perception begins.[1]

Learning to read Orkney is essential to understanding the writings of
George Mackay Brown. He emerges from an Orkney patrimony to lead
the way to an articulation of its special perception of sacramental time,
within which the symbols swarm. Orkney as wilderness: Orkney is wild
everywhere; the Orkney rhythm gathers momentum with its experience
of islands, hills and valleys close to the sea, its quick-flowing waters
and wave surges. Readers are touched directly by the primal power
of nature, understood by Mackay Brown as sacrament. The natural
perception of God in an Orkney wildness commits to a supernatural
Christian perception which 'presupposes a dogmatic knowledge'[2] that
affords Mackay Brown the 'swarm of symbols' that are uniquely the
Christian vision of primary forms of faith preserved in metaphors,
symbols and myths. Mackay Brown has earned his bardic credentials
and as he basks in the medieval sensorium that is his Orkney, he enters
the ecclesiological door of Catholicism where he finds kindred spirits
in John Henry Newman, Gerard Manley Hopkins and Duns Scotus.
All his creative tensions sharply honed in the psychological turmoil
expressed in the prose poems allow him to give voice to a style that
will be as tersely skaldic as it is pre-theologically artistic.

The Craft of Restoration

In his critics there is a great loss of the reality of the 'Faith' and its
connection between a code of morals and a mystical vision of nature.

There is a subjectively sensuous appreciation of the natural vision but the crossover to the Christian supernatural perception is seen as deeply suspect. There would also seem to be the suggestion among some critics that the Mackay Brown writings are an expression of subconscious conflict and an instability for which religion is neither legitimate consolation nor catharsis.[3] The rejection of a Christian epistemology that informs every word and phrase stemming from the Logos, Christ, the Word, leads to an arbitrary mistrust of Mackay Brown's sincere faith commitment. Mackay Brown was already moral and intellectual upon his 'conversion' to Catholicism. Like Muir he had been nurtured in the Bible Christianity of the Kirk and there is no doubt it is here he first soaked up the great stories of Scripture. His intuitions wanted more, and he sensed 'inscape' by 'inscape' that there was a harmony, an 'instress' which ultimately drove him to the periphery, keeping one foot within the natural wildness of Orkney and its configurations of family, friends and community, but simultaneously his inner nature compelled him to open the door to a higher reality. This created social tensions in a post-Reformation Orkney[4] but Mackay Brown sought to reclaim, and then reconfigure, the medieval world that had been closed so convincingly at the Reformation. He rediscovered the medieval rhythms and moods in modulations of pre-theological thought and feeling in startling new patterns of imagery, language and metre. Mackay Brown finds in Catholicism, and specifically Newman, and also the distinctive blend of Hopkins and Duns Scotus, justification for his own poetical consciousness and awareness of the objective world. His growing attitude to life becomes a personal dialectic that is more complete and intimate because he has made it his own, rather than importing the ideas of others into his artistic endeavours.

As Hopkins had discovered, Duns Scotus is not a popular and accessible philosopher. His arguments are long and subtle but for Hopkins and Mackay Brown his analysis of beauty, individuation and knowledge are explicitly and implicitly well understood because of an 'attitude' that has been lived for a good long while in their respective journeys. This attitude is contemplative and sacramental. Scottish-born Scotus, the philosopher of the particular, insists that the process of being created is the same as the substance of created being. Hopkins gives this a special resonance in his idea of 'stress'. The relation between nature and self, nature and selvèd Hopkins, nature and selvèd Mackay Brown, is a real union between the individual and the object of knowledge. The 'stress' of the object forms an 'instress' on the individual. If the nature of each human is the Nature of all the world, this commonality, which is an elemental, sensitive and vegetative individuality possessed by means of the margin in which the infinite is lacking. This metaphysical deficit tends towards that which redeems it and draws it towards the God that made it. The physically felt outreach towards harmony and completion is a sympathy that stresses itself upon us. The redemption of our unconscious nature is felt intensively in Hopkins and Mackay Brown. They both find an affinity in Duns Scotus that empowers the redemptive release of the Holy Spirit into their style of patterning word and phrase.

Certain strands of Scotus's philosophy are embedded into the 'attitude' or the way of seeing and living so vivid in Hopkins and also Mackay Brown. There is a convergence of thoughts on individuality, intuitive knowledge and the will, which once taken into account, give a commanding insight into the poets' fullness of meaning and significance. The swarm of symbols are pre-theologically holding centre ground at the core of their writings. The pre-Reformation Scottish Scotus influence permeates their mind and work. It blends with the Jesuit Hopkins and Mackay Brown's Jesuit sympathies. This influence does not induce or inspire the originality in either Hopkins or Mackay Brown. Those definitive sparks of originality, already their own, are deepened and enlarged, within the Scotus system of thought. Hopkins is explicit about such an influence, Mackay Brown implicitly so by his heartfelt devotion to Hopkins who would give him great solace throughout his life-long psychological turmoil.

Scotus is not prescribing ideas of inscape and instress or notions of the individual essences of things. Those belong to Hopkins alone. Hopkins came to Scotus with the provenance of the inscape, stress and instress well established. Hopkins's natural perception of God in the world had made the crossover to the supernatural, to the point of Christian perception where the impact of God as unique being, upon himself, he is now able to articulate as inscape, stress and instress. Mackay Brown for his part comes to Scotus through Hopkins, but equally in possession of stylistic credentials that deepen and enlarge and make their own distinctive path. Mackay Brown's writings are invested with a Scotist philosophy and the Hopkins vocabulary. Therein are many unconscious echoes of Scotist teaching and startingly similar Hopkinsesque terms.

Scotus has the distinctive univocal idea of being that suggests complete dependence of creatures for their very existence. Univocity is the idea that the difference between God, who by nature is possessed of all perfections, and creatures, who by their nature are possessed of limitations, is ultimately one of degree. Whatever attributes we ascribe to God are possessed by God infinitely, whereas creatures possess these attributes in a limited way. Language assigned to these attributes is used univocally. So an individual feels a personal lack of the infinite and that part of his individuality is this degree of distance from God. Not-being is a want of one-ness and inscape is the proportion of that mixture of Being and not-being. Being is and not-being is not and all things are upheld by instress and are meaningless without it. A simple *yes* and *is* in the depth of the instress is required for how fast the inscape holds a thing. The truth in thought is being, stress and each word is one way of acknowledging being.[5]

The impact or stress of individual nature on the perceiver implies something is behind and beneath the inscape of the object, for example Hopkins looks at a bluebell. Mackay Brown looks at a daffodil, to know the beauty of Our Lord by it. This 'knowing' is an inscape or form mixed of strength and grace. Mackay Brown, like Hopkins, understands from long experience that the raw materials for poetic images are the

> busy working of nature wholly independent of the earth and seeming to go on in a strain of time not reckoned by our reckoning of days and years but simpler as if correcting the preoccupation of the world by being preoccupied with and appealing to and dated to the day of judgment was like a new witness to God and filled me with a delightful fear.[6]

As Hopkins recognises in Scotus a sympathetic mind, so too does Mackay Brown firmly attach to this sympathy. But in each, their 'attitude' is prior and well formed. An intense awareness of beauty, not just as strong feeling or melancholy, leads to the self-discovery of inscape and its power to instress. The poetical sensibility is made strong by the reasoned philosophical velocity of the instress that seeks answers to questions. Is it the instress that individualises things?[7] Scotus organised and explained reality for Hopkins, and subsequently for Mackay Brown, in a way that was compatible for them both and their own already finely honed experience, not only of nature and the created world but also of their own psychological turmoil. Kindred spirits, both dead and alive, together within the ecclesiological submission of Catholicism, gave them a metaphysics that would hold. The outward face of the institutional Church held their allegiance especially because of this inner metaphysics.

Mackay Brown is content to let lie the questioning Hopkins, who agonised over the tension between Jesuit poet and Jesuit priest. Hopkins's harrowing battles, won through for himself gave heart to Mackay Brown to find his own existential and stylistic 'Way'. The poet driven to give voice to the depth and urgency of the poetic vision requires a philosophical attitude to give reasoned rigour. Hopkins won that battle for Mackay Brown, who could give equal balance to the Orcadian medieval, pre-Reformation sensorium with his embracing of the Norse skald. Just as Hopkins was able to go to new depths with his study of the Welsh patrimony, Mackay Brown could open the doors into the vista of the world of the sagas. Scotus ploughed the furrows to break up the intractable earth of his times to make seeds available to Hopkins, who nurtured and brought to fruition what Scotus could see from afar and with great penetration.

Hopkins, in the poem 'Duns Scotus's Oxford', gives the English pre-eminence in the power to speak and write of the doctrine of the Immaculate Conception, 'a not rivalled insight, be rival Italy or Greece; who fired France for Mary without spot'.[8] The English language, rooted in its Anglo-Saxon formation, absorbs a blend of the ideas and thought of the Scottish Scotus and the inflected nature of Welsh. An intimate use of a vocabulary and grammar is deepened and enlarged by its at times startling patterns and arrangements to capture the nuances of the inscape, deeply instressed in the subjectivities of consciousness. The English language is empowered to give voice to high and sweet Catholic doctrine lived so convincingly by ordinary laity in medieval devotions. So it is not just a matter of the quintessential English spirit of Oxford which has its part to play in the English language and its power to communicate ideas. Welsh, Gaelic and Old Norse are gathered in to reinvigorate the English language, and Muir and Mackay Brown, from their Orcadian sensibilities, could give this the respect it warranted. Mackay Brown, by his Catholic intuitions and commitment, immersed and stabilised as he was in the kindred spirits that he found in Catholicism, was free to allow the instress to navigate his inner world and dialogue with subtlety in thought and expression within 'a great company of minds and hearts ... set on a quest for the ultimate meaning of things.'[9]

If Mackay Brown is considered obscure, he is in good company, as Scotus and Hopkins were too in their times. Mackay Brown could under such instress be an original and powerful poet and thinker working in the old tradition, but producing and heralding something new. As a poet Mackay Brown was drawn to give voice to the distinctiveness, the difference and individuality of things. The Orkney inscape, its impact upon his perception, developed over many years of struggle, enabled a bardic power to hone down to the internal principle of a thing, the thing which makes it what it is, and put this into language. The particular essence, given expression through his poetical mind, is not separate from its external unity. The Mackay Brown trademark, 'no separation', is a Scotism, a Hopkinsism, a Catholic trademark surely absorbed at the Bible's 'knee': 'They ploughed my back like ploughmen drawing long furrows', Psalm 128. The intrinsic form of Orkney, and all its myriad phenomenological stimuli found in its natural configurations, became the Mackay Brown inscape, the index of Orkney's unique individuality as a whole. The Orkney inscape, finding in Mackay Brown a soul able to withstand the tensions perceived in its essence, also discerns its moral pitch or *haecceitas*. The universal and the particular, distinct as they are, have a formal reality in God's creative mind. Essence has its being first as an object of the divine mind. It does not subsist by itself apart from God. But since essences are objects of the Divine Mind, they must have the being that belongs to objects in a mind. It is very small, but it is something. It has some reality. This is the univocalism of Scotus. Both the object outside and inside the mind are said in the same sense and mean the same thing. Mackay Brown starts to see and know that this is how symbols participate in their reality.

The power of seeing and writing, shared by Hopkins, Scotus and Mackay Brown, is arrived at in two ways. Through stopping or stalling the abstractive process so that the inscape, the individualised nature, is grasped in sight or vision, and the result is a glimpse of the ideal nature, of which all other natures are a pale reflection. Equally, through the study of the individual aspects of the existing being, the selfhood of a thing (what makes it different), to the exclusion of what is common to it and to other things, so that the unique relationship between the thing and its source of its individuality is perceived. This is inscape as the object known in action. The knowledge secured assures the mind of a direct contact with reality, a bridge linking the mind with the reality outside it. This is the vision of existence that is the foundation of all knowledge and provides the raw materials from which clear and distinct concepts, universal ideas, are formed. To Scotus, Hopkins and Mackay Brown, individuality is a positive determination not knowable in isolation, yet knowable directly in conjunction with the universals.

The inscape is that experience common to all creation. It is the soul that receives knowing power from the creative mind of God. This innate power of knowing, used to know particular things, is a type of underlying illumination from God. It is by this Scotus-Hopkins-Mackay Brown way of threading of ideas that a theory of knowledge emerges fundamental to a pre-theology wherein there is a bottomless pool of nature from which the swarm of symbols can emerge, the sensations of which command a poetical sway always tending towards God by this underlying illumination invested in them. It is in this primal rawness that originality is given expression by the symbol already present in the mind. Innate images and symbols precede all knowledge and help to cause such knowledge.

The common nature of the inscape confirms a unity in the real union between the knower and what is known, between the knowing subject and the particular object known. The intellect and memory are threaded cognitively together and find fulfilment, not in the particular object itself, but in its cause and motivation. That the particular object 'is' gives way to 'why' it is. The 'instress' embraces the 'how' of a particular object in nature, but goes further to its 'why' and as Hopkins writes: 'As we drove home the stars came out thick: I leant back to look at them and my heart opening more than usual praised our Lord to and in whom all that beauty comes home.'[10] So too for Mackay Brown, whose heart opens often in the Orkney 'green-fields kirk'. Biblical burning bushes are never, for him, in short supply.

The Scotus-Hopkins epistemology gives firm grounds for the Orkney pre-Reformation sensorium that can walk on to the Nordic corridor and make good the 'particularity' in the Orkney tapestry. There is here a banquet to be had as the abstractive process is delayed and the poet can have insights into what is going on behind the swarm of symbols, the images and ideas in the act of creation. For Hopkins 'The world is charged with the grandeur of God',[11] 'There lives the dearest freshness deep down things'[12] expresses the startling and surprising delight in natural beauty and the immanence of God and simultaneously a direct but brief glimpse of nature being created. 'I walk, I lift up heart, eyes down all that glory in the heavens to glean our Saviour.'[13]

Difference in Unity

The selvèd Mackay Brown is no mimic of Hopkins. But the Scotus-Hopkins influence is palpable. The deep affinity with Hopkins and thus Scotushe makes his own, but more. The self of Mackay Brown, in Orkney, resonates and reasons towards other particularities. Mackay Brown ultimately had no choice but to explore and preside over the intrinsic possibilities that Orkney extrinsically offered. He receives them into his whole being, his very individuality, his self, the source of his distinctiveness. Orkney stimulates an understanding of God, and the bonding between Mackay Brown and God, delicate and ephemeral, even nonsensical, as it may appear to others, was enduringly strong enough to see him through, 'all things counter, original, spare, strange; whatever is fickle, freckled (who knows how?) ... He fathers-forth whose beauty is past change ...'[14]

The Mackay Brown individuality and intuitive cognition are specific Scotus markers and have theological consequences. Philosophically and theologically Mackay Brown had room to breathe and explore. He was deeply touched by distinctive patterns in Orkney, within which he was profoundly aware of his own individuality and struck by the intensity of pitch in its language and history and social groupings. Being Catholic is his pitch and instress. It made him an object of suspicion and awkward distrust for many locally, but he needed an epistemology to give his writing an enduring style that could take command of the theophany that Orkney manifested itself to be to him.

Individuality, the self, and its logical development, the theory of intuitive cognition, the perception of inscape are Scotus-Hopkins-Mackay Brown markers that individually and jointly depend on the primacy of the will. Stress is the inscape or nature which is the principle of action. Pitch has the same relation to stress as self or *haecceitas* does to inscape, and instress is related to intuitive cognition as the completion or fulfilment of the knowing process. An existing being is an individualised nature, the sum of all secondary acts taken together, which as such are the reality of the thing. Mackay Brown, like Hopkins, 'is' and actively so as a poet. The Mackay Brown stress is his making himself more of what he already is as he struggles through writing to bring out his own fullness of nature, and in so doing he brings out the fullness of Orkney in all its particularities threaded in the Mackay Brown tapestry. The exploration of the Orkney inscapes brings out their nature. Hopkins models for Mackay Brown how to delve into the 'sakes' of things because they are doors and windows into the inscapes of things. This is also a Mackay Brown marker:

Thus Hopkins writes of sakes of things in such patterned phrases as:

> the dappled-with-damson west
> skies of couple-colour as a brinded cow
> fresh firecoal chestnut falls
> rose-moles all in a stipple upon trout that swim
> Whatever is fickle, freckled … with swift, slow; sweet,
> sour; adazzle, dim[15]

In like manner Mackay Brown writes:

> Let the corn have gentle falls of wind and rain[16]
> Ripening corn from green shimmers to gold[17]
> Buttered the marsh with marigolds[18]
> A thin wash through the pebbles[19]
> Corn-patched Orkneys[20]
> Barbarous with gulls[21]
> Ritual stars[22]
> But the night was a funnel of darkness roaring with stars[23]
> Restore to that maimed rockpool, when the flood
> Sounds all her lucent strings, its ocean dance[24]

These inscapes of particular things give fascinating expression to their outward appearances, which are more or less static. The second phase of interest is the greater intensity of interest in particular things in action. These too are Mackay Brown markers.

For example, Hopkins writes of particular things in action:

+ Rivers, pools and streams in the poems 'Penmaen Pool', 'The Loss of the Eurydice', 'Inversnaid'.
+ Of all growing things in the poems 'Spring', 'May Magnificat', 'Binsey Poplars'.
+ Of birds in the poems 'The Windhover', 'The Sea and the Skylark', 'Henry Purcell', 'As Kingfishers Catch Fire'.

Particularities of action are worded at different times, in different seasons and in all weathers.

In like manner Mackay Brown writes:

+ Of water 'Sea's cold fermentation' in the poem 'Orcadians: Seven Impromptus'.
+ Of seasons in 'Harlequin spring' in the poem 'December Day, Hoy Sound'.
+ Of water, season and bird in 'From the loch's April lip a swan slid out' in the poem 'Dream of Winter'.
+ Of light in 'Pale wick of the sun' in the poem 'Daffodils':

> Splash our rooms coldly with
> First grace of light, until
> The corn-tide throb, and fields
> Drown in honey and fleeces

Of even more interest is what Hopkins classifies as 'selves', because they have the power of choice, self-determination, and pitch. Layer by layer and as fascinatingly lovely and fresh as particular objects are in their sakes and motions, it is through the 'selve' that Hopkins argues that one finds oneself: 'I find myself both as man and as myself something most determined and distinctive in pitch, more distinctive and higher pitched than anything else I see.'[25] Selfhood and pitch cannot exist separately. It needs a nature (Scotus's *ecceitas*), a stress through which to work. 'It is the self then that supplies the determination, the difference, but the nature supplies the exercise, and in these two things freedom exists.'[26] The will is the highest sphere of consciousness, the noblest of the soul's powers because it is free to choose even when there is no alternative. In the prose poem 'Man into Oak' Mackay Brown's will has freedom of pitch and play, but not of field. The affective will is drawn towards the good. Mackay Brown like Hopkins had seen what was good for him and he held on to it in the face of temptations drawing him elsewhere. These too are Mackay Brown markers: for example, Hopkins writes of selves in the following: 'Felix Randal', 'Brothers', 'Tom's Garland', 'Harry Ploughman'; Mackay Brown writes of selves in the 'Orcadians: Seven Impromptus' series in 'Lifeboatmen', 'Fisherman', 'Crofter', 'Doctor', 'Saint', and in 'The Death of Peter Esson', 'The Old Women', 'Gregory Hero', 'Thorfinn' and 'Hamnavoe'.

When Mackay Brown, poet, stresses himself, his selvèd nature, he uses the Scotus parameters which Hopkins so articulately modelled. Mackay Brown finds himself in the 'stress' and wills himself into a like manner of expression. It was within his nature to do so, giving particularity to Orkney, continuing to express himself as he always had but now it was stronger and better. His soul had found its 'pitch' in the supernatural stress of Catholicism. His instressed will apprehended the feeling of God's will within himself inseparably from particularities of Orkney. He discerned an understated Trinitarian understanding that the divine stress is the Holy Spirit and, since it comes through Christ, is Christ's spirit. The priest Hopkins would write, 'that is Christ being me and me being Christ'.[27] Mackay Brown would never be so direct about Christ. He was not a priest and his audience, Orcadian and further afield, as Marwick taught him, would never countenance such deliberate assertions. It would be incomprehensible to them, if not abhorrent.

But there is undoubtedly a power in Mackay Brown that can impress his Christ inscapes on others. This is the instress which conveys the individual object to the perceiver as present and existing. The instress is the act of will fixing and completing the inscape in the poet's crafted network of sign and symbols. It gives an intuitive knowledge of something as present and existing in a willed crafting which, properly attended to, leads the mind back almost instantaneously to the most distinctive self of whom all other selves are only pale reflections. The unlimited being of the most distinctive self is the only focus of the will wherein it attains in union the infinity, the 'heave' for heaven. This is the joy and truth of poetry through the swarm of symbols: 'My silver spirit swims from my body over the darkling hills.'[28] Whose silver spirit? This is vintage Mackay Brown soul.

Unity in Difference

Mackay Brown had already embraced inscape and instress intuitively and implicitly before his encounter in the way of literature to what Hopkins had articulated and given a thorough expression to. He had already worked out the philosophical weave of Scotus through the medieval sensorium vividly alive in his grasp of pre-Reformation Orkney. He was aware of nature's distinctiveness in Orkney and from his childhood days had observed Orkney in a very attentive and retentive way, always curious and alert to the Orkney 'particularities'. The idea of creation as a reflection of God and of human beings as images of God is not peculiar to Scotus, it is the essence of Catholicism and Mackay Brown was undoubtedly intensely alive to the divine communication in visible creation from his earliest beginnings.

Mackay Brown is an intricacy of puzzle pieces. I am giving emphasis to those deep Hopkins and Scotus pieces that are foundational. Mackay Brown brought questions to the way of literature, but also some tentative answers. Whatever perceptions Mackay Brown had worked out for himself were deepened by the Scotus-Hopkins alliance and at this fountain Mackay Brown drank, to great effect. The natural and human world of Orkney as a system of divine communications sharpened his organisation of their patterns. He was enabled to give 'particularities' special emphasis in literary style and content. His Catholic attitude and allegiances gave him scope to lose himself in the detail of Orkney, natural and social, giving distinctive expression in crafting the precise tinge of form and colour of a cloud or a buttercup, or the precise configuration of rain, or sea or sunset, or the very feel of them, or the soundings of birds, or the textures of fish. The 'sakes' of these particularities is inscaped into the Orkney tapestry, a seamless garment. Appearances caught in text with a truthful precision are given to their particular principles of action in time and seasons. These things are lovely in themselves because they are themselves, but even more importantly they are the 'good news' of God.

The processing of the sensations of Orkney act in the intellectual memory as inscapes or imperfect approximations of the particular objects giving rise to the particular sensations. The poet has an intuition of an indivualised nature, a particularity, but before abstraction begins to dominate the powers of perception, there is a fleeting glimpse of a nature that is universal and actively participating in the particularities of creation. This insight into what is going on behind secondary images and sensations (or the swarm of symbols that is Mackay Brown's fountain and forge) is Being itself, in its infiniteness. This is no natural insight, it is supernatural: 'It is impossible to say where the natural perception of God in the world ceases and the supernatural, Christian perception begins ...'[29] The power of knowing the universal nature in intellectual memory is Christ, the Word of God, who is the innate substance of all created things.

The poet's craft is to seek the exact word to convey precise feeling. Hopkins found great delight in this and so did Mackay Brown. It was in his craft that he most truly was and is. Artistic demands need philosophical reinforcement to have authenticity. To produce the thing exactly was the only way to present the thing to the reader. A proper apprehension of the thing is necessary for the apprehension of the divine communication behind and in the thing. Feeling for external pattern expressive of internal form is the Mackay Brown craft, and he acquired much from the Scotus-Hopkins affinities. It was important for Mackay Brown to know and transmit his Orkney perceptions properly apprehended because they not only will his mind to Christ and to God but also elicited degrees of assent from readers. He can rely on readers having the experience of unity in the Mind of God expressed in nature as the common element. It was an inscape shared with, and loved by many, an irresistible consolation in which they found psalm-like rest.

The will of God is something else for readers where the distinctive action of the individual is the stress of characters and their degrees of self-determination, their pitch. It is notable that the Mackay Brown characters with the most degrees of pitch are those who live on the margins of society in more ways than one, those who live in accord with what Mackay Brown perceives to be the natural rhythms of existence. The tinker, tramp, beachcomber, the blind fiddler, and the everyman 'Mansie' (a diminutive of Magnus) emerge from a composite of inscape, stress and pitch, abled to quietly glorify God by a distinctive merit or worthiness. Character is a means by which human difference is explored in the deep faith allegiances of Mackay Brown. Character is an appearance in society of something deeper. Character is drawn from the primal well within which energies radiate from the universal in particularities. Everyman steps from the Logos-Christ-St Magnus-Mansie and variations on Mansie in their guise of brother, priest, abbot, fisherman, lifeboatman, farmer, crofter, doctor, librarian, minister, kirk elder, mariner, publican and so on.

Everywoman is there also to complement and partner the masculine identity. Ever the helpmate, variations and particularities are drawn from universal woman: Eve, Mary, bride, wife, mother, widow, barmaid, teacher and so on. Mackay Brown rests his readers in a cosmic man-woman interplay that is biblical and Catholic. Our Lady, the Virgin Mary, Mother of God, is not artificially elevated, but walks with us in the fabric of the everyday. Man and woman, wounded with original sin, walk on into the great Redemption project to which Mackay Brown gives his faith allegiance and from which he unfolds his sacramental vision of a consecrated Creation in the distinctive particularity of Orkney. The Latin word *sacramentum* means 'a sign of the sacred'. There are seven sacraments, each a visible sign of an inward grace. They are special occasions for experiencing God's saving presence and these set forms were immensely satisfying for Mackay Brown.

The Incarnation, so intimate to Scotus, Hopkins and Mackay Brown, is given a pre-theological tapestry of poetic statement. The Word of God, the grace of Christ, working in nature (and human nature) is the bridge of re-establishment of the primordial harmony between the Mind of God which projects the divine idea of the nature and the will of God working through matter, through life, and through free selves which are separated and reflected in created things in time or duration, but which are inseparable in eternity. The Scotus-Hopkins-Mackay Brown act of 'saying' is what has to be said (the content) and has to be dictated by how it is said. The imagery, the swarm of symbols that are the Mackay Brown corpus, when analysed, indicate a poetical method and its philosophical system that combines to form a resonating pre-theologics. Any distinctive twist of syntax was to bring about some precise rhythmical or rhetorical effect to integrate object, experience and language in the intense beauty of the inscape. This is the 'no separation' speaking truthfully to literature. Language is so deeply penetrated by idea that the words are animated by the life principles that are so freely accessed in Orkney. A beautiful sparseness captured and articulated by the Mackay Brown poetic inscape is the instress of the shared space that is in his mind and that of the reader. Such a combination owes much to the philosophy of Scotus and the disciplined breath-of-life Hopkins to which Mackay Brown aligned himself so naturally. But he could also go his own way into the nordic complementarity that came to make its historical mark in Orkney and on its peoples. Catholicism is its seamless garment, according to Mackay Brown and his illumined Orkney poetics.

Notes

1   Hans Urs von Balthasar, *The Glory of the Lord. A Theological Aesthetics. III: Studies in Theological Style: Lay Styles.* San Francisco: Ignatius Press, 1986, p. 396.

2   *Ibid.*

3   Fergusson, *George Mackay Brown. The Life*, pp. 281–2.

4   Murray, *Interrogation of Silence*, p. 95.

5   Gerard Manley Hopkins, 'Parmenides', in *The Note-Books and Papers of Gerard Manley Hopkins*, ed. Humphrey House. London: Oxford University Press, 1937, pp. 98, 100, 101.

6   *Ibid.* pp. 128, 129, 134, 135, 140.

7   *Ibid.* pp. 153, 154, 161.

8   Gerard Manley Hopkins, 'Duns Scotus's Oxford', in *Poems and Prose*, ed. Gardner, p. 40.

9   Mackay Brown, *Vinland*, p. 211.

10   Hopkins, *Note-Books*, p. 205.

11   Gerard Manley Hopkins, 'God's Grandeur', in *Poems and Prose*, ed. Gardner, p. 27.

12   *Ibid.*

13   Gerard Manley Hopkins, 'Hurrahing in the Harvest', in *Poems and Prose*, ed. Gardner, p. 31.

[14] Gerard Manley Hopkins, 'The Wreck of the Deutschland', 'Pied Beauty', in *Poems and Prose*, ed. Gardner, pp. 12, 30.

[15] Hopkins, 'Pied Beauty'.

[16] George Mackay Brown, 'The Old Woman in the Kirk', in *The Collected Poems*, p. 322.

[17] George Mackay Brown, 'Chorus: Soon Spring Will Come', in *The Collected Poems*, p. 6.

[18] George Mackay Brown, 'Lifeboatman', in *The Collected Poems*, p. 10.

[19] George Mackay Brown, 'Fisherman', in *The Collected Poems*, p. 10.

[20] George Mackay Brown, 'Thorfinn', in *The Collected Poems*, p. 20.

[21] George Mackay Brown, 'Hamnavoe', in *The Collected Poems*, p. 24.

[22] George Mackay Brown, 'Dream of Winter', in *The Collected Poems*, p. 31.

[23] George Mackay Brown, 'The Shining Ones', in *The Collected Poems*, p. 33.

[24] George Mackay Brown, 'Chapel between Cornfield and Shore', in *The Collected Poems*, p. 35.

[25] Gerard Manley Hopkins, 'The Principle of Foundation', in *Note-Books*, pp. 309, 325, 328, 323.

[26] *Ibid.*

[27] *Ibid.*, p. 332.

[28] George Mackay Brown, 'Death by Fire. A Newbattle Legend', in *The Collected Poems*, p. 9.

[29] von Balthasar, *The Glory of the Lord III*, p. 396.

✛ 6 ✛

The Virgin Mary

I delight in those parts of The Canterbury Tales that I know: Lines like these, about the Blessed Virgin:

Within the cloistre blissful of thy sydis [womb]
Took manes shape the eternal Love and Peace.[1]

Mariology

Mentored by Hopkins and Scotus, Mackay Brown configures his own intricate weavings of metaphor, imagery and wordplay with an incarnational vision. He recaptures the medieval lyric's complex theology as he rises up from his sure ground of complete attentiveness to Orkney where he is immersed in an utterly objective contemplation of the primal power of nature, reading and writing in its language. His senses, schooled in Orkney, embrace the medieval world where Mary is everywhere with the power of what Hopkins called the 'new Nazareths' and 'Bethlehems'.[2] Mackay Brown's aesthetics stands or falls with its avowed but understated Mariology. The courtly charm of the medieval love lyric (I sing of a maiden that is makeles ... Maiden and moder Was never such but she Well may such a ladye Godes moder be)[3] tenderly saturates the swarm of symbols, gives them a hidden theological centre where the incarnation and biblical typology holds a crafted mastery. Orkney in all its natural noisy and stormy joyfulness, romping pillows of clouds and swathes of rains and winds, is literally a manifestation of God's grace. Mackay Brown does not turn his back on the material world, the truths of nature inform all his work in their reflective participation of the Creator. Wind and rain and clouds and sea have a real sacramentality. They are life-giving, essential and necessary to being.

Mary is the medium through which God flows. Mary is the immaculate, the mirror of God's light, similied and metaphored as moon, star, blue sky to the sun. All creation, all laws, do not preclude the existence of the Creator, they find in the Creator their origin. Natural beauty and natural fact, poetry and science do not contest each other. They give evidence and witness to a God who is divine and personal and Creator. Mary may be 'hidden' and understated but still essential as air is unobserved and yet indispensable. Mary as Mother is not a cosmic force separate from the Creator. Mary is our 'atmosphere' as Hopkins and Scotus and Mackay Brown express it: 'I say a Hail Mary whenever I remember—ungrateful ungracious creature that I am—and feel a sense of peace afterwards.'[4]

Mackay Brown excels in the articulation of the how and the why of 'no separation' within the Trinitarian community of love. There is a numinous sacramental vision that Mary ministers to. This is no sentimentalised Mary, no goddess of myth, no mere symbol of some female life principle. Mary of Galilee is Mary of Orkney as a woman of flesh and blood, an individual who gave her assent to her active participation in our redemption. Her cooperation makes our God the sweeter and clearer with her mothering care. As Christ's limbs were moulded within her womb, so too are we moulded in the exacting naturalness of reproduction. Hers is a high motherhood that has a natural and supernatural defence. Mary is the model and prototype of the members of the body of Christ. In her we can see what we can become by giving our *fiat* or cooperation moving towards our redemptive end. We can bear the Word in spirit becoming more Christ-like and in so doing more ourselves. The dignity of the human person is lovingly given special prominence. New Bethlehems and new Nazareths are made in us.

It is from this incarnational theology that Mackay Brown can capture in language a joyful and childlike delight in beauty: 'there lives the dearest freshness deep down in things'. He may have the appearance as being physically frail and inept, socially at odds, retreating from literary mores of the day, given to spiritual and mental anguish but nevertheless putting pen to paper shows an intensity and determination and giftedness to express as powerfully as he can the startling truths of Orkney and Christianity as being one and the same. There is a tensely tempered degree of cosmic rapture worked into his crafted texts that holds within it the intimate dialogue of the sinner and the crucified Redeemer, hence his devotion to the Stations of the Cross and his explicitness as to their being all he ever intended to mean in his writing as a whole.

There is also the muted solemnity of Mary, without which our redemption is not graced. Mackay Brown can hold the tensions and give them warp and weave in the 'seamless garment' of Catholicism because he works unobtrusively and undogmatically within the tradition while holding the uniqueness of his Orkney selvèd-ness so apparent in his writings. Applying pen to paper resolves the inner contradictions. Being 'shipwrecked' early through disease and suffering (given testament in the 1940 prose poems) opens the 'way' for those original experiences to breathe everywhere the patch-worked fields, the strong winds, the driving clouds, the closeness of the sea and wave surge. This is a world wild everywhere and its literalness enters the written word with an original purity. Orcadian distinctiveness blossoms in the rediscovery of a pre-Reformation Orkney. The world is a surprising place and as Duns Scotus and Hopkins pioneered the path, Mackay Brown can go that 'way' and find freedom to radiate the glory of the Lord.

Hopkins is in tune with Scotus's basic idea that the sacrifice of the Son is God's first thought of the world. The actuality of the world is his focus from which Hopkins speculates,

> that the first intention of God outside himself ... the first outstress of God's power, was Christ: and we must believe the next was the Blessed Virgin ... to give God glory and that by sacrifice, sacrifice offered in the barren wilderness outside of God, as the children of Israel were led into the wilderness to offer sacrifice ... It is as if the blissful agony or stress of selvèd in God had forced out drops of sweat or blood, which drops were the world, or as if the lights lit at the festival of the 'peaceful Trinity' through some little cranny striking out lit up into being.[5]

Hopkins saw the eucharistic presence of Christ to be present throughout the cosmos, which as a whole possesses Christological form. The creation of the world seen in this way allows for 'no separation'. Through all the raging of the elements, all the wildernesses of matter, all the tragedies of human 'wreck and ruins', Christ is coming by implication of the incarnation.

Incarnation

The incarnation is the theological centre from which Mackay Brown is 'foredrawn'[6] by the swarm of symbols and his writing gives testament to an aesthetics thoroughly Catholic, thoroughly Orcadian. Christ is truth and all beauty belongs to him. This truth and beauty is actual and invitational. The poetical vision is imprinted with seraphic signs and the Cross emerges shining through phenomena. Mackay Brown gave his assent (prose poems) and in so doing received the 'stroke and stress'[7] of the Cross sealed in a divine and human way (his stigmata). This is not a 'happy-ever-after' life story or one of dogmatic assertion at all times and places. But there is a deep and intense emphasis more clearly on God through Christ. Incarnation is the mark of the man and his writing, his 'signature', which takes considerable legacy from Scotus and Hopkins but is nevertheless his own literary configuration. The sacramental poetry that emerges is Christ-centred but it does not compel readers to read it as such if they do not wish to, or if they are not able to. The interweavings, the grace, the assent, embedded as they are in the personal life of Mackay Brown do not impose their inscape and instress but their possibilities are textualised. The Incarnate God is given by Mackay Brown the truest and most inward glory of forms symbolised with special reference to Orkney in its convergence of nature in history that he is privy to by craft and content. This is the pre-theologics of the poet. The Christian can read this glory and can surrender in this reading to be inspired, nurtured, and to give praise to the special configuration of beauty and love. The reader can interpret symbols rather than concepts and arrive at the orthodox creativity of Catholicism (and Mackay Brown was orthodox in his choice and practice of religion): 'Without the Creator, the lesser creatures—poet, artist, musician could not be.'[8]

But there are other readings. They are not my concern here. The sheer loveliness of Mackay Brown's reading of Orkney is enough for many readers in itself without having to acknowledge that this reading is subsumed into the higher Christian law. The sun, moon, stars, corn-patched Orkneys, the wildness of the sea, can be 'read' for the beauty that they are and great respect can be given to ancestral patterns of living in all its historical permutations. But fervour such as Mackay

Brown's for the subjective rewards of aesthetics and style, capturing the enchantment of the natural world, would be a misunderstanding of his 'no separation' of form and content that belong to his own existential anchorage in Catholicism. This does not mean he has to be titled a 'Catholic writer' with a 'Catholic imagination' at work. This is too exclusive a stereotype and his pre-theological quest belongs to the world of poetry where many can feast and find in the 'swarm of symbols' a door into an original and primal being. As Newman observed, a Catholic literature, 'is not exclusive or primarily of Catholic matters, of Catholic doctrine, controversy, history, persons, or politics; but it includes all subjects of literature whatever, as a Catholic would treat them, and as he only can treat them'.[9] But Mackay Brown did find himself 'in a current in the direction of Catholic truth, and the waters are rapidly flowing the other way'.[10]

It is enough for the poet to leave the mind of the reader on the 'quiver'[11] as Hopkins intended and perhaps Mackay Brown too, for his craft is in that suggestive style through the 'swarm of symbols'. Is this purely technique or an understanding of the way the mystery of God takes form in the world? Within the sacrament of the Word symbols are subsumed and symbols can well contain within themselves a likeness to the original, the primordial, the stress. There is a muted and understated cosmic rapture at work in Mackay Brown, held and 'hidden' within his craft in the manner of the post-Reformation Catholic who has learnt to keep his head down in an immediate society that is more about the suppressions of the times. These are the 'currents' Newman refers to, for the writer at large in the world Catholicism is counter-culture. But Mackay Brown is true to his quest and treats the world as only he can treat it going as honestly as he can where the swarm of symbols takes him. He could do no other.

Christ's cross is no mere natural fact in history, it is fundamental to understanding all of nature and its processes. The beauty of the world, of Orkney in particular, is a 'shining' summer glory on harvest day with many a silk-wind walk and silk-sack cloud that lifts the heart and eye to praise. Here is the signature of Christ as in Psalm 128: 'They ploughed my back like ploughmen drawing long furrows'. The seamless interchange or oscillation from field furrows to Christ's scourging, Christ's back to earthy field leads to the perception 'It is impossible to say where the natural perception of God in the world ceases and the supernatural, Christian perception begins.'[12] The inner condition in the Orkney 'reading' moves from sacramental sign and symbol to the mystery of salvation. The fallen world gives way to the 'dearest freshness deep down in things'[13] and our natural mother, the unfallen Mary, the air we breathe, elicits through her intercessory mediation the possibility of new Nazareths and Bethlehems in our nobler selves. Variation on the Mackay Brown incarnation signature 'always Christmas' is the lit barn within us wherein is the sacrament of the Incarnate God. This is no reverie or giddy enchantment but a tightly crafted aesthetic rapture composed of many shades of Christian obligation and inclination, an ethical self-transcendence, ultimately underpinned by the fact that 'Christ opened himself to the worst rejection, pain and desolation.'[14] Furthermore:

> In the Mass the sacrifice is repeated, over and over, every second of every day, all over the world; but Golgotha is made beautiful and meaningful by 'the dance at the altar', the offering of the fruit of the people's labour as they themselves journey to death, suffering and rejoicing: the bread and the wine.[15]

And so the 'swarm of symbols' gives way to the sacrament of the world, a world perishing as it is ascending to God: death as resurrection. Resurrection is in death. The existential experiences of the prose poems of the 1940s gave Mackay Brown his 'single eye' to interpret the formless chaos of his 'night' as his rightful place within which he could summon an assent in the midst of those questions of who and why he 'is'. Here he is found 'in a current in the direction of Catholic truth ... where the waters are rapidly flowing the other way'.[16]

The Immaculate Conception

The Christological basis for Scotus's theology on the Immaculate Conception is fundamental to understanding how the Virgin Mary figures in the understanding and literary expression of Hopkins and Mackay Brown. The privilege of the Immaculate Conception of the Virgin Mary required its correct theological setting. Scotus, in the medieval stream of thought about Mary, articulates to great effect a rational argument, centred upon Christ, who is eternally predestined by God the Father to assume human nature in the Incarnation.[17] According to Scotus the incarnation was not primarily intended to be the condition for the redemption of humanity from sin. In God's provident plan, the Incarnation of the Word in the person of Jesus Christ was, first and foremost, at the heart of the act of creation by God the Father. All creation has been patterned and designed according to the image of the Incarnate Word and is the result of a pure and free act of love on the part of God. Creation, in this way, enters in a mysterious but real way into a loving relationship with God as a trinity of persons. Each and every creature, being complete in itself and unique in its essence, is a model of God the Son, who became incarnate in order to glorify his father for the beauty of creation. It is true that, in the history of redemption, the Incarnation was then orientated toward the salvation of humankind from sin, but this aspect, important though it may be, could not be the only reason for the Incarnation. It is because of this trinitarian expression of overflowing love that God holds within His nature the primacy of the free will. His love for us is such that it invites but does not force or compel against out free will.[18] For a Christian, free will is definitive. We see this modelled for us throughout the Bible and especially in the Fall, Gethsemane and the Annunciation. Saying 'Mary' is really saying 'Jesus' and 'Father' through the Holy Spirit.

It is in this Christological view[19] of the world and of redemption that Scotus speaks about the Virgin Mary as mother of Jesus Christ, the incarnate Word of God. She becomes the embodiment of all perfection in creation, freed from sin and from its effects through the saving power of Jesus Christ, the universal mediator between God and humankind. It was fitting that God would choose for His Son a mother who would be totally free from any stain of original and actual sin, in order to become a channel of grace to us all.

The key notion in understanding Scotus's theology, as indeed in all his arguments in this question on the Immaculate Conception, is the verb 'to preserve'. Christ *preserved* his mother from original sin, according to Scotus. In other words, the Blessed Virgin Mary, like every other human person, was bound to be conceived in original sin, but she was *preserved* from it through the merits of her Son. The Virgin Mary had been purified of sin and in this *preservation* Christ assumed human nature in a purified mother. It is of course impossible to say exactly within the processes of natural reproduction how this *preservation* took place. But the word *preserve* holds within its conceptual grasp an understanding that at some point Mary was defended and protected from original sin which enabled her Immaculate Conception. It is by faith that our natural perceptions of how God works in the processes of the world are inseparable from supernatural Christian perceptions. This interchange of perceptions is based on our faith in an all-powerful and all-knowing God, some of whose processes we do understand but a point is reached where we do not literally understand and have proof, so we trust and believe because we can recognise that our human nature has creaturely limitations.[20] Mary models this for us so powerfully at the Annunciation.

In the constitution *Ineffabilis Deus* of 8 December 1854, Pius IX pronounced on the Blessed Virgin Mary:

> To the honour of the holy and undivided Trinity, to the worthiness and splendid beauty of the Virgin Mother of God, to the upholding of the Catholic faith, and to the furthering of the Christian religion, with the authority of Our Lord Jesus Christ, with that of the holy Apostles Peter and Paul, and with Our own authority, we declare, we pronounce and we define the doctrine which holds that the most Blessed Virgin Mary, in the very first moments of her Conception, through the singular grace of Almighty God, and through the foresight of the merits of Christ Jesus, Saviour of the human race, was preserved immune from all stains of original sin. We furthermore declare, pronounce and define that this doctrine has been revealed by God, and therefore has to be strongly and always believed by all the faithful.[21]

The high language and conceptualisation of the Church document is rooted in a long gradual development of doctrine (marked by controversies) but enthused and inspired by an early established childlike pious love for Mary by the lay faithful that emerged—and continues to do so—from revelations and apocryphal legends. Scotus refers to the liturgical practice of the Church in his times, which celebrated the feast of the Nativity of the Virgin Mary, but not that of her conception, because Mary was not believed to have been conceived immaculate. Scotus is referring to a commentary on the *Decretum Gratiani*, which mentioned the feast of the Conception which was celebrated particularly in England, but did not encourage it, since it was contrary to the Church's official teaching. St Anselm, in *De conceptu virginali*, writes: 'It was fitting that the Mother of Christ would have a purity greater than which nobody could think of'.[22]

Duns Scotus was able to lay the foundations of the true doctrine so solidly and dispelled the objections in a manner which was so satisfactory because he was able to show that Mary's sanctification followed the order of nature rather than a time sequence. Her preservation from sin was a *mystery* and the natural limitations of human understanding gave way to the supernatural understanding that it is in God's nature to be able to act within his power to preserve Mary from original sin, it was fitting for Him to do so, therefore He did it. Mary's Immaculate Conception is not contrary to faith and reason.

Mackay Brown does not need to articulate his faith in Church doctrine and the intricacies of Duns Scotus's arguments. By means of his pre-theological poetic sensibilities, enriched by his childlike piety and courtly love for Mary, he could compose well for Our Lady of Orkney, surrounded as he was in an ever-expanding interdisciplinary evidence base of place names, archaeological remains of stones, wells and chapels, buildings and dedications and shrines found in the altars of the medieval St Magnus's Cathedral and throughout the islands, with each having their own ecclesiastical history.

From Mary to Everywoman

Mackay Brown's powers of compression and command of using 'essences', scaling them up and down, oscillating them from within the cosmic rapture of God's glory to their profane shadows, are *katalogically* (as von Balthasar formulated) or 'on the quiver' (as Hopkins articulated) at work in his novel *Time in a Red Coat*. This dynamic interplay that can be confusing and demanding of its readers, is the tale of:

> A girl in a white gown that is in need of bleaching and stitching is afloat on the river of time … Nor is she alone. In a sense—in the poetical way of looking at things, which packs a whole world into a symbol, in order to make simple and joyous and comprehensible the manifold confusions of life—in a sense the young girl in the boat

crossing the river is not only all the young women who have crossed the river in time past and who will cross it in time to come. She is all the young women in the world verging on love ... She is more, she is all women, all the girl children and the old ones who have added their salt drops to the sweet on-flowing river of life, and who hate war and war-makers with a bitter hatred.

This girl is all women, princess and peasant-lass and fish-wife, who have lived or who will live in time to come (if indeed there is much time left—perhaps the river is nearer the bitterness of the end than we think. A few have heard, they say, breakers on rocks, far away, the cry of a seabird).[23]

Mackay Brown takes up the Orkney 'fable'[24] bequeathed to him by Edwin Muir and takes it to a universal stage. It is 'against war'[25] and as such prayer for peace. 'Women have always been the chief sufferers in times of war, and so this story is the story of Everywoman'.[26] 'The princess, branded at birth with the sign of war ... wanders through history';[27] she brings to the 'most terrible human situations' her 'wealth of the world to be shared (the money-bag) and that art (the flute)' to 'bring the kiss and consolation of peace'.[28] 'The girl in this fable—Everywoman—may save the generations at last. The book is intended as a gesture to the untapped potential of woman as healers and restorers and guardians'.[29]

He squinnied at the icon on the wall, the Blessed Virgin and the child. So: an inn, an inn in midwinter, and in a crib in that inn had begun the true history of man, after the false start in Eden. Yes, with that sleeping infant the world had woken to a full knowledge of itself. There, on the Virgin's arm, silent, reposed The Word was to flood the whole universe with meaning ... A wintered inn, with soldiers all around: that was where the great story had its second beginning. There, unheard, except by angels and a few shepherds, the music had had its pure source.[30]

... in the sea village called Ottervoe ... At last they were all there, the women standing a little back from the men-folk, around the well in the centre of the village; that being a familiar place to the women in any case.[31]

Woman's place in Orkney is honed down to essence and symbol. The Everywoman essence and symbol can then be scaled up from the particularity in an Orkney Tapestry to a universality that is cosmic and metaphysical. The natural becomes seamlessly supernatural. The feminine in the poetical way of looking at things, the Mackay Brown perception always pursues the origins of the modern period, in order to weave back together the irrational fragments that particularities are when they are ruptured and fissured from their universality. The rupture at the Reformation weighed heavy on Mackay Brown. Gladly he puts his hand into the fire of images to rediscover the interpenetration of sources that lost their connectedness to the cosmic universality in 1560.

The Mackay Brown Mariology gives to Mary a place of silence where rigid principles and stereotypes just do not work. Mary, her stance in silence and hiddenness, a little removed from that of the masculine, centred at the 'well' so familiar to women in general. She has no neat definition or formula. Mary is a process that oscillates, taking up her biblical points of reference as Virgin, Mother of God, Mother of the Church, source of the race, Pieta. Mary is answer and face, man's delight, his help and security, the home or 'house' he needs, the vessel of fulfilment specially designed with a preserved purity for her Son. She will bear fruit, Jesus, the fruit of her womb. Together in their nuptial complementarity, man and woman are the image of God. She received the seed of the Divine Word, carried it in her womb and gave it its fully developed form. This is the Incarnation, 'always Christmas', the Mackay Brown signature, one of the many, wherein questions arise about the nature of Mary as woman who is 'helpmate' both personally and socially.

Mary, has her role and purpose in the redemptive plan re-encapsulating Eve 'the tall unfingered harp',[32] pointing the way to an understanding of the relationship between man and woman to be an ultimate one. The varied status of woman is Mary as person in her own right, Jewish and Israelite, participant in the origins of humankind, participant in the Fall proving her solidarity with humanity. But her destination, our destination, is an ultimate one in the passion, death and resurrection of her Son (every time we say or turn to Mary we are really saying Jesus in the unique intimacy of their relationship).

The Mackay Brown litany of titles that venerate Mary ebb and flow with his perception of her, in her stance of silence and hiddenness, emphatically suppressed at the Reformation. He is in accord with the great theologians of his times, and the devotion that goes back to the beginning of Christendom. Mackay Brown does not trade in rigid conceptual categories as he is in tune with the 'oscillation' within the woman herself: man and woman are equal before God, equal but different, sharing in the same free human nature; her lowliness and nothingness as helpmate and handmaid makes her Mary of the Bible, belonging as she does to the Old and New Testament.

But it is Mary's freedom that brings all the reflections in Mackay Brown's poetical mind distilled from the crucible of Gospel texts and Catholic tradition to form a constellation in his own writings. She is for him the 'the air we breathe' as Hopkins joyously proclaims:

> Wild air, mothering air,
> Nestling me everywhere ...
> And makes. O marvellous!
> New Nazareths in us,
> Where she shall conceive
> Him, morning, noon and eve;
> New Bethlems ...
> Be thou then, O thou dear
> Mother, my atmosphere;
> My happier world ...
> Stir in my ears, speak there
> Of God's love, O live air,
> Of patience, penance, prayer:
> World-mothering air, air wild,
> Wound with thee, in thee is led,
> Fold home, fast fold thy child.[33]

Mackay Brown can lose and find himself in the wild exhilarating beauty of Orkney, having been conceived and mothered into the silence and salt of Our Lady, Mary, and the liturgy of the elements: of land, sea and air. The 'feminine', not element but essence, 'woman' is a compelling study and one that Mackay Brown explores alongside and inside the ecclesial concerns of the twentieth century that saw an ever increasing Catholic articulation of an anthropology that is able to speak the truth about being man and woman.

Liturgy and Litany

Learning to live as a Catholic in Orkney, or elsewhere after the Reformation, was the taking up of an inferior status in society. Newman and Hopkins did it as clerics and writers in nineteenth-century England. As the Oxford Movement called forth the reawakening of a Catholic past they were called to the task of bringing forth what was lost to spirituality and its expression in language. An Orkney poetics in its own distinct way also brought forth much that the Reformation and its Scottish Calvinism had dismantled and suppressed. Mackay Brown took this call as his own and worked on where others, Edwin Muir in particular, had brought this path to our attention. The re-invigoration of language brought into a new light the Orcadian dialect and gave it an international appreciation as well as a local one. This re-opened world view picked up where in hindsight the medieval period could be re-examined and interpreted from the purest of Orkney sources and phenomena. Mackay Brown's perceptions of these sources and phenomena as the 'swarm of symbols' took the set forms of a Catholicism that had been articulated from the outset of Christianity as in the brief and accessible formulas of the liturgical form of the litany. The litany is a series of prayerful petitions that alternate between clergy and laity. The litany was as clear and dear to Mackay Brown as the Nordic kennings. Its 'set form' was rooted in the psalms and canticles of the Bible, and Mackay Brown develops a distinctively devotional way of capturing the cosmic essences specifically in relation to the Virgin Mary.

Mackay Brown moves seamlessly from the familiar to the unfamiliar, the simple to the complex, the natural to the supernatural. Mary has special months and feast days in the liturgical calendar. Mackay Brown can use this 'set form' for his perception of Mary within a liturgical calendar of the months and seasons of the natural world. She is not some sort of gnostic emanation or pantheistic mother earth. Mary embodies and enshrines the natural world of land and sea and sky, but always pointing elsewhere. Saying 'Mary' is really saying 'Jesus'. Our origins in the dual narratives of the Genesis creation accounts are feasted upon in the Virgin isles.[34] Mary is her own feminine and free person standing in her silence, raising us through her grace to the glory of the Lord. She is human, living as we do, and dependent on the structures and material being of the universe; yet more, preserved as she is from original sin and its worldfall apples[35] And Eve, 'a tall unfingered harp',[36] is redeemed in her definitive pronouncement of the feminine.

Line by line, image by image, we find the Mackay Brown threads in the Orkney tapestry. He stitches by means of the 'set form' her embodied soul that finds its pivot in the passion of her Son: 'A red rain bursts about her' held in the composition of her silence: 'Her hair is glory about her quiet throat'.[37] The Mary 'symbol' is Orkney rain conflated with the red blood of the crucifixion; hair is conflated with Orkney phenomena of sky, sea and land. The contemplative quiet stills the rawness of the throat into the silence that goes deeper than words ever can, to more than we know. Then there is the release of enlightenment: 'My silver spirit swims from my body over the darkling hills.'[38] Mary's spirit, Mackay Brown's spirit, the reader's spirit: embodied souls released towards resurrected souls, partial and incomplete until Parousia. The Mackay Brown eschatology is embedded in the Mary 'symbol', resourcefully ecclesial and biblical. The threads are Orkney ones, alive to the glory of the Lord, a raptured and reasoned theophany embedded in the creation story of the natural world.

For woman, the essence of which is 'an undersong of terrible holy joy'[39] is that pain of tragedy that cuts to our centre. It is the essence of woman, also the essence of being human, but Mary-woman gives us an insight into her nature. Here as natural biological 'motherer' of the species, she is giving birth to Jesus, incarnate in the Virgin Mary, embraced as this is in the quiet, silent and patient walk through *Time in a Red Coat*. This is the Way of the Cross, the Christian walk, a way of pain Mackay Brown knew intimately to his core. He could see how woman in her complementarity, standing a little back nearer the well, could give face and voice to the silence that must bear all, and walk on. Orkney culture, cut off as it was at the time of the Reformation, saw women immersed in the day to day struggles, unsanctified and suppressed by Calvinism, as regards their inner nature. Before the appetites of secularism completely took over, Orkney women, or women in Orkney, could go on pilgrimage to the old chapels and lochs and islands to participate in pre-Reformation rituals. The ancient memories lived on that spurred a woman in times of infertility and sickness to find a way through prayer to tenderness and consolation that resonated with her ongoing existential crises.

Mackay Brown moved seamlessly from the ancient world of Troy to Orkney, 'Before the ploughman chants across the glebe'[40] giving symbol to essence as he draws in and re-weaves the 'ploughman', 'chant' and 'glebe', his eye perceiving that they are one, the ancient and ever new, primal perceptions which come to the fore. No secular sham, no psychological suppression, can quell the spirit of reasoned enquiry to articulate and recraft 'no separation'. Particularity is reconnected to the universal, the cosmic. The universal and cosmic is reconnected to the particular. The ploughman as symbol: 'His liturgy of spring, turning a page With every patient furrow Or the sudden image of a woman weaving.'[41] The chant is a psalmic one, 'They ploughed my back like ploughmen drawing long furrows', Psalm 128. The Orkney ploughing ceremonies[42] that were once pagan fertility rites were absorbed into the Christian liturgical calendar, subsumed into the higher Christian law, to the point where, 'It is impossible to say where the natural perception of God in the world ceases and the supernatural, Christian perception begins.'[43]

Complementarity of the 'particularities' of woman and man are nuptially at one with each other, 'Women scanning the sea'[44] ... 'They trembled as their lips / Welded holy and carnal in one flame.'[45] Mackay Brown returns for his textual authenticity to the Bethlehem Incarnation narrative, 'If the queer pair below will pay their lodging.'[46] Mary and Joseph, woman and man; does 'queer' mean that they are at a tangent to the secular world, or is the tangent the secular world? Their son, the Son of God, is told: 'And you must hang on your own tree.'[47] Mackay Brown found the 'Tree of Life' in the 'Man into Oak'. It is the cross where in the, 'five gates of your blood',[48] the Christian walks as a 'Passion partner' on towards the light (of that other place) that embeds a cheerfulness that 'worm' and 'scarecrow' and 'rag', real as they are in the Mackay Brown psychology, cannot eclipse. 'I heard my mother calling.'[49] Is it the Virgin Mary, Mhairi (Mackay Brown's own much loved mother), or the feminine? All and each are assimilated into symbol and essence and oscillation. There are no rigid conceptual categories, just the perception of wave upon wave of redemption.

Openness to the 'other place' where 'the Byres stood open,'[50] where 'The red ploughs cleave their snow and curve forever / Across the April hill'[51] is Bethlehem in the Orkney winter, the Orkney farm. The 'red ploughs' will bloody the purity of our origins but give birth to new life from the wintered heart that is empowered to 'curve forever'. The April Easter hill, Calvary, Orkney and Jerusalem are conflated into symbol. Mackay Brown is masterly at this assimilation and conflation working the reader seamlessly towards something new and renewed. He opens out the 'other place' with his own perceptions. The symbol holds together the holistic oneness of the body and soul, man and woman, sexual and nuptial, the seasoned cycles of birth and death, seed to harvest, 'The ploughman turns / Furrow by holy furrow / The liturgy of April'.[52] This is our liturgy, the set form of which has a realism and beauty threaded as it is with paradox. Seeing from the point of view of the 'Cornstalks, golden conspirators'[53] bringing 'Ripeness and resurrection / How the calm wound / Of the girl entering earth's side / Gives back immortal bread / For this year's dust and rain that shall be man'.[54] The sadness of the elegy grieves for the furrows that have been and will be ploughed with the best and worst of what humans can do. The way through, the Resurrection 'Cornstalk', comes at a wearing cost. But it is always darkest before the dawn, consolation is ever close by. 'The girl' helpmate and partner, equal but different, a little at remove, is integral to the human story to raise 'the dust and rain that would be man'.[55]

'But the night / Was a funnel of darkness, roaring with stars.'[56] These are Orkney nights resplendent with stars. They are spiritual dark nights of the soul from which Mackay Brown emerges to find the glory of God in 'The sky grew tall as lupins. Far below Wave and boat swayed like familiar dancers. That sea must hold him now …'[57] Creation walks with us with its urgent reasoned perceptions that are biblical and prompt explanation and interpretation. But Mackay Brown makes sure we come back to his 'core' his 'seeing' of daffodils, 'Heads skewered with grief / Shawled in radiance / Tissue of sun and snow / Mary Mary Mary'.[58] This is our liturgical walk always towards the Light. The three Marys, the company of the Virgin Mary, the company of the Mother of God, the Mary-woman oscillation, 'To the seven dark shawls'[59] to the 'The seven sounds of the sea';[60] 'The sea lay round the isle, a bright girdle'.[61]

Moving in and out of history the cosmic tapestry documents the inner and outer face of woman, 'Weaving, she sings of the beauty of defeat'.[62] The Christian paradox of 'the beauty of defeat' won on the

Cross, gives the stance of silence to the 'Figure of Our Lady'[63] 'Blessed Lady',[64] 'Holy Mother',[65] 'Sweet Virgin',[66] 'Queen of Heaven',[67] 'Guard the plough and the nets', 'Star of the sea, shine on us'.[68] 'Our Lady of the Waves' gives the Mackay Brown litany an Orcadian exquisiteness from the Mackay Brown devotion. He knows about the Virgin Mary, he knows about woman's essence, where he feels 'at home' in the 'swarm of symbols'. He derived a lot of complementarity from many women; women liked and loved him, for his tenderness and support and much else. But ultimately his interior life was one fiercely guarded in order to open his perceptions and insight where, 'She guards the field, the river, the birds'[69] 'The dark hills roll across her silence',[70] 'she sees',[71] 'Stone and litany fold her now'.[72] This is no plaster statuesque Mary put on a hierarchical pedestal of the unattainable (often the critique of the Catholic Mary). Mackay Brown's Mary was deeply earthed, deeply human, deeply reasoned, deeply questioning, deeply faithful, deeply doctrinal, deeply experienced in all her 'oscillation' across the centuries. Women resonate with their primal and first beginnings, their aged selves: 'The girl sang from another shore / And the tranced oars beat on, / And the old woman's fingers wend / Like roots through the gray stone'.[73] Orcadian women had been forged on the edge of the elemental world where the boundaries between life and death formed a perception; 'The wind that sweeps like an angel's wing'[74] cautioned them about their beginning and end. Mackay Brown writes substantively of the past that never really changes, no matter how thoroughly modern life tries to suppress the cosmic tapestry. He teaches us how to 'see' and again be at one with the miracle of life.

Mackay Brown had a great devotion and respect for Orcadian women; he knew their history, rooted in essence and symbol. He gave me a great tirade once (1995), perhaps tongue-in-cheek, that the motor car and learning to drive was the cause of the demise of Orcadian women, as was their turning away from the farm and its traditions. He was quite vehement about it and I was quite shocked at the time. Was it tongue-in-cheek? I can't say but he was very aware of what Orkney had lost. The Reformation was a raw and real focus of discontent for him, for good reason. But he has done much to restore the balance, to breach the fissure, to re-open the medieval world view in particular and give it and its pre-Reformation Catholicism its rightful place in the scheme of things.

What he had learned in this process was that he could now use a finer power to 'see' events in modern twentieth-century life and apply his Orkney poetics. For example, the assassination of the first Catholic president of the United States of America, John F. Kennedy, prompted a poem sent, along with the local parish of Our Lady and St Joseph Mass offering, to Jacqueline Kennedy on Sunday, 24 November 1963. The parish had the official reply card from Jacqueline Kennedy, signed by her personally and framed to record the occasion. The assassination of Kennedy held great significance for Catholics worldwide. Given what we know now about his private life has no real significance here. His presidency was intensely supported by Catholics worldwide because he was a Catholic from an Irish Catholic family who in the New World had, after the suppression of Catholic life after the Reformation, found again the high status of public and political life. His death was felt bitterly by Catholics, including Mackay Brown. Kennedy was one of 'our own'.

The Mackay Brown poem uses the set form of the litany to encapsulate the timelessness of the event, setting it in the context of Catholic essence, 'House of the Womb House of Birth House of Man House of Corn and Grape House of Love House of Policy House of History'.[75] The play and interplay between womb and birth, corn and grape and love, policy and history give praise and acknowledgement to the Virgin birth, holding within it every birth, the death of Christ holding within it every death, the vocation of public life embedded in the notion of bringing Christ into the marketplace of ideas and society. This poem is very much in the spirit of Vatican II, which was underway at this time, to look outwards as well as inwards, to give the Church new impetus. The poem is not one of Mackay Brown's best in the sense that his best is the Orkney theophany where the glory of the Lord is exquisitely made manifest. But this poem does fulfil the duties of the 'makar', to try to sanctify or set in context, the meaning of historical events, for the 'tribe'. Opportunities to 'put one's hand into the fire of images' for public or commercial ventures never quite had the same grace and glory of the natural rhythms sprung from the Orkney stimulus. They seemed contrived and half-hearted in comparison, to my way of thinking. President Kennedy is more of a conflict-ridden King David than a modern-day St Magnus.

It is the introspective attunement to the profound rhythms of life and death where the contemplative Mackay Brown can find in this inner world prismatic symbols that work various dimensions and time-shifts to great effect: 'Their queen is a stone woman / Their lord a scarecrow with five red tatters'.[76] He has a theory of knowledge, an epistemology, not that of a 'closed society', or a 'surreal ... clashing of different realities'.[77] 'You must dance in a beautiful coat',[78] 'The lady cried in the straw'[79] line by line, both within a text and across texts, the symbols fulfil their purpose to open perceptions, minds and hearts to what may at first glance be ephemeral and fragile: 'Perhaps this kingdom does not exist. Perhaps we found it and did not recognise it. Perhaps it is hidden so deep in birth and love and death that we will never find it.'[80] Mackay Brown always returns to the essences that he 'reads' in the wild beauty of Orkney, wrapped as they are in a Catholic understanding. The set form of the litany reminds and renews the great Christian narratives but also gives them a salty Gospel originality:

> Our Lady A Jar of Salt Our Lady of the Inshore Our Lady of the Atlantic Our Lady of Cornstalks Our Lady of Flail Our Lady of Winnowing Our Lady of Querns Our Lady of the Oven Blue Tabernacle Our Lady of Five Loaves Our Lady of the Boat Our Lady of Oil and Salt Our Lady of Silver Dancers Our Lady of Nets Star of the Sea Our Lady of Lent Our Lady of the Last Snow Our Lady of Muirburn Fold of the Agnus Dei Our Lady of Quiet Waters Our Lady of April Our Lady of Vagabonds Our Lady of Fishbone and Crust Our Lady of Ditch Fires Pieta, quiet chalice Our Lady of Pilgrims Our Lady of the Wind and Sun Our Lady of the Pool Make clean our hearts Lady Clother of the Christ Child Preparer of linen for the unborn and the dead Our Lady Immaculate Our Lady of the Last Oil Our Lady of Silence Our Lady of Two Candles Mater Dolorosa Our Lady of Dark Saturday Stone of these stones Our Lady of the Garden Our Lady of Dark Ploughs Our Lady of Furled Boats Our Lady of Kneeling Oxen Our Lady of Perpetual Vigil[81]

This is the Mary story, the Orkney story, the story of birth and love and death repeated over and over again as the monotoned chant presses us towards 'the other place' in a stream of consciousness. Mary is our Gospel salt, calmly standing with us in the inshore but ready to do combat with Atlantic storms and tides. She is earthed as are cornstalks, open to the harvest processes, to be cut down, and shaken and ground, ready for the Christian forge and formation with her Son preparing to give himself in the eucharistic bread. She is our sparkle and shine of the sun dancing on the waves, adept with Gospel boats and nets, moving liturgically through the calendar of the life seasons. She is impelled towards the gutting of fish and sacrifice of Passover lambs, an outcast on the margins sending invitations to hedgerows and ditches, the mother who will cradle her dead son. She is a prayered centre of quiet, there for those who journey with her welcome and nurture, of wind and sun, the air we breathe, giving healing miracles in sacred waters, helping us to be clean again. She is the tragic griever, knowing the bitterness of death and its rituals, where silence becomes the only rite of passage. She is our garden and guide to her Son where dark ploughs become furled boats to our Bethlehem hearts where we keep vigil. Saying 'Mary' is saying 'Jesus'. This is the Catholic intimacy of prayer that here is a Mackay Brown gift for Orkney.

This is a knowledge that is accessible, and using so many dear familiar Orkney ways of life. It is a child's catechesis where 'Daffodils at the door in April', are seen as the 'Three shawled Marys' and the natural world and its creatures, 'A lark splurges in galilees of sky[82] our Holy Land. Mackay Brown never made that physical journey. Orkney was the Holy Land in more ways than one and the Orphir round kirk, built as a replica of the Church of the Holy Sepulchre in Jerusalem, was testament enough for him. That whole medieval atmosphere enshrined in the *Orkneyinga Saga* opened out the pages of the Bible with a new life-giving vibrancy.

Mackay Brown gave the Virgin Mary her Atlantic credentials, 'Our Lady of the Waves'[83] is the Orkney *Stella Maris*, the Orkney Star of the Sea. The idea of Mary as a guiding star for seafarers has led to devotion to Our Lady, Star of the Sea in many Catholic coastal and fishing communities. This ancient title emphasises Mary's role as a sign of hope and is a guiding star for Christians. Originally it was used especially for gentiles. The Old Testament Israelites metaphorically referred to anyone beyond the Israelite 'coasts' and their Mosaic law as 'the sea'. Under this title, the Virgin Mary is believed to intercede as a guide and protector of those who travel or seek their livelihoods on the sea. So that includes Orkney for Mackay Brown, and as much as he is inspired by the set form of the litanies and hymns to Mary, he creates a very distinctive Orkney version.

The Rackwick Madonna

Medieval Orkney was well endowed with chapels and statues dedicated to Mary. Only archaeological and documented traces remain. But we do have the Rackwick Madonna or *Untitled Tryptych* by Sylvia Wishart. This Madonna is painted in the Byzantine iconic style, the statue in the wall presides over Rackwick fishing and farmlands. Rackwick is well documented as a place of enchantment for both Mackay Brown and Wishart, and the time that they shared in the early 1960s clearly led a rich visual and symbolic and spiritual complementarity. For poet and artist there was a coming together and a giving to each other recorded here in the Triptych. Their relationship was for a time enough to reinstate the Virgin Mary, Mother of God, 'House of Bread'[84] attended to by the priesthood in the order of Melchizedek. Catholicism did not last for Sylvia; her road configured with visual symbols took her elsewhere. Mackay Brown meanwhile always returned to 'A wintered hovel' where 'Hides a glory Whiter than snowflake or silver or star'.[85] His allegiance did not waver as he could not forsake incarnation, atonement, Eucharist, or his Mary love. 'Inside one chamber, see A bare thorn Wait. A bud breaks. It is a white rose. We think, in the heart of the house A table is set With a wine jar and broken bread'.[86] This is no romantic idealism, no golden age that never existed in reality. Orkney never stopped being a stimulus to the 'other place' where 'At midnight I dreamed / Of a thin lost child in the snow'.[87] A bourgeois domesticity was never for him. He was always the scarecrow, the rag, the worm, the lost child in the snow. As such he could not lose the vision, 'In radiant tatters they robe / The Winter King'.[88] And we thank God that he found and walked the Orkney Way of Beauty at peace with himself and the social complexities of Orkney.

> Where does the glory come from, that streams forever through the firmament and the world of nature with its endless variety of creatures, and maintains them and keeps them in their courses, and has a keeping of them always, beginning to end? It comes from God: the marvellous bounty comes from God and belongs to the glory of God.[89]

Notes

[1] George Mackay Brown, in a letter to the author 15 April 1982 (Eve of St Magnus). Also in Mackay Brown, *For the Islands I Sing*, p. 56. Quoted from Geoffery Chaucer's *The Canterbury Tales*, 'The Second Nun's Tale'.

[2] Gerard Manley Hopkins, 'The Blessed Virgin Compared to the Air We Breathe', in *Poems and Prose*, ed. Gardner, p.. 54.

[3] *Ibid.*, p. 55.

[4] George Mackay Brown, in a letter to the author, 28 April 1980. See Appendix.

[5] Hopkins, 'Parmenides', in *Note-Books*, p. 254.

[6] Hopkins, *Note-Books*, p. 127.

[7] Hopkins, 'The Wreck of the Deutschland'.

[8] Mackay Brown, *For the Islands I Sing*, p. 154.

[9] Newman. 'English Catholic Literature', pp. 178–9.

[10] *Ibid.*, p. 185.

[11] Gerard Manley Hopkins, letter to Robert Bridges, 24 October 1883, in *The Journals and Papers*, p. 201.

[12] von Balthasar, *The Glory of the Lord III*, p. 396.

[13] Hopkins, 'God's Grandeur'.

[14] Mackay Brown, *For the Islands I Sing*, p. 185.

[15] *Ibid.*

[16] *Ibid.*

[17] Pope John Paul II, *Address* at Blessed Scotus Beatification Ceremony, 20 March 1993. http://w2.vatican.va/content/john-paul-ii/en/homilies/1993.index.4.html.

[18] Broadie, *The Shadow of Scotus* , p. 50.

[19] Pope Benedict XVI, 'John Duns Scotus', in *General Audience*, 7 July 2010. http://w2.vatican.va/content/benedict-xvi/en/audiences/2010/documents/hf_ben-xvi_aud_20100707.html.

[20] St Thomas Aquinas, *Summa Theologica* III q27, 'Of the Sanctification of the Blessed Virgin of Saint Thomas Aquinas' as translated by the Fathers of the English Dominican Province, and from the works of Blessed John Duns Scotus as selected and arranged by Jerome of Montefortino and as translated by Peter L. P. Simpson. Texts are taken from the *Opus Oxoniense* and the *Reportata Parisiensia* of the Wadding edition of Scotus's works: http://www.franciscan-archive.org/scotus/opera/Monte-ST3–27.pdf.

[21] Pope Pius IX, 'Constitution', in *Ineffabilis Deus*, 8 December 1854: http://www.papalencyclicals.net/Pius09/p. 9ineff.htm.

[22] *Ibid.*

[23] George Mackay Brown, *Time in a Red Coat*. Harmondsworth: Penguin Books, 1986, p. 33.

[24] George Mackay Brown, 'Time in a Red Coat. For Karin Meisenburg, German translator'. Orkney Archive, George Mackay Brown Collection, D124/2/2/6.

[25] *Ibid.*

[26] *Ibid.*

[27] *Ibid.*

[28] *Ibid.*

[29] *Ibid.*

[30] Mackay Brown, *Time in a Red Coat*, p. 49.

[31] *Ibid.*, p. 232.

[32] Mackay Brown, 'Death by Fire', pp. 7–8.

[33] Hopkins, 'The Blessed Virgin Compared to the Air We Breathe'.

[34] 'Saint Magnus in Egilsay', in Mackay Brown, *The Collected Poems*, p. 32.

[35] Mackay Brown, 'Death by Fire', pp. 7–8.

[36] *Ibid.*

[37] *Ibid.*

[38] *Ibid.*

[39] 'The Old Women', in Mackay Brown, *The Collected Poems*, p. 16.

[40] 'The Night in Troy', in Mackay Brown, *The Collected Poems*, pp. 17–18.

[41] *Ibid.*

[42] 'The plough ceremonies, held on the first working day after Christmas, were fertility rites, when the young men of the village harnessed themselves to a plough which they dragged about the parish ... these patently pagan observances were absorbed into the religious calendar: many churches had a "ploughlight", perhaps burning before the Sacrament or the Rood' (Duffy, *The Stripping of the Altars*, p. 13). When the guilds were suppressed at the Reformation the plough plays were ended. 'The absence of Plough Plays from Scotland may also be attributed to the prevailing system of small-scale farming and, therefore, the absence of sufficient numbers of young farmworkers to make up the play teams. The result has been that the ritual, the 'streeking of the plough', continued in the same form until eventually, with the passage of time and the enlightenment that came with education and agricultural progress, the ceremony has fallen into desuetude' (Thomas Davidson, 'Plough Rituals in England and Scotland', in *The Agricultural History Review* 7 (1959), p. 37). A remnant remains today in the boys' summer ploughing matches in South Ronaldsay, when boys plough miniature furrows on the beach and boys and girls dress up as plough horses in intricate costumes.

[43] von Balthasar, *The Glory of the Lord III*, p. 396.

[44] 'Themes', in Mackay Brown, *The Collected Poems*, p. 21.

[45] *Ibid.*

[46] 'The Lodging', in Mackay Brown, *The Collected Poems*, p. 28.

[47] 'The Redeeming Wave: Part 3 The Heavenly Stones', in Mackay Brown, *The Collected Poems*, p. 20.

[48] *Ibid.*

[49] *Ibid.*

[50] 'Dream of Winter', in Mackay Brown, *The Collected Poems*, p. 31.

[51] *Ibid.*

[52] 'Elegy', in Mackay Brown, *The Collected Poems*, , p. 32.

[53] *Ibid.*

[54] *Ibid.*, pp. 32–3.

[55] *Ibid.*

[56] 'The Shining Ones', in Mackay Brown, *The Collected Poems*, p. 33.

[57] *Ibid.*, p. 34.

[58] *Ibid.*

[59] 'Shipwreck', p. 38.

[60] 'Horseman and Seals, Birsay', p. 41.

[61] *Ibid.*

[62] 'Culloden', p. 41.

[63] 'Our Lady of the Waves', pp. 44–5.

[64] *Ibid.*

[65] *Ibid.*

[66] *Ibid.*

[67] *Ibid.*

[68] *Ibid.*

[69] 'The Image in the Hills', p. 12.

[70] *Ibid.*

[71] *Ibid.*

[72] *Ibid.*

[73] 'The Sailor, the Old Woman and the Girl', pp. 53–4.

[74] 'A New Fishing Boat', p. 59.

[75] 'The Seven Houses. In Memory of John F. Kennedy', pp. 60–1.

[76] 'Viking Testament', p. 65.

[77] Murray, *Interrogation of Silence*, p. 95.

[78] 'The Coat', p. 67.

[79] 'Lord of Mirrors', p. 72.

[80] 'King of Kings', p. 77.

[81] 'Our Lady Jar of Salt', pp. 98–100.

[82] 'A Child's Calendar', p. 122.

[83] 'A Shipwreck in Shetland', p. 158.

[84] 'Desert Rose', p. 280.

[85] 'Christmas Poem', p. 283.

[86] 'House of Winter', pp. 284–5.

[87] 'The Child in the Snow', p. 285.

[88] 'Snowman', p. 285.

[89] Mackay Brown, *For the Islands I Sing*, p. 152.

✛ 7 ✛

Reading Orkney

> Some disturbing thoughts visited me last month. I grow more and more sick of the Church of Scotland. By nature I'm interested in religion (if not strictly speaking a religious person) and the pale watery Calvinism of present day Orkney frankly disgusts me ... I could live cheerfully in a Catholic country, or in pre-Reformation Orkney; if that were possible; The present day organised religious life here is shocking; much worse than atheism.[1]

Mackay Brown makes the most subtle distinction: 'By nature I'm interested in religion (if not strictly speaking a religious person)'. He does not carry the external trappings and stereotypes of 'the religious person' but by his nature he was always clearly directed to what Edwin Muir called 'the other place'. Reading Orkney is a labour of love and many are attentive to its wildness, its gentle presence, its spur and spark to the aesthetic, its truth about the natural-cum-supernatural world. This attentiveness is no romantic fantasy. It is grounded in Christian asceticism within which Mackay Brown is imprinted with the pattern of the Cross. He starts from the central image of the Cross, and returns there. Within this pattern and formation he plays out a convergence and confluence of all the ideological tendencies from the many sources embedded in the twentieth century. The 'swarm of symbols' are held pre-theologically to a theological standard of the Cross. He is able to give form and content, method and subject matter that are maintained across his writings with a tension that can be awkward at times. The unity that he is able to embrace is the freedom to express himself, which he found in a pre-Reformation Orkney. This is the unity which contains all else. He could be deeper and bolder with a license to explore the sources with an epistemology that remained open-ended and tolerant of interpretation.

Revisionism Studies of the Reformation

Mackay Brown, nurtured and reared in Orkney, learned to be aware of difference, to live with it, to oppose it, to embrace it, but most of all to work out how to live in Orkney in a reasonable way that accorded with the faith he had chosen in spite of obvious religious frictions which clearly troubled him. The Reformation debate has been subject to polarising extremes, both in England and Scotland. There has been considerable revisionism, a 'critical construct' of the historical processes, which strikes a balance between 'clearly recognisable approaches' where on the one hand there are 'happy medieval Catholics visiting their holy wells, attending frequent masses and deeply respectful of Purgatory and afraid of hell' and 'Alternatively, ... oppressed by corrupt churchmen. They yearned for the liberty of the Gospel.'[2]

Duffy asserts in *The Stripping of the Altars* that the Reformation 'represented a deep and traumatic cultural hiatus',[3] as does Michael Lynch, who uses for Scotland the word 'fissure'[4] instead of 'hiatus'. Contemporary scholarship gives greater emphasis to an interdisciplinary approach that is able to explore new questions, as in Thomas Clancy's reclaiming of a 're-opened world view', a time of 'earlier development'.[5] Barbara Crawford in *The Northern Earldoms* equally pursues an interdisciplinary approach to greatly enhance what was once a 'narrow historical focus'.[6] Archaeology, place names, saga literature and cults of the saints bring a freshness and new quality to understanding the pre-Reformation world in Orkney, an understanding that can also highlight the 'hiatus' and 'fissure' asserted by Duffy and Lynch. Similarities, differences and continuities become prominent and recognisable for what they actually are, rather than reconstructed to perpetuate highly secularised post-Reformation stereotypes.

Mackay Brown, more than able to take up the 'hiatus' and 'fissure' in literary terms, challenged the ignorance of Orcadians, and of his readers in general, both Scottish and world-wide, of Orkney's Catholic past and heritage. His questions and concerns were literary and pre-theological to bring to the fore a coherent and less repellent understanding of a different religious tradition by means of compelling symbols and images. This was his way of giving heart, soul and voice to what historians articulate as 'broader questions of social and psychic continuity and disjunction under the dynastic and ideological shifts'.[7] He was able to sense with his eye for the 'other place' through the suppressions of the Reformation, a world of which there were no clear memories prior to 1560 and its lack of religious confusion. This was a time of a communal solidarity celebrated in outward ceremony, where there was a holistic balance between good and evil.

> Saints and fairies, prayers and charms, larks and wormsall had their part to play in the overall design of community life. The relationship between the visible and the invisible was permeated with sacred imagery and meaning. Before the Reformation, the devotions, including the popular charms and spells of the people, were not in opposition to the official form of worship of the church. They shared much the same ground but they were distinct. The break-up of that symbolic world set adrift its elements and coherency but these elements still surged up from time to time to be demonised by the Kirk.[8]

Pre-Reformation Orkney

Mackay Brown was compelled to trace the origins of a specific place, Orkney, nurtured and reared as he was among archaeological relics embedded in the natural wild beauty of the Orkney Islands. The greatest pleasures of his writings could well be said to be 'a going back' in history and time, but there is a simultaneous forward motion that carries the reader in a cosmic and prophetical current that tries always to make sense of a fragmented and relativistic world that the author and his readers are at odds with. But is the reader's greatest source of pleasure to be found in a monotheistic vision set in the medieval period where Mackay Brown found peace with himself and the social realities of Orkney? Spurred on by St Magnus as he was, he finds an expansive freedom received and developed from the classical experience of a world which reveals God. There is an understood salvation history to draw upon within a comprehensive and cosmic context. He finds in its universal categories of beauty a conceptual language totally immersed in the revelation of God, the centre of which is Jesus Christ. It is a vision where the Christian can dare to assert that the reflection of the eternal goodness and beauty (that God is) is perceived in all that He has made. The Creator is reflected in His Creation. Mackay

Brown works avowedly in that tradition set by Thomas Aquinas in the realism of Aristotle imbued with the light of Plato, Dionysius and Augustine. The inheritance of antiquity in its entirety is embodied in Catholicism by Aquinas and there have been no imitations since that command such depth and breadth within the history of philosophy and religions. Faith and reason find their specific Catholic synthesis in the works of Aquinas, within which there is a dynamic interrelationship of classical theo-philosophy and Christian theology of revelation. It is this interrelationship that is instilled in the 'no separation' Mackay Brown signature.

How far Mackay Brown can be said to follow the Scotus model where 'being as a concept'[9] specifically in 'haeccitas' or 'thisness' is a difficult question but it is fair to say that he found, as did Gerard Manley Hopkins, a very modern perception and understanding in the face of the wild natural beauty of Orkney, that was able to see the glory of God in the things of creation that He had made, and find his path in the 'swarm of symbols'. Mackay Brown is not following the traces of the Scotus model to an empiricism, a materialism, a positivism, that found their impetus in 'things' themselves, the details of which could be examined only in their material aspects. The Scotus God, beyond the limits of all knowledge, brought an emphasis on a distinctive understanding between God as Creator and what He had made. Hopkins mastered this distinctive understanding in the seeing, the knowing, the praising, the loving of God, linguistically integrating by means of his poetic sensibilities.

Mackay Brown endeavoured to do the same by means of his literary responses but to, and in, a very different natural environment. Orkney does not have the nature of Oxford or English countryside.

> Nature is an infinite feast. For look: we speak of grass, and falcons, and soldiers and stars. But it is wrong, in a sense, to speak so generically— given our cast of thought, it is necessary to make such simplifications, but every blade of grass differs from the other grass-blades; a falcon is not only different from every other falcon, it changes from second to second, splendours never on earth before the flash from its pinions, as it turns in the changing light of a morning (and no two dawns are ever the same either); a Highland burn is superficially like streams and rivulets everywhere on earth, yet it is unique, changing with glooms

and gleams and burn-music (and even when we say 'moment; it is an arbitrary measure and division of time, for the behaviour of the burn is outside time altogether, it is set in an altogether more marvellous framework).[10]

As Aquinas found the particular in the universal, Duns Scotus found the universal in the particular, but Hopkins could mentor Mackay Brown in how to give importance and emphasis linguistically to the principle of individuation and 'thisness' by means of the inscape and instress of a thing. Hopkins in the nineteenth century was closer to the reactiveness of the Romantic period and Victorian Oxford Movement with its rediscovery of the dynamics of a suppressed Catholic past. Deep-seated principles of sacramental teaching and spirituality once again could legitimately take their place in society through literature. The introspective world of poetry reacquainted itself with the contemplative spirit of Christianity. Scotus had also given an emphasis to the personal where the human species holds within it the importance of this 'particular man'. Hopkins's appreciation of Duns Scotus and his focus on the personal 'thisness' was also a dynamic at work in the Oxford Movement and John Henry Newman's method of personal being, personal liberalism and personal certitude. Throughout the nineteenth century and into the twentieth, personal being and personal relationships found its time and development.

A soldier, a ploughman, a farrier—so we give the richness and uniqueness of a soldier glimpsed in the street, Harry and his horses and plough cleaving the earth, Felix Randal between his forge and his anvil? A poet can faintly celebrate the mystery that man is – 'immortal diamond.'[11]

Scottish Reformation studies have not always fully appreciated and understood Catholic factors in Orkney history but with new interdisciplinary approaches and a return to sources, fragmented as they are, a more accurate picture is emerging that challenges the accepted view that Catholicism completely disappeared for long periods after the Reformation in the Orkney Islands.[12] Mackay Brown gave heart, soul and voice to a proper understanding of the immense legacy, heritage and continuities of Catholicism, not in asserting himself as a 'Catholic' writer but in his pre-theological response, in his master-crafting of the 'swarm of symbols', by which he was able to bring Orkney into the modern period with its pre-Reformation past intact. Locally this is still to be acknowledged. William Thompson, as recently as 2008, and Simon Hall in 2010 have taken a suppressive tone:

> It was a monolithic society which, at an organisational level, dissent was unknown … although the Rev John Brand was obviously right when he noted that a popular attachment to pilgrimages, penances, votive offerings, the observation of saint's days, the use of holy water, the habit of signing the cross, and the veneration for local chapel sites represented a tenacious devotion to a degenerate form of Catholicism, long unsupported by any priesthood.[13]

> Roman Catholicism had been the historical religion of Orkney for centuries prior to the Reformation and is in this respect deeply embedded in Orcadian history. Although the Reformation in Orkney was less traumatic than elsewhere in Scotland, and in post-reformation times, Roman Catholicism has not suffered from any marked prejudice or sectarianism in Orkney, it is nevertheless a marginal, eccentric aspect of modern Orcadian religious practice.[14]

There is still much work to be done to inclusively examine the history of the land, people, and literature of Orkney and its uniqueness embedded in the wider shifts from centre to periphery and vice versa, in the constantly shifting panorama of the history of the area with all its borders, frontiers, allegiances and suppressions. Even to examine the place names in the Orkney Islands that still, to this day, mark out clear identifiers for Catholic beliefs and practices gives evidence of the revisionist view: 'The Reformation was a violent disruption not the natural fulfilment of, of most of what was vigorous in late medieval piety and religious practice.'[15] The Scottish Reformation after revisionism and the growth and development of interdisciplinary studies re-opens an intrinsic interest and vitality in what Thompson describes as 'a tenacious devotion to a degenerate form of Catholicism'[16] and Hall as 'a marginal, eccentric aspect'.[17] Mackay Brown takes his literary experiment 'back before Scottish Literature' until we see 'a recognisable mirror to our modern, multi-cultural, hybrid-identity literary scene'.[18] A re-opened world view is in keeping with Clancy's 'back before Scottish Literature'[19] to more fully appreciate where we are now, who we are now.

Duffy writes: 'a Catholic background can be an advantage to the historian of this period, enabling them to see late medieval religion as 'more coherent and less repellent than may be the case for historians formed in a different religious tradition'.[20] This stands for Scotland and Orkney as well, in spite of the very different Reformation history that has marked Scotland and Orkney so profoundly. The heart, soul and voice of Mackay Brown, so sharply condemnatory of Calvinism (and he was well qualified to be so given his theological and existential credentials firmly formed by his environment) found stimulus for his imagination. The highly local, highly specific materials from the medieval period that remain in Orkney are a constant primary source that for Mackay Brown posed the question, where does Church tradition stop? Survival, loss and change and their legacy of disempowerment forced him to evolve and emerge and endure but able to contest the conformist pressures of the past and present in his multi-volume and multi-genre literary experimentations and achievements.

Restoration and Realignment

'Reading' Orkney in the modern period of the twentieth century, clearly a labour of love for Mackay Brown, was in keeping with the most ancient impulses of Catholicism stretching back to the Bible and the Church Fathers. He was energised by Newman and Hopkins with the reactive energy of the Oxford Movement to reintroduce 'transcendence' into Orkney poetics in the company of others locally and internationally. What he was able to learn from literature became his catechesis and formation, that could vehemently put Calvinism to one side (for the moment anyway) and imaginatively find a redemption and ascendance in the craft of mastering the 'swarm of symbols'. His consciousness of this is one that does not explicitly set out to dogmatically assert 'I am a Catholic writer', or 'I am a religious poet'. That would have been anathema to him. He found a place where he could 'be', within which the exercise of his linguistic giftedness was enough for him. He says himself in the BBC Scotland documentary *One Star in the West. George Mackay Brown at 70*[21] 'if it wasn't fun I wouldn't do it'; 'intricate word games appeal to me enormously', and he says that he finds 'the mere sound of them (words) intoxicating', and furthermore, 'without set forms life is a meaningless drift'. It is the 'doing', it is the 'act' of writing that he is compelled to pursue, this is his literary apostolate that works in the 'deep quarry of images'.[22] Readers can make of it what they will, and they do. The Mackay Brown 'project' is a realignment of his life and being that goes counter to the modernism and liberalism of his day, a legacy of the dominance of Kantianism and its separation of reason and emotion. The dominance of rationalism, that saw emotion as a distortion, was not going to help Mackay Brown find himself and release him from his dominant depressive temperament configured by nurture in a damning anti-life-giving Calvinism, from which he wanted to escape till the day he died.

Many of the period were also realigning theology against the backdrop of loss of orientation in a fruitful aesthetics. Mackay Brown knew about perception and faith, and knowing these things he was able, by means of the wild beauty of Orkney, counter the powerful inhibitory force he experienced Calvinism to be. He was in a position to interpret symbols, not only through responsiveness to the wild beauty of Orkney, but he was specifically forced into so doing by a psychological struggle for his sanity brought about by illness and the closeness of death. Such symbols were the 'set forms' by which he could counter the 'meaningless drift'. The 'set form' of the symbol comprises 'a complex of gestures, sounds, images and words, that evoke, invite and persuade participation in that to which they refer'.[23] A symbol is always more than its 'set form'. What better way to read Orkney with its polyvalent materials, which make demands on the human psyche to the extent that Creation itself takes on an explanation, that many in past and present times have discovered is a transcendent one. From its earliest beginnings of civilisation, Orkney is testament to many layers of explanation that tend towards the supernatural. Images, whether they be the natural phenomena of land, sky and sea, or the archaeological remains of civilisations or the architecture that still survives, refer back not only to prehistoric periods, but for Mackay Brown to the medieval period where he found 'the sweetness of the old religion'.

The twentieth century has been specially marked as a linguistic being, conceptually driven but, equally, as non-conceptually creative. Mackay Brown speaks evocatively about heraldry and has a preference for the world of the poet, wherein he has personally found 'more satisfaction, nourishment', a place where one must use 'finer tools', the results of which are 'more precious in your own mind'.[24] Orkney was 'the only place he could write in'.[25] It is here in this time and place that Mackay Brown could read Orkney to write of Orkney, to be its heart and voice. He is not adding religious values to the content of a symbol. He quarries the images in their original state, the materials so near at hand, in fishing and farming. In the natural world he came to discern the Form that a theologian such as von Balthasar, who in another country at that time, would articulate by means of a theological aesthetics.

Mackay Brown, not a theologian, but a poet, works unselfconsciously in a pre-theological domain, having discovered for himself, the true, the beautiful and the good in all their 'particularities', just as Hopkins had before him. These are the transcendental values that emerged from the ancient classical world and were deeply embedded also in the Bible. Christian symbolism combines the Old Testament Jewish eschatological typologies with New Testament categories by means of a Neoplatonic understanding that gave a profound unity to the monistic vision of Christianity. It is within this vision that Mackay Brown had made the movement of his whole person that led away, from a 'self' that he more often than not could not bear, to an invisible God. This response is intellectual and cognitive as much as it is emotional and affective. The journey is a faith one, possessed of its own language which opens the way forward for the entire person rather than closes off, and is what Calvinism would consider to be the idolatrous aesthetical path of art and creativity. Calvinism to Mackay Brown was a constant source of psychological harshness that scarred him for life with sadness and depression.

> 5 October 1991. I was suffering from a deep depression and recently spent 3 weeks in hospital in Aberdeen' but I am fortunate in having so many good friends who set the fire for me, do my shopping, invite me for meals ... Maybe all this kindness isn't altogether good for me. I am losing my cooking skills, for one thing ... I haven't been to Mass for some weeks but I'll try, I think, to go tomorrow. The Calvinistic inheritance of the 'angry God' is hard to shake off, having been in the bloodstream for 12 generations. The God of Joy, the Lord of the Dance, is what we need increasingly.

That was his experience, his inheritance of the Reformation period. Mackay Brown existed in a set of surroundings, most notably and decisively the Orkney Islands. What matters is the character of those surroundings to which his life and work give testament. This life is inflected by a totality of events in his time and place, and he is not alone in his critique of Calvinism, which he experienced first-hand. His critique is a literary one, a pre-theological one that has a firm structure, a specific gravity, a love of the particulars, a complex interrelatedness, a keen spirit of inquiry that all held together in a fragile but serenely tender balance of forces and tensions. The Form is always material and particular and is irreducibly incarnational. The 'glory' of the Form is come to by means of the Cross and the disfigurement of Christ. Disfigurement is always a Mackay Brown signature, as is the Cross. He has intimate associations with both, as documented in 'Man into Oak' and 'Summer Day'. First the vision then the rapture. Here is the documented source of an intrinsic attractiveness, a luminosity that is never content to stay with the material alone. There is always the 'other place'. Mackay Brown was at ease with a revitalised metaphysics expressed once again by means of the twentieth-century existentialist development that could still hold the unity of person against a century of deconstructive fragmentation of society and person.

Symbols, as they swarm, were specially understood and expressed by the Church Fathers, and once again find the power of communication in 'set forms' that still speak to us today. The interpenetration of emotion and reason, reason and faith, the material and the immaterial, for Mackay Brown are resonant of an epistemology, a theory of knowledge, that can be traced back from a theological aesthetics via Newman and Hopkins and the Oxford Movement, to a re-opened world view where 'symbols are free to swarm'. The sensorium of the medieval period is the missing piece in the jigsaw, the door that opens out for von Balthasar, the authentic quest to express the glory of revelation, of the Lord, from the experience of the laity. This group of laity perceive well that 'the run-of-the-mill clergy'[26] are no-longer able to defend this quest and as poets and artists their engagement with Primary Form (God) make accessible for others, through the secondary form of words, concepts, images and patterns. The Mackay Brown project is metaphysical and cosmic with insights wherein the readercan rest and be sustained by the single powerful and original vision which was won in the prose poems of the 1941–51 period, and enshrined in the poem, 'Summer Day', the energies of which were revisited and reworked until the very last Mackay Brown breath of life. As Mackay Brown himself acknowledges: 'Yet, in that decade, I had certain very intense experiences that became part of the fabric of my life. I did not will them and I did not go in search of them.'[27]

The Power of Symbols

I include here some telling thoughts about his preoccupation with symbols. Writing about Edwin Muir's text on growing up in Wyre, Mackay Brown says: 'but if a symbol is not held onto, as the first good impulse of creation, and its final perfection, then man's existence on earth is a mean and cruel and pitiful thing indeed'.[28] On Ecclesiastes, he writes: 'the words sank deep and seemed to illuminate a huge tract of darkness.'[29] He was also attentive to the power of reason in his writing and how emotion is given its rightful place within the symbol: 'a true poet never wallows in emotion … very quietness of his writing carries power'.[30] In a BBC educational radio transcript he says, 'the class of writers to which I belong goes into a kind of mild trance, and if you're lucky, into the blank of his mind comes an image, more alive than the living.'[31] These insights are absolute gems. Who better than the poet himself to articulate his creative processes at work within his inner life? His faith is authentic and credible and he acknowledges the tradition within which he found such deep and sustaining nurture:

> In principio erat verbum. Our western form of religion, Christianity, thinks of the Word as illuminating all history with beauty, wisdom and truth. For poetry and the other arts, to be handmaidens of that supreme word is a worthy enough calling.[32]

> I find difficulty in the ancient theory of 'inspiration'. If, sometimes, I write at a higher plane than I had thought possible, it is only that the ground has been well prepared. It is possible for an artist or writer, preparing for the day's work, to go into a quiet trance, that need not last five or seven minutes. A word, a phrase, or an image, or even rhythm, enters the silence. Other words and images gather about it, a rhythm begins to pulse through the ordered cluster of images—it

is the beginning of a new story or poem. It doesn't always work, of course, but it has worked for me, often enough: then 'the complete consort dances together'. I am not foolish enough to think that the muse is overmastering me. But something mysterious, and beyond the reach of the conscious mind, is happening.[33]

There may be no meaning in our life at all: though I think there must be. Some great writers have faced the emptiness, and wrung a barren beauty from it: Kafka, Beckett, Sartre. In one sense, each individual is alone in the labyrinth of himself. He may be lost and uncertain: he may think of himself as being in the quest of an unimagined beauty and truth. In the old Greek myth a monster dwelt at the centre of the labyrinth. Perhaps only by confronting and coming to terms with this terror or ecstasy—whatever it may be—can we become truly human; and so find our way out into the light of common day, and add, a hard-won iota to the sum of human experience.

But no man is an island. Everything we do or speak or think—however seemingly unremarkable—may set the whole web of existence trembling, and affect the living and the dead and the unborn. It is an awesome thought, that we should not let burden us overmuch. It manifests itself in a religious image of great simplicity and beauty: the cornstalk rising into sun and wind from the buried seed, the offered bread and the hallowed bread, all humanity sitting down at last to share a common meal.[34]

Mackay Brown is analysed and critiqued with great sympathy and it is acknowledged that he goes beyond the conventions, 'Despite the scriptural allusion in the Loaves and Fishes, not much contained therein expresses the kind of faith and hope one might normally expect of Christian poetry'.[35] The 'kind of faith and hope' he knows about is first and last 'Orkney' and its place in the cosmos. This is a big canvas but he patiently works the many layers of Orkney within his own inner life demonstrating the tense dynamic at work in a distinctively Orkney poetics.

It cannot be denied that the Reformation and its suppressions and new energies were intensely difficult for Mackay Brown, but he did square up to what he understood to be its effects. His sanity did prevail and it will never be justifiable to sideline a physical predisposition to his form of depression. Depression takes many forms and has a causal interactivity that is physical and existential. Nevertheless Muir and Mackay Brown are right to give voice to what was lost in the sixteenth century in Scotland and re-open the earlier historical period to reclaim their heritage. The Oxford Movement with the special voices of Newman and Hopkins had done the same in England and it made a deep impression upon Mackay Brown. Muir left Scotland with his strong marriage and purposefulness found elsewhere but Mackay Brown was different:

> the cause of Brown's depressions may derive from the insecurities of his conversion to a religion that was the historical antithesis of Scotland's more 'patriotic' Calvinism; and the overlay of an ancient Catholicism of crosses and contradictions upon a traditionally hell-haunted Presbyterianism may have been more than Brown's personality could bear.[36]

It was always going to be hard for Mackay Brown to be Catholic in Orkney. To get close to the real Mackay Brown one cannot do better than turn to Ernest Marwick and what he wrote about his reception into the Catholic Church:

> For one thing, it has meant that certain negative elements in his work, induced by his distaste for Calvinism and its fruits, have been replaced by a positive philosophy. The receptive attitude of mind, the instinctive identification with the old faith, had long been there ... After his submission to the church, which followed prolonged and agonising thought, he began to look more deeply into the spiritual realities that give meaning and potential to the life of man ... He returned, as he has often done, to his beloved St Magnus, ... and he began to explore in symbolical terms the problem of sanctity: what it is that makes a man sacrifice himself and others that some ideal of duty may be fulfilled, some identification of his purposes with those of God achieved ... men hoard life until it becomes dry and sour, or actively deny its wonder and fruitfulness, by adopting false patterns of living.
>
> In his early callow verse, of which he published little, he was inclined to blame 'Knox and his wild hogmanay' for our spiritual predicament. The kirk elder, the merchant 'holy with greed', the censorious old women—ever present representatives of those who followed a smug, humourless and repressive mode of existence—were repugnant to

him in that they denied to themselves and others the opportunity of savouring the richness and variety of life. He looked around, both in actual Orkney of today and in the Orkney of history and tradition, for the kind of people who had, consciously or unconsciously, discovered their true identity and who lived by instinct instead of by rule. The types he celebrated, included those not normally esteemed in a Presbyterian community—the tinker, sitting easy to life, asking little from it, yet rejoicing in a lusty freedom; the local romeo. Taking his pleasure without any sense of guilt; the farm girl, vaguely aware of her destiny as a woman viewing with complacency and utter content a body big with child.[37]

Reformation and Orkney

Marwick gives a reasoned and balanced insight but perhaps it is fair to say that Mackay Brown's reading of Reformation history, as it pertained to Orkney and Scotland, as a 'Time of bitterness and degradation' where 'accomplished tyrants' quickly institutionalised the new regime was overly extreme. But was it? My own study of the transition of Orkney from the medieval period to the Reformation and beyond from a Catholic point of view[38] makes 'a strong case for challenging many of the conventional assumptions made in the past by Protestant writers'.[39] These 'conventional assumptions' give a picture of the Catholic Church in Orkney as 'a debased clerical and financial institution that depleted and neglected parishes in favour of drawing all the resources to the Cathedral'.[40] However, contrary to this view, 'there is more than enough evidence to indicate a very strong religious culture that embraces every aspect of daily life. Liturgy, music, education, law, banking, public health and recreation are all the remit of the Church and well understood by every level of society'.[41] Catholicism was 'sufficiently incarnated among its adherents to the extent that it surfaces in subsequent centuries demonstrating vigour, adaptability and popularity'.[42] The old Church and its worship did not die out. There was a dismantling of medieval culture and its onset was sudden. The Reformation Parliament of 1560 forbade the Mass; tradition has it that the last Mass was officiated at Rapness on Westray.

The break-up of Catholic Orkney was led by Bishop Bothwell, who quickly reorganised land ownership, personnel and family power.

Bishop Bothwell astutely 'reformed' from outside the Church whereas his predecessor Bishop Reid had led reform from within the Church. Bishop Bothwell achieved with considerable success a break with abuses and inadequacies of the church at that time, but conversely this 'break' or hiatus and fissure severed all outward links with the flowering and achievements of later medieval Catholicism. Regional study of parish clergy and their deployment at the Reformation has always laid great emphasis on the conforming of Catholic clergy in Orkney to the reformed church: 60 per cent of the thirty-four clerics is one of the two highest percentages in Scotland. Galloway recorded 50 per cent. Both Orkney and Galloway were both dioceses whose bishops actively supported the Reformation and as such hastened a smooth transition by taking a stable body of clergy with them who were able to implement the new order, at least on the administrative level. In spite of the efficient reorganisation the 'medieval catechesis with its emphasis on the visual, ceremony and ritual lingers through the imagination … there was considerable cultural retention in chapels, pilgrimages, penitential and votive practices'[43] throughout the Orkney Islands.

Mackay Brown works from the historical fragments of this period, dispersed and fragmented as they are, to rework them through his imagination and bring them to life in a later period. His reading of history is true to its sources and the exploration of the emotional character of these sources is right and necessary, even if it is hard for his local audience to accept. But Marwick worked hard to temper Mackay Brown's first 'callow' literary efforts and lead him to a maturity that was more palatable to the audiences available to him. If Mackay Brown's 'tone' was overly emotional, revealing a bitter sense of loss, then this is the reality of reading history and coming to terms with the past.

> The cruellest thing of all was that the people's ballads were broken and trampled upon … the Presbyterian churchmen of the time did their thorough best to rid the islands of its native folk culture. The ballads and songs went down before the rants of John Knox. In St Magnus Cathedral … Cromwell's men tied their horses to the pillars, and the glowing walls were deadened with whitewash … It is a time of great ugliness and squalor … Fragments of their ballads survived … The Play of the Lady Odivere … And whenever they were sick, it was not the Presbyterian ministers they went, but to the old Catholic chapels

crumbling to ruin all over the islands. Among the broken stones they knelt and asked the Virgin and Saint Magnus to cure them … the utilitarian heresy is the curse of modern Orkney.[44]

Mackay Brown was not a Catholic writer or a Catholic poet, but his strong literary responsiveness was how a Catholic would respond. He was not on a mission to convert readers but his steady spirit that weaves the Orkney tapestry draws his readers into his inner world where

> In narrative terms, then, Brown's world is offered to us in fragments, like the tesserae of a mosaic we are invited to assemble, or to reassemble. It is unhelpful to read his espousal of Catholicism … as a genuine desire to convert his readers. The point is perhaps rather that readers will not share his value or belief system, and that this divergence between the poet and the reader will highlight the role of ideology, and of the associated narratives, in allowing meaning to be conferred upon experience.[45]

Marwick mentored Mackay Brown in the art of how to cultivate a relationship with an audience, and Whyte validates how successfully Mackay Brown achieved this. Ascherson judges Mackay Brown to be 'the least tormented, the most spiritually secure'[46] in his contribution to the *Seven Poets*, a perceptive study of Mackay Brown and his literary peers. Schmid has pointed out that there are those who have 'argued that his religious outlook and didacticism led to a restricting of his literary ability'.[47] His Catholicism is acknowledged but has been held at a distance in favour of a more immediate interest in Orcadian and Nordic studies. To do justice to Mackay Brown one must square up to his choice of religion as anything but a degenerate form of restricting eccentricity.

Universal Parameters

There is something about Orkney, steeped as it is in primal sources, which Mackay Brown capitalises on. It is precisely these primal sources that pressed him and others, and subsequently many others in and outside Orkney, towards their origins. The 'hiatus' or the 'fissure', the imbalance in the dismantled world that was the case after the Reformation, in itself pressed for a correcting reconnection with traditional roots. This same impetus drove forward the Oxford Movement, and learning much from Newman, Mackay Brown too adopted the 'phe-nomenological attitude' that resonated so strongly with the reactive ethos of the twentieth century. Newman saw far in advance of his time and was instrumental, along with others, in re-opening a prior period of history that now could emerge for further development. Mackay Brown's reading and re-readings of Newman's *Apologia* did not dwell on the points of nineteenth-century ecclesiastical history. He found in Newman confirmation of how one can be certain of the truth in one's inner world so marked by doubts and contradicted by one's own social surroundings. Like Newman, an initial vehement tone and hypersen-sitivity released energies that carried one forward into a movement towards a special 'work'. For Newman it was the Oxford Movement; for Mackay Brown it was an Orkney poetics.

Orkney could be in touch with its own great past and also with modern intellectual life and developments. Mackay Brown felt the urgent need of the full metaphysical range and the unity of knowledge that had been dismantled at the Reformation and subsequently broken up throughout the Enlightenment period, when Scotland had carved out a special prominence. Mackay Brown, it can be argued, as much as he is motivated by a sense of fun and word-games, achieves much in setting the record straight, giving great measure and credence to a restoration process, to a balanced interpretation of Orkney with all its varied layers of life and civilisation. But his natural context is not a pre-historic or pagan one. The Christendom of the medieval period with a special loving focus on St Magnus, gives him a unity of knowledge and the full metaphysical range, from which the 'fun and games' of naming, arranging, patterning, the phenomena that surrounds him, the signs and symbols are more fruitful ways of knowing and understanding. The separation of faith and reason that underwent a profound disengage-ment throughout the Enlightenment, subsequently placed the source of authority not within original patterns of agreement as held and lived by the ancient world religion of Catholicism, but in the Renaissance mind. The simple teachings of the Galilee fisherman, Peter, the first pope, ploughed deep furrows into the instabilities and incoherencies of Mackay Brown securing him in a life-long faithfulness. He under-stood the profound evidence of the descent of the Catholic Church on his own doorstep to be traceable to the presence of Simon Peter, the Fisherman who shimmers from the beyond, to what he perceived to be our deepest truth.

His powers of perception rose up over the educational system he experienced and seemingly abhorred with its rationalism and utilitarian intentions. A primal authority was sensed to be found elsewhere. Liturgy, firstly in the set forms of the natural world, his 'greenfields kirk' and later in the Catholic Church with its sounds, its rhythms and lexicon soaking deep into his mind. He had already discovered a vast sacred space for his 'silent foundations of speech', a 'deep listening' and more fruitful ways of knowing and believing. Here was the principal reservoir from which religious paradigms and beliefs were 'quarried' for himself and his readers, drawing people into a careful balance of faith and reason rooted in primal agreement, Scripture and tradition lived out in the Liturgy.

Mackay Brown set his own parameters as a literary antithesis to narrow intellectualism, a separation between faith and reason, a denial of the senses, an interpretation that emotions were dangerous sources of distortion, a preoccupation with self and ego and the priority of subjective psychological states. The full metaphysical range, with its parameters falling outside a materialistic and empirical narrowness, inevitably leads to a tender and gentle grasp of religion with a literary imperative to give signs and symbols their rightful place locally and further afield. Many important religious concepts are expressed through signs and symbols and the post-Reformation legacy from which we seem to be legitimately emerging, gave an overemphasis on texts and the written word. This overemphasis could be a consequence of a life-denying rationality and a dominance of Calvinistic theological determinism. This dominance has been expressed in the lowering of the status of sign, symbol, images, ritual, shrines, artefacts and buildings associated with the Roman Catholic tradition.

Gently, Mackay Brown leads us 'back' and 'towards', to the 'beginning' and to the 'end', to the origins. This is a process by which his perceptual attentiveness takes the reader beyond arbitrary moments and phases of 'time' to the timeless. These 'particularities' are rewoven in to the cruciform, the returning to the Cross where all manifestations of the 'particular' 'flashed with a leap and lance of nails', 'over the lambing hills', 'the thousand candles of gorse', the sea- organ and pipes—wailed miserere', 'that Godsent storm.'[48] We are held within the unity of that Form that is the glory of the Lord selvèd as it is in the poet Mackay Brown. Likewise in the Eucharist Mackay Brown makes available to readers the 'Way':

> ... a pure seeking past a swarm of symbols, the millwheel, sun and scythe, and ox, and harrow, Station by station to that simple act Of terror or love, that broke the hill apart but what stood there—an Angel with a sword Or Grinning rags—astride the kindled seed? He knelt in the doorway.[49]

This is a deep intimacy between Mackay Brown and Christ, born of an authentic personal contemplative relationship. This intimacy is no sham, no literary artifice. As Jesus says in John 10:14, 'I know my own and my own know me'. Catholic readers, Christian readers, readers who sense the transcendence, are in a shared deep reality.

And as for the Reformation, for all Mackay Brown's rejection of it, his life and work found their purpose: 'Restore to that maimed rock-pool, when the flood sounds all her lucent strings, its ocean dance.'[50] To read and write Orkney, according to 'all her lucent strings', to restore the beauty and truth of the 'ocean dance' was his destiny—to go further and deeper than those who became before him in Orkney, and those that were around him in Orkney, in a distinctive Orkney poetics. The 'wreck' and 'storm' that he understood the Reformation to be, 'That swung Iona, like keel of Scotland, Into the wrecking European wave,'[51] he squared up to and set about the discipline of a slow and patient reworking of the labyrinthian odyssey in which he was to find his giftedness and 'the only thing I could do'. 'The wind that sweeps like an angel's wing'[52] was enough for him to be getting on with.

Notes

[1] George Mackay Brown, undated (probably 1947) letter to Edwin Walker Marwick. Orkney Archive, Ernest Walker Marwick Collection, D31/30/4.

[2] Norman Jones, *The English Reformation: Religion and Cultural Adaptation.* Oxford: Blackwell Publishers, 2002, p. 1.

[3] Eamon Duffy, 'The English Reformation after Revisionism', in *Renaissance Quarterly* 59 (2006), p. 721.

[4] Michael Lynch, *Scotland: A New History.* London: Century, 1991, p. 104.

[5] Clancy, 'Scottish Literature before Scottish Literature', p. 23.

[6] Barbara E. Crawford, *The Northern Earldoms. Orkney and Caithness from AD 870 to 1470.* Edinburgh: Birlinn, 2013, p. 4.

[7] Duffy, 'The English Reformation after Revisionism', p. 727.

[8] Alison Gray, *Circle of Light. The Catholic Church in Orkney since 1560.* Edinburgh: John Donald, 2000, p. 42.

[9] Broadie, *The Shadow of Scotus* , p. 7.

[10] Mackay Brown, *For the Islands I Sing*, pp. 151–2.

[11] *Ibid.*, p. 152.

[12] See the earlier work of Alison Gray, *The Circle of Light.*

[13] William P. L. Thomson, *Orkney Land and People.* Kirkwall: Orcadian, 2008, p. 196.

[14] Hall, *The History of Orkney Literature*, p. 144.

[15] Duffy, *The Stripping of the Altars*, p. 4.

[16] Thomson, *Orkney Land and People*, p. 196.

[17] Hall, *The History of Orkney Literature*, p. 144.

[18] Clancy, 'Scottish Literature before Scottish Literature', p. 23.

[19] *Ibid.*

[20] Duffy, 'The English Reformation after Revisionism', pp. 720–31.

[21] BBC Scotland, *George Mackay Brown 70th Birthday. One Star in the West.* Broadcast on BBC Scotland, April 1996.

[22] *Ibid.*

[23] J. A. Komonchak, M. Collins and D. A. Lane, ed., *The New Dictionary of Theology.* Dublin: Gill and MacMillan, 1987, p. 997.

[24] BBC Scotland, *George Mackay Brown 70th Birthday.*

[25] *Ibid.*

[26] von Balthasar, *The Glory of the Lord II*, p. 15.

[27] Mackay Brown, *For the Islands I Sing*, p. 79.

28 George Mackay Brown, 'Edwin Muir', *Glasgow Herald*, 21 Nov. 1988. Held in Orkney Archive, George Mackay Brown Collection, D124/2/1/2.

29 George Mackay Brown, 'Predicament of the Writer', *Scotsman* 22 Feb. 1986. Held in Orkney Archive, George Mackay Brown Collection, D124/2/2/5.

30 George Mackay Brown, 'Treasures beyond Price'. *The Sunday Mail Story of Scotland*, vol. 4, 1988, p. 48. Held in Orkney Archive, George Mackay Brown Collection, D124/2/2/13.

31 George Mackay Brown, transcript of unpublished BBC Educational Radio, 'Silver: A Commentary on a Story', 1988. Held in Orkney Archive, George Mackay Brown Collection, D124/2/2/16.

32 Mackay Brown, 'Poetry Keeping the Flame Alive'.

33 Mackay Brown, 'Thoughts of an Old-Age Pensioner', pp. 17–18.

34 *Ibid.*, pp. 18–19.

35 Joseph Reino, 'George Mackay Brown', in *The Dictionary of Literary Biography*, vol. 27, *Poets of Great Britain and Ireland, 1945–1960*, ed. Vincent B. Sherry, Jr. Michigan: Gale, 1984, pp. 31–9. Held in Orkney Archive, George Mackay Brown Collection, D124/1/5/12.

36 *Ibid.*, p. 35.

37 Marwick, 'Profile of George Mackay Brown'.

38 Gray, *Circle of Light*.

39 *Ibid.*, p. 12.

40 *Ibid.*

41 *Ibid.*, pp. 12–13.

42 *Ibid.*, pp. 12–14.

43 *Ibid.*, p. 23.

44 George Mackay Brown, 'Living in Orkney', *Saltire Review* 2/6 (Winter 1955), pp. 55, 58.

45 Christopher Whyte, *Modern Scottish Poetry*. Edinburgh: Edinburgh University Press, 2004, p. 170.

46 Neil Ascherson, *Seven Poets. Hugh MacDiarmid, Norman MacCaig, Iain Crichton Smith, George Mackay Brown, Robert Garioch, Sorley MacLean, Edwin Morgan*. Glasgow: Third Eye Centre, 1981, p. 23.

47 Sabine Schmid, *Keeping the Sources Pure. The Making of George Mackay Brown*. Bern: Peter Lang, 2003, p. 15.

48 George Mackay Brown, 'The Storm' (1954), in *The Collected Poems*, pp. 3–4.

49 George Mackay Brown, 'The Masque of Bread' (1959), in *The Collected Poems*, pp. 18–19.

[50] George Mackay Brown, 'Chapel between Cornfield and Shore' (1959), in *The Collected Poems*, p. 35.

[51] George Mackay Brown, 'Culloden: The Last Battle' (1965), in *The Collected Poems*, p. 40.

[52] George Mackay Brown, 'A New Fishing Boat' (1965), in *The Collected Poems*, p. 59.

Conclusion

It seems fitting to complete the Mackay Brown faith story with a fuller appreciation of his death and the rites and rituals that gave him a Catholic farewell. His life as a Catholic parishioner has not been given the fuller disclosure that his thirty-five years of attending Mass deserves. The Church of Our Lady and St Joseph, Kirkwall, was where he was baptised, confessed and confirmed by Fr Cairns SJ in 1961. I met George at the Church in 1976. I had first come to Orkney with a New Zealand friend whose Orcadian grandparents had emigrated to New Zealand. For a while when I lived in Harray I used to get a lift to Mass every Sunday with John Broom and George, meeting them on the Kirkwall Road. I visited George at Mayburn Court regularly until I returned to New Zealand in 1978. We would sit in his small workaday kitchen or in front of the sitting-room fire. Sometimes, weather permitting, we would sit down on the seat at the museum frontage looking out over the water. We then wrote to each other over a period between 1979 and 1995. Excerpts of this correspondence are transcribed in an appendix. Here George speaks for himself about his life as the 'parishioner'.

As a Catholic parishioner George was public as well as private in his worship and devotions. He sang well and also took the Offertory baskets around the congregation during the Mass taking them up in the Offertory procession to the altar. He was participant in the rituals of the Mass. In 1976 to 1978 I do not recall him receiving the Eucharist. The church had yet to undergo its Vatican II reconfiguration and this meant at this time the Mass was celebrated by Fr Bamber with his back to the congregation. He stayed for coffee after Mass and was very sociable. That is how we met. In fact, he had many friends, and one can truly say he had a great capacity and gift for friendship with those near and far away. Yes, he was a private person, but he was also very interested in people. In the early days of his Catholicism he had house Masses at his home in Mayburn Court.

It is important to understand that he was not treated in any special way in the parish. We all are one before Christ and the communion we share through the Eucharist is a great leveller. We are all sinners, and confess privately and as a community. Catholics in all their variety emerge from Holy Communion, having received the body and blood of Our Lord, the food and drink our hearts and minds cannot forget, as one in Christ. There is no distinction between the highs and lows of social class. This is so compelling, and it was so for George. He loved the oneness as all Catholics do. The intimacy of this time with Christ spurs us on to use our gifts and talents, to develop our vocations in this world. Even more assuredly we are prepared for the afterlife. It is in the silence after Holy Communion that Catholics most truly encounter and know this. In the Communion of Saints there is no separation between this world and the next, between the living and the dead. In fact as I heard an Irish priest preach in Orkney once, Catholics are more 'at home' with the dead than the living. George knew that only too well and his writings are testament to this understanding.

It is also important to understand that Catholics are a 'hedgerow' people invited and called from all directions. George was very committed to this New Testament understanding with his understanding of those who live on the margins. There were many parishioners across the years who helped him in many ways but remain anonymous in their respect for him. Within the Church of Our Lady and St Joseph Kirkwall there are those who have a very developed spirituality and the Catholic tradition of prayer is alive and well, hidden as it is in a humble penetrating silence.

When I returned to Orkney in 1995, Renee Simm would drive him to Mass, sometimes to Kirkwall for Holy Days of Obligation, but Sunday Mass was then also celebrated at Braemar on a hill overlooking Stromness and then the newly built house, Our Lady, Star of the Sea. Both were owned by a parishioner. George did receive communion, the body and the blood, regularly at this time in his life. A Stromness parishioner, and also a eucharistic minister, drove him to Mass at times and took him Holy Communion at Mayburn Court on occasion.

George died on 13 April 1996. He had gone into hospital on Friday, 12 April. I had seen him a week before on the street where he was deep in conversation or some kind of interior dialogue. I do remember he looked very disconcerted when I greeted him and he was somewhat awkward about being 'caught' in this situation. I did not know he had gone into hospital. I was rung by the sacristan on Saturday with the news that he had died. His death was not something I was sad about. This was a time of joy. I have always felt close to him in matters of faith and even more so since his death.

The following Monday his body was received into the parish church of Our Lady and St Joseph in Kirkwall and mourners, Catholic and non-Catholic, attended for the meditation of the rosary, as is the custom in Catholicism on the eve of the Requiem Mass. The coffin was open and from my point of view his body looked the husk shed upon departure of the soul. This was intensified as he was always in life very animated facially and in death this animation was absent to the point of realisation that life had now departed, the soul well on its way in the afterlife. George spoke often about Purgatory, and he was always clear that was his destiny until purification was complete. Any physical repose of the body was one of a noticeable absence of life. Rene Simm asked Bishop Conti if she could take a photograph, consent was given and she did so.

The Requiem Mass at St Magnus's Cathedral was a joyous occasion, a celebration of his life and a most fitting farewell. I participated by doing the first reading from St Paul's letter to the Romans. In the company of St Magnus's relics, entombed in a pillar of this medieval cathedral with all its long history before the Reformation and since, the liturgy of the Requiem Mass embraced him, releasing him into the afterlife. There again lies the perception so familiar to him in his life and writings, 'It is impossible to say where the natural perception of God in the world ceases and the supernatural, Christian perception begins.'[1] As Bishop Mario Conti (now Emeritus Archbishop of Glasgow) said so well in his homily:

> I remember George describing the earth under the farmer's plough as being scourged—or was it the back of Christ he saw being ploughed? If my memory falters, it is because of George's characteristic interchanging of images, which revealed, not only the twin source of his deepest inspiration, namely his native Orkney and his adopted Catholicism, but also his easy integration of what for so many remain separate orders of life and faith.[2]

George had imbibed early the biblical 'seeing' and 'knowing' in Psalm 128: 'They ploughed my back like ploughmen drawing long furrows', interchanging the fields and ploughs of Orkney with the Holy Land fields and ploughs of the Bible. In fact they were for him not only the *cruciform* of his writings, but the actual body of the crucified Christ. Jesus taught us 'see' the natural simple things of life as they are. Seeing God in the things he has made resides in their original configurations. Duns Scotus and Hopkins reinvigorated this 'seeing' drawing us back to the enduring weave of the 'particular' never eclipsed of its distinctive 'thisness', embedded as it is in the Creator God who made it, who caused it, who ordered it, leaving patterns and contours of naturalness by which one could find their origin.

Bishop Mario continued:

> This is why his death at this season seems so right, for this is the season when the life of faith and the life of nature so marvellously correspond; when He who was hung upon the bare wood and moistened it with his blood, made it to flower as the instrument of salvation; when He who was buried in the dark earth and shared its apparent sleep, burst forth from it revealing the new life of grace.[3]

Bishop Mario then read 'The Harrowing of Hell' from the Easter edition of the *Tablet*, which only days before he had

> read and re-read … and it sweetened the dreary wait at Schiphol Airport yesterday afternoon—before a paper on the next flight told me of his death. Permit me to share this poem with you as a testimony not only of his poetic artistry, but to his Christian faith.[4]

> ### The Harrowing of Hell[5]
> He went down the first step.
> His lantern shone like the morning star.
> Down and down he went
> Clothed in his five wounds.
>
> Solomon whose coat was like daffodils
> Came out of the shadows.
> He kissed Wisdom there, on the second step.
> The boy whose mouth had been filled with harp-songs,
> The shepherd-king
> Gave, on the third step, his purest cry.

At the root of the Tree of Man, an urn
With dust of apple-blossom
Joseph, harvest-dreamer, counsellor of pharaohs
Stood on the fourth step.
He blessed the lingering Bread of Life.

He who had wrestled with an angel,
The third of the chosen,
Hailed the King of Angels on the fifth step.

Abel with his flute and fleeces
Who bore the first wound
Came to the sixth step with his pastorals.

On the seventh step down
The tall primal dust
Turned with a cry from digging and delving.
Tomorrow the Son of Man will walk in a garden
Through drifts of apple-blossom.

Years ago in the early 'callow' prose poems George had become the Oak Tree, his Tree of Life, his 'Dream of the Rood', and he the narrator taking readers into a dream. In this dream or vision he is speaking to the Cross on which Jesus was crucified. George learnt at first hand the Christian rite of passage, how to interchange Christ's suffering with his own, how to see the purpose of suffering. From this vantage point he became inwardly strong where the harrowing of 'rag' and 'scarecrow' and 'worm' could inspire some of his finest writing.

George went to his beloved Warbeth 'tomb' in the funeral cortege vividly accompanied along the Old Finstown Road dazzling with its 'Resurrection ditches' and 'blaze of Solomon-coated-daffodils'. The sun enhancing the light, the glory of the Lord that day so evident, the wind caressing the mourners as angels' wings. The parish priest, Fr Michael Spenser SJ, not known for his careful driving, having read out George's last column from the Orcadian; he had given a special emphasis to George's use of brackets and shared the consolation he always felt in common with George in residence in Stromness. He concelebrated at the Mass, and in characteristic form, had after the funeral homily made an audacious journey at speed down the Old Finstown Road in his car with the two altar boys, on the wrong side of the road, in order to get behind the hearse.

At Warbeth, there were many mourners, the weather sunny and windy, the roar of the Pentland Firth and the eagle-capped Hoy Hills, attuned in the set form of the burial liturgy. Priest and altar boys, incense and candles adrift at the graveside as the pall-bearers lowered George into the family plot. The sacramental solemnity was very dramatic. Where was George? His body now going down into the dust at Warbeth, site of a pre-Reformation monastery which to this day retains the immortal intimations of its prayer, its *Vinland* sanctity where:

> an Irish monk who had stayed for a while with the brothers at Warbeth had told him the marvellous tale of the voyages of Saint Brandon who had sailed out to find the Island of the Blessed in the western sea; and of how in this hut by himself, so that he could solve the riddle of fate and freedom, and so make preparations for his last voyage upon the waters of the end.[6]

George's body lay in the night and sleep of the grave, his soul abroad on the ocean of God's love. George, the solitary, had sat at his candle, and commended us to this silence, as it is engraved on his tombstone, 'Carve the runes and then be content with silence'. His life had been a 'harrowing' both internally and externally, but it was in his mastery of the interior life where his contemplative attunement could see the patterns. He went down the first step 'clothed' in Christ's wounds, returning to the New Covenant of the Cross where on 'the second step' he discerned and interchanged Solomon and daffodils to the point where there is no separation. On 'the third step' the conflict-ridden David found in death humanity, made in the image of God, fragrant with what of this image is now 'dust of apple-blossom'. Deeper into the Old Covenant 'the fourth step' George-dreamer is witness, as was Joseph, to the good, elicited as it is from evil. On 'the fifth step' George 'wrestled with angels' on Jacob's ladder to find his King. On 'the sixth step' the concept of sin ravaged the body and soul with fratricide, consequent of 'the seventh step' where the 'cry' from 'tall primal dust' reminds us of that original 'garden'. The Garden of Eden fragrant with 'drifts of apple-blossom', where one can 'dig and delve' in the 'unsullied vision' was George's life-long project. He makes 'sweet' for us, digging and delving, with the sweetness of the old religion. He re-opened the world view suppressed and scorned since the Reformation.

So the George Mackay Brown story is a faith story. Orkney is his glory of the Lord where he found the eucharistic Jesus. His writings not only give testament to his faith, but also how to 'read' as one would read the Bible, turning the 'pages' of its historical phases set in a wild beauty still to this day so vividly tangible. George Mackay Brown, Orkney poet, presided with a universal spirituality that from its first 'rapture' saw far and wide, with an ever deepening insight into things that remain alive and unchanging. He brought a freshness to many standard teachings of traditional thought in philosophy and history. His 'attitude' was contemplative and attuned to a positivity and open-ness towards changes in society and ways of living. He discovered for himself the patterns of 'orthodoxy', Orcadian and ecclesial, in the 'swarm of symbols'. He saw no separation between them, and their textured interchanging perceptions were evidence enough for what he considered to be the most convincing expression of a life-giving meaning.

He resisted being labelled one way or another and he was right to do so. Being described as an Orkney poet was enough. He is not a Catholic writer, but as Newman pointed out his reactions and literary responses are as a Catholic would react and respond. Von Balthasar had perceived that 'the run-of-the-mill clergy',[7] no longer philosophers, are reinvigorated by the 'ressourcement'[8] of the poets:

> Now it is primarily laity who, out of an adequate theological culture and with a more powerful vision and deeper creative insight than the theologians of the schools, carry forward the concern and guarantee of its effectiveness with a breadth and depth that escapes the profes-sional theologians.[9]

Mackay Brown ultimately made the judgement that 'the old wals of Churches and Monasteries, the defaced ruines of altars, images, and crosses do cry with a loud voice, that the Romain Catholique faith of Jesus Christ did tread this way'.[10] He had been bitter about it, vehe-mently giving voice to views not well understood in Orkney. But he carried his religious experience, serenely tempered and textured across the years, to readers near and far, with a consistent conviction always true to his sources. In re-opening the pre-Reformation world view he is in fact engaging with the modern world and through the power of symbols he is able to overcome the radical dichotomy that existed between the world and God, between the natural and the supernatural. His contemplative reading of Orkney is true to its nature and its grace. An Orkney poetics commands his writing with a pivotal impulse for reform, for 'ressourcement'. Simultaneously that same pivotal impulse deep within the very heart of the Catholic Church was blossoming into ecclesial renewal and reform. The current shape of Catholic theology, spirituality and ecclesial perspective is a direct product of this movement. George Mackay Brown went where he was led by his conscience through his existential struggles for meaning and truth in his writing. He brought an Orkney poetics into the shared metaphysical workspace quarried by many before and after him.

His contemplative spirit, as expressed in his observation: 'One must be passive, often, to let the swarming delights of the world in, and things beyond',[11] led to an exquisite exposition of the pre-theological poetic art 'In the fire of images, / Gladly I put my hand'.[12] George Mackay Brown, we also are very *glad* (as in the the Old English *glæd* with its sense of 'bright, shining' and related to the Old Norse *glaðr* meaning 'bright, joyous'). You are a bright, shining joy.

Conclusion

Notes

1   von Balthasar, *The Glory of the Lord III*, p. 396.

2   Bishop Mario Conti, 'Sermon at St Magnus Cathedral on St Magnus Day, 16 April 1996. Funeral of George Mackay Brown'. Reproduced in Appendix 2 of Gray, *Circle of Light*, p. 104.

3   *Ibid.*

4   *Ibid.*

5   Reproduced from Mackay Brown, *The Collected Poems*, pp. 400–1.

6   Mackay Brown, *Vinland*, p. 254.

7   von Balthasar, *The Glory of the Lord II*, p. 15.

8   *Ressourcement* is a movement of twentieth-century Catholic theology (back to sources).

9   *Ibid.*

10   Eyston, *A cleer looking glass for all wandering sinners*, cited in Shell, 'Abbey Ruins', p. 23.

11   George Mackay Brown, letter to the author, 2 September 1983. See Appendix.

12   Mackay Brown, 'Hamnavoe'.

Appendix

Excerpts from the Letters of George Mackay Brown to Alison Gray, 1977–1993

Parishioner: Our Lady and St Joseph, Kirkwall

The bonds of the Catholic community stretch far and wide and deep. The outward manifestations of George Mackay Brown's Mass attendance are recorded here. He did as all Catholics do, living out his day-to-day existence understanding and committing to the authority of the original patterns of Christ in the sacraments amidst the trials and tribulations of life. It was the liturgy that lay at the heart of his religion wherein the Mass occupies a unique centrality. The world was redeemed in the Good Friday Crucifixion once and for all and regularly George Mackay Brown was transported to Calvary on the altar of his parish church. He knelt alongside the congregation across the years and with his community was gathered into the passion and resurrection of Christ. Within the fullness of salvation history he was renewed as an individual and as a believing member of the community. The unity of the Mass and the bonds of love wrought in him fellowship, affection, loyalty, acts of charity and works of mercy within the community and beyond. His consciousness of sin, dread and doubt became his sweet joyous peace through Christ. The extracts that follow are testament to his much loved religion which guided and nurtured his soul and his literary audaciousness.

Fr Bamber

21 September 1979.... the church on Sunday mornings has been crowded for months past. Then Father Bamber goes to Flotta.

3 July 1980. Father Bamber: I like him very much, there's something of great charm about him, and he has a kind generous nature. He is eccentric, but in a good English tradition.

3 September 1980. Mass on Sundays is always full to overflowing—many tourists of course. Father Bamber had to show the Queen Mother the Italian Chapel last week. Then he went for a short holiday to Blackpool.

31 July 1981. Father Bamber was 70 last Friday. His flock presented him with a fine new bicycle; that seemed to please him.

14 February 1982. Fr Bamber was here the other day—having been a victim of the flu that is ravaging Orkney—and thinks he'll be leaving Orkney in about a year's time. He is 70 now, and has been here for over 18 years. I shall miss him. This week he is off on one his frequent jaunts to the South. Many of the people who attend mass nowadays are strangers. The little church is full to brimming every Sunday morning. In summer, with all the tourists, there are two masses ...

28 X 1982. Fr Bamber has been 'on retreat' for 3 weeks but returns, I think, tomorrow. Meantime we have had a Jesuit from Glasgow who preached excellent sermons; though people—used to Father Bamber's—complained about their length. I think it was a sad day when the Latin Mass was abandoned. The heart of it remains, of course, untouched: but much majesty and mystery has been lost.

13 January 1983. I had a visit from Father Bamber yesterday—he stayed to drink tea and chat.

3 February 1983. Fr Bamber preached in St Magnus 2 Sundays ago! John Broom and I didn't stay, after Mass, to hear him. Now Fr B. is off south on one of his brief rambles ...

24 February 1983. I wonder who we will get when Fr Bamber goes?—he seems to be sure that this is his last year in Orkney. It will be another Jesuit, I think (and hope).

6 June 1983. Father Bamber thinks he won't be in Orkney much longer, after 20 years. The Kirkwall people will miss him, he seems a part of the fabric of the community.

2 September 1983. Father Bamber, I hear, is leaving Orkney in October, after 20 years. I don't know the name of the new priest but I hear he was a ship's officer once. Probably he's a Jesuit … the little church seems to get more and more people all the time. A Catholic man with wife and 7 children are coming to settle in Stromness any day now.

6 October 1983. Father Bamber left Orkney on Wednesday, and all Orkney (including of course the Catholic community) will miss him).

24 November 1988. Fr Bamber returns from time to time to see his old friends. There were Masses in the Episcopal church here during the summer, but so meagrely advertised that hardly any tourists showed up … You'd hardly recognise the interior of Our Lady and St Joseph in Kirkwall, it's been so extensively renovated. It was lovely having Masses in St Magnus while the work was going on.

18 August 1990. Fr Bamber is here at the moment; he loves making frequent returns to Orkney.

24 July 1991. Father Bamber will be 80 tomorrow. I hear there's to be a party for him in Kirkwall. I think, as I'm not one for parties, I'll stay at home. Our priest, Fr Spencer, likes parties very much.

15 March 1992 Father Bamber died last month, in a school near Sheffield, aged 80. He was an eccentric priest but very well liked by most Orcadians. R.I.P.

Fr Spencer

8 September 1983. Our new priest is a Father Spencer, a Jesuit. There's to be a party for Fr Bamber and a presentation, end of September.

21 April 1988. Now they have renovated the church and presbytery in Kirkwall and it looks good. While the renovation was going on, Mass was said in St Magnus.

15 March 1992. Our new priest—well, 8 years he has been with us—Fr Spenser, S.J., is quite different: good devoted man, too.

Good Friday [1 April] 1994. Fr Spencer S.J. is still our priest. Some sheep drift from the flock and others join it. So, I suppose, it always has been.

Bishop Conti

13 September 1992. Last week we had Bishop Conti saying Mass in Stromness. Some Catholics falling off, new Catholics appearing. I suppose it was ever thus.

John Broom

1 March 1979. For lots of Sundays, John Broom couldn't make Kirkwall for the snow. But last Sunday we got there, at last. The church was crowded—how will it be when the thousands of tourists come? Father Bamber read a letter from John Paul II.

25 September 1981. The church is full most Sundays. One Sunday Mass we had an Australian Jesuit, while Father Bamber was visiting contemporaries in Wales. John Broom the librarian drives me in but last Sunday morning was too stormy (O Broom and Brown of little faith!)

28 November 1981. Tomorrow, as usual, John Broom drives me to Mass. The little church is full to brimming every Sunday; in summer there has to be two Masses. And always it lifts the heart: *sursum corda*. As we used to chant in the beautiful Latin Mass.

17 December 1981. John Broom and I haven't managed to get to Mass for 2 Sundays past, because of frost and snow. I hope the roads are clear for Christmas. I always like to see Father Bamber with his flock at the Nativity.

18 November 1982. John Broom and I still go, Sunday after Sunday, to Mass at Our Lady and St Joseph's.

24 February 1983. Now that the snow has gone for good—I wonder?—John Broom and I get to Mass every Sunday morning. The little Catholic church is almost full—in high summer, it is full to over-flowing at 2 Masses.

6 February 1985. John Broom doesn't go to church any more and so—until my friend with the car returns from France—I only get to Mass once a month when Fr Spenser comes to say Mass at Weber's house.

7 May 1989. John Broom is busy at the bookshop and studying in Kirkwall library.

Pope John Paul II

23 November 1978. I was immensely pleased that a non-Italian was chosen to be Pope. He seems a good man in every way.

Midsummer Day 1982. Midsummer here! Midwinter with you. The sun has been poured upon us, lavishly; especially during John Paul's visit—which thrilled the whole nation. Such a marvellous presence! Truly he brings hope and joy and quickening to all the nations of the earth.

9 July 1983. We may be thankful that we have such a Pope as John Paul to confront the evils of our time. How rapturously he was greeted in Britain last year!—and the young folk led the singing and the cheering.

Sunday Mass

16 August 1979. I suppose we are all meant to be parents—it opens the door into the future, in which our dust and blood will have a part to play in the great mystery drama of time and Eternity, long after we are dead. For such as me, that door is closed: I sit and brood in the present and the past, and try as best I can to see a meaning and a pattern. My black depressions have lifted a little. Maybe I'm to be allowed a little field for sun and a dance, before Old Age. I go to Mass occasionally. The church overflows most Sundays. Father Bamber is still there. (My faith is still a feeble flicker. But it hasn't gone out.)

28 April 1980. John Broom drives me to Mass whenever a car is available. I feel more at peace afterwards; even though I don't communicate. Fr Bamber is still in Orkney ... I say a 'Hail Mary' whenever I remember—ungrateful ungracious creature that I am—and feel a sense of peace and sweetness afterwards, sometimes.

28 April 1980. [After Mass] I feel at peace afterwards even tho' I don't communicate ... I say a 'Hail Mary' whenever I remember—ungrateful ungracious creature that I am—and feel a sense afterwards, sometimes ... Orkney has little yellow tarns and lakes of daffodils along the road-side, wind-ruffled.

20 April 1981. Yesterday the 11 o'clock Mass was full to overflowing. Outside, masses of daffodils and the sun shining, and inside the joyful ritual, with children's voices. It was the first time in 9 weeks that I'd been to Mass. My health had been bad all winter and in the middle of March got so bad—lungs and heart—that I was taken into hospital for 12 days. Everybody in the hospital was most kind. Now I am out in the world again and seeing with joy the awakening life everywhere.

18 August 1981. So many go to Mass on a Sunday now, Fr Bamber has to have 2 Masses. Of course tourists swell the ranks of the faithful.

27 March 1982. I go to Mass most Sundays, driven by John Broom, and the little church is overflowing, with all the English who have come to live in Orkney. Fr Bamber thinks this will be his last year of exile. We shall miss him in many ways. Susie is still at the organ.

Midsummer Day 1982. I have just come back from Mass and Benediction in Kirkwall. The little kirk, as always now full to overflowing ... Father Bamber went to see the Pope in Glasgow: but John Paul didn't pick out Father B in the huge crowd, he reported.

22 July 1982. The little church in Kirkwall is full to overflowing these days. Fr Bamber has to say 2 Masses on a Sunday—and another last Sunday at the Italian chapel.

7 August 1982. Mass at 11 every Sunday is overflowing, of course ... Last Sunday, John Broom and I took a pleasant French girl called Katin who with her boyfriend is translating some of my poems.

24 February 1983. I agree with you—the Latin Mass is a miss. The majesty of Latin has been cast aside for a dull drab contemporary English. Of course, the central core of the Mass remains untouched. But I miss the grave and lovely dialogue of priest and acolyte, and those mysterious silences when each silent heart was a loom of prayer.

26 January 1989. You wouldn't recognise the church in Kirkwall; it has been completely restored, with carpets and new furniture and the altar at the other end. Not being a driver, I rarely get to Mass. Otherwise I don't waver in my allegiance.

7 May 1989. Today is Sunday and I was hoping to get to Mass in Stromness but somehow I don't like being in a tiny congregation, in a drab place that isn't really a church. I know this is all wrong of me. Soon, perhaps, I'll find a way to Kirkwall on Sunday mornings.

18 August 1990. The little church in Kirkwall—nicely renovated—has been full these 3 past Sundays; many tourists of course.

15 March 1992. 'Sunday morning here—letterwriting day. Then up the hill to lunch with an old friend. Mass in a Stromness house in the evening, if there's a car.

Lent

21 February 1980. I still go to Mass in Kirkwall some Sunday mornings, when John Broom calls in the car. Father Bamber is still there. Yesterday was Ash Wednesday. I remembered not to eat steaks or sausages, but only a tomato omelette. Then, alas, went to the opening of a photograph exhibition; after which whiskey flowed. Not the best thing to start Lent.

2 June 1980. I went to Mass (Trinity Sunday) with John Broom yesterday. Father Bamber filled his sermon with humorous sallies; I suppose religion has a place for fun and self-satire, as well as for 'external verities' … These Sundays, the little church is full to overflowing. When the tourists begin to flood in, there will have to be 2 masses. (Of course, Fr Bamber says Mass in Flotta every Sunday afternoon.)

7 February 1991. On 15 April (eve of St Magnus) there's to be a Mass in St Magnus Cathedral. Only 6 days now till Ash Wednesday.

27 March 1993. I'm afraid I haven't done much in the way of Lent fasting: except to read the daily office from the pre-Vatican Council II missal. Some great Old Testament stories: Susannah and the elders, Joseph and his brothers, Naaman's leprosy and the cure, Elijah and his

bringing back to life, the widow's pots of oil. Now there are Catholics in many islands here; Father Spenser has a busy time of it. There's been a little Mass—house outside Stromness for 2 or 3 years past. There are fallings-away, adherences, always; as happen, I suppose world-wide.

Easter

15 April 1982 (St Magnus Eve). The peedie kirk was overflowing for the Mass of Easter day—a brightness of daffodils and faces and candles and the words of scripture … Fr Bamber is away for a week or two—a priest with an Irish name is coming to hold the fort.

4 April 1985. Today's Maundy Thursday. Our new priest may be coming to say Mass in Stromness on Easter day. I'd rather go to church is Kirkwall.

Easter [11 April] 1993. I am hoping to go to Easter Mass at Braemar at 6pm … Fr Spenser hasn't been well for weeks but he battles on. In addition to all his other duties, yesterday he had a wedding at the Italian chapel (And of course 3 masses today, starting with the Easter Vigil at midnight.) … 5 more days till St Magnus day (16 April) … Duns Scotus: Gerard Manley Hopkins held Blessed D.S. 'most swayed my spirit to peace' … They were dunces themselves who put that label on him.

Christmas

24 November 1988. Christmas cards arrived in two parcels. It's a thought, all that addressing and scores of envelopes. The commercialism—TV advertising, etc.—is rampant. A far cry from the Child in the crib.

27 December 1989. We're just getting over the festivities here: which means for most of us too much to eat and drink. However, I got to Midnight Mass and the little church in Kirkwall was full to overflowing.

St Stephen's Day [26 December] 1991. Here—as always—it was mostly the mad splurge in commercialism and glitter. But those pretenders to the places of the Magi never get near the meaning of the time. I did a bit of splurging myself yesterday in turkey and plum pudding, wine, cognac: but not too much—I'm too old a hand at the game of excess.

Nor will my spider-web-frail physique stand up to too much of that kind of punishment. Thank God, I'm still able to sit down after breakfast and enjoy work at the writing-table. A blank sheet of paper and the feel of pen in hand fills me with joy. The Catholics in Orkney ebb and flow. New faces appear, old adherents drift into apathy or unbelief. That's the way it has always been. I think the Church always at its best in poor and dangerous places—not among the smug and affluent (like Europe in the 90s and vast bloated America. The Russians are a spiritual people and there may well be an opening of ancient springs there).

30 December 1994. Christmas—the commercial part of it—is over, let it go. The eternal part of Christmas endures for ever.

Braemar and Our Lady Star of the Sea Stromness

18 August 1990. Fr Spenser says Mass in a house in Stromness on Sunday evenings.

7 February 1991. I forgot to say there's a Mass in Stromness every Sunday evening in a small house on the outskirt.

26 May 1991. This afternoon I'll have lunch with a 90 year old friend. Then she'll drive me to Mass to a peedie house just outside Stromness.

24 July 1991. Now Mass is said at a peedie house a mile out of Stromness every Sunday evening. (A nurse from Glasgow lives there).

Good Friday [1 April] 1994. Stromness is beginning to fill up with Easter tourists. I have had a bit of bronchitis but I must try to get into Kirkwall for Mass this evening. A little chapel is being built outside Stromness one mile, by Mary Firth.

17 July 1994. The new little Catholic chapel goes up slowly—there has been some official objection to the red tiles on the roof. It will be called Our Lady Star of the sea, I think ... Fr Spenser is on holiday; last Sunday we had an American Jesuit who preached a rather brief beautiful sermon.

Depression

29 September 1977. The rain is knocking on the window and I sit writing letters, letters. Nothing much has happened to revive the Catholic flame. Instead, I think more of such august 'eternal truths' as Courage, Pity, Mercy, Beauty, charity. These have always been there and always will be, while generations come and go. To be sure, this is a cold and abstract way of looking at things, but it's all I can subscribe to at the moment. If you knew me, you would discover an unpleasant self-absorbed cowardly creature. But of course, like everyone else, I suppose I have my bearable moments.

Any inner sanctuary I had is all a heap of stones these days. I must gather the scattered blocks together and try, somehow to build anew.

16 March 1978. I have been suffering from an intense depression (a highly neurotic state) but I am calmer now because I've had two libriums. I hope this journey of mine through gorse doesn't go on too long—I had 2½ years of it already, sometimes bearable, sometimes anguished. And there seems to be no reason why I am taking that direction. Enough of grousing. I eat and sleep and manage to live an apparently normal existence. The spring is coming, little hints and intimations: longer light, daffodils on the table, a faint infusion of warmth. One sure road at least is taking us to the heart of summer.

1 March 1979. I am experiencing, off and on, some dark things in recent years. A little patience, a little endurance, and the sun may come again. (I've been through these dark times in earlier life. Now I can partly understand them—but at the age of 15–17 it was all a nightmare. The nightmare passed then. It will now too, sooner or later). But I'm still able to eat and sleep and drink and create and laugh; so you shouldn't think life is all misery. It isn't, at all.

26 March 1978. As you might have seen from *The Orcadian*, I have been suffering from 2 bugs simultaneously, plus a dark depression. But I am a bit better now. (I wished to be at church Easter Day, but physical weakness kept me at home.)

10 April 1979. Still the weather keeps cold and dull. It seems to put a weight on all our spirits. I seem sometimes to be living at the bottom

of a dangerous pit. The light of faith burns very dim. Today—so cold and wet!—I lay in bed till 3pm: having taken a valium tablet when I first woke up earlier.

8 June 1979. I felt I had to get away, or something would give in my mind.

December 1979. I am quite busy writing: Some days it goes well, some days not. (This is part of our human condition.)

29 December 1979. Little happens except that I write most days: poetry, stories, little scenes for plays. It keeps me from thinking dark thoughts.

21 February 1980. I woke thoroughly miserable after a sleepless night and decided to write the misery away with letters; since I was in no mood to work on poem or play or story. And now I am more cheerful.

3 July 1980. These days I have lost relish for reading and even writing (my dearest joy it is, the putting of pen to paper.) It is as tho' I'm walking in a gray menacing mist, with ugly shapes here and there ... Some friends from Aberdeen are staying with me. Some French friends ... to stay a month ... but I fear they won't get much joy out of me, in my present state ... I might have been in Melbourne now: but here I exist, grayly ... PS Writing 3 letters and an 'Orcadian' article has cheered me a little!

18 August 1981. My health varies from day to day. I am not as fit as I was 2 years ago. What I dread most are the dark 'inscapes'. One must try to accept those, and bodily weaknesses as well, as one's just share of humanity's burden.

15 April 1982 (St Magnus Eve). I was recovering from the first cold of 1982—cured quickly enough by antibiotics, but the cure induces such dark depressions that life seems to be a poor thing, a handful of barren dust instead of a sheaf of golden corn. However, the dark days have gone again—I wish I could say, forever ... Now the sun is growing and broadening, and the air is like cold wine, full of promise.

2 September 1983. There is that dour old Scottish Calvinist in me that yells—'Work, work!' that's what you're here for, *Work* ... which is not true at all. A little work, true. But then one must be passive, often, to let the swarming delights of the world in, and things beyond.

4 April 1985. 'I have been busy, fighting depressions (that come and go) with work and tranquillisers. I'm very grateful for the tranquillisers.

5 October 1991. I was suffering from a deep depression and recently spent 3 weeks in hospital in Aberdeen but I am fortunate in having so many good friends who set the fire for me, do my shopping, invite me for meals ... Maybe all this kindness isn't altogether good for me. I am losing my cooking skills, for one thing ... I haven't been to Mass for some weeks but I'll try, I think, to go tomorrow. The Calvinistic inheritance of the 'angry God' is hard to shake off, having been in the bloodstream for 12 generations. The God of joy, the Lord of the dance, is what we need increasingly.

23 February 1992. The light grows every day. I grow weary of strangers coming to visit. Even now, in winter ... In summer it's nigh unbearable, for a solitary like me. I ought to be thankful: but sometimes clouds come and settle on the mind, like last autumn when I had to go to hospital in Aberdeen ... today I'm going to have lunch with a remarkable old lady, aged 91. I hope, if I feel well enough, to go to Mass in a house a mile from Stromness, at 6pm.

17 July 1994. I go one from day to day—'one step enough for me.'[1] I suppose many would think me fortunate, doing the work I like and being moderately successful at it. But the 'making of things' has its flip-side: clouds and fogs in the mind, and unknown menaces. Not all the time, thank goodness.

11 September 1994. The little chapel in Stromness goes up slowly, after a few hiccups.

30 October 1994. The new Chapel of the Sacred Heart is going up, ever so slowly, among the fields a mile from Stromness. The local planning office objected to the colour (red) of the roof tiles: that held things up. The builders come for a few days, then disappear for weeks ... Sunday morning here. I've just had toast and marmalade and tea. After letter-writing, I must tidy this filthy kitchen (washing-up, putting papers in order), then go out for lunch, then maybe watch football (Celtic v Rangers), then mass at 6.

Reflective Comment

18 August 1981. Dryden, at his best, is marvellous. But so much of his verse is contemporary satire, we of the 20th century miss the point. His craftsmanship is superb: *Ode on St Cecilia's Day*, etc.

At the moment I am reading that pessimistic poet with the pity for poor suffering humanity and his hostility to God. Again a marvellous craftsman in the art of verse; but, As G. K. Chesterton said, he likes to pose and posture as the 'village atheist'.

1 March 1984. Never forget: in silence is the movement of purer deeper thoughts, that words only stain and obscure, mostly.

18 August 1990. I keep well clear of all kinds of Catholic controversy. I think the Church seems full of energy nowadays (some misdirected, but that's the way it has always been).

7 February 1991. The Orkney Catholics seem to increase, though there are always a few who 'lapse', of course.

15 November 1991. I had a happy birthday surrounded by friends. A Dominican priest in Dublin—remembered me in his Mass that day. No harm in studying the scriptures, so long as one knows what one is about. It is such a richly poetic-symbolical body of work, some people read into it (especially a book like Revelation) all kinds of meaning. The Reformation happened because people were making private inferences. The Church is there to prevent such strayings. 'This is what scripture means', the church is never tired of saying, 'this and nothing else, unless the Holy Spirit unfolds some new meaning ...' it shouldn't be forgotten that the scripture we have is only a translation of translations—and meaning alters subtly with each translation. I have been writing Christmas stories. The fire and the teapot, books and music and friends are delightful these early winter evenings. I am going out for lunch today to a kind house. *Pray for me as I will for thee, that we may merrily meet in heaven* (St Thomas More) ... I saw the marvellous new film about St T. M, 'A Man For All Seasons' on TV last Sunday, before going to Mass in the tiny cottage Braemar outside Stromness. Now I've discovered a copy of the play and look forward to read that. A saint to rejoice in and to pray to for help, as I do daily. That was

a wonderful quotation you sent, of Cardinal Newman. He received Gerard Manley Hopkins the Jesuit poet in the Church—there's a good new biography of GMH.

15 March 1992. Catholics everywhere, it seems, are great at squabbling. The wonder is they haven't torn themselves apart many times since the reformation: I suppose the wind of the Holy Spirit keeps the ark from the rocks ... I'd never belong to that Lefébrist lot ... As for my spiritual state, I'm inclined not to worry about it as much as I used to. God knows, I have problems, difficulties, sins that I cling to: on the other hand, we may all have gifts that are hidden even in the eyes of our own spirits. And we must hope and pray that light never goes out; even while we seek here and there with the lamps we think we have been given to use ... It is all a great mystery. Cardinal Newman was quite right: we ought to rest in faith and trust. I myself don't have one iota of Newman's marvellous power of reason—but I do have a certain measure of imagination, and I seek out my way by that light. The truth is, I think, that I'm not a very spiritual person. The beauty and poetry of Catholicism attracted me when I was quite young, and the riches have grown since then. The certainty too: insofar as one can be certain of anything, in 'this brief transit'.[2]

25 April 1992. I was much intrigued by the extracts from Newman you sent. He was a wonderful man, maybe a Saint. I read a biography of the Jesuit St John Ogilvie who was martyred in Glasgow, early 17th century such bravery, patience, constancy! I think (being such a coward) I'd have signed any document the heretics pushed in front of me. But maybe we all have more hidden strength than we know. In Catholic Orkney, there is (it seems) a constant leaking away but also there is a continuing stream of new people coming in. It is a highly secular age we live in—little in the way of awe or imagination. But the ship ECCLESIA must endure all weathers, droughts, and tempests.

8 Oct 1992. John Brook's *The School of Prayer*[3] ... I have dipped into it and hope to return to it again and again: there are many things to be learned and relished ... The Catholic community in Orkney seems to shrink: fallings off and desertions. But then suddenly new faces appear, a family settles in from the south. So the well is always renewed. And

I'm sure many of 'the deserters' come back. As Father Spenser says, 'A Catholic is always a Catholic'. A New Zealand priest, a Carmelite, Father Shaa, was relieving Fr Spenser a few weeks ago—a fine sermon he preached; the way he conducted Mass was beautiful too. I am going to be 71 in a few days' time—I feel sometimes 'grown old in iniquity' but then alight breaks in from time to time ... I feel sure The School of Prayer will be a great help. Everybody here speaks of 'recession' but still how affluent they are, most of them: it is just, I expect, what people want more and more luxuries on their plates, forever and ever ... The true Kingdom is everywhere around, unacknowledged.

13 December 1992. Our Catholic population suffers lapses, but there are always new streams feeding in. The Kirkwall church has been completely transformed ... I don't know if there will be any movement Rome-wards of the Orkney Anglicans—I hear the Anglicans here have an Evangelical priest nowadays.

Notes

[1] John Henry Newman, 'Lead Kindly Light', a hymn with words written in 1833 within a poem entitled 'The Pillar of Cloud' (in *The Oxford Book of English Mystical Verse*, ed. D. H. S. Nicholson and A. H. E. Lee. Oxford: Clarendon Press, 1917; also at http://www.bartleby.com/236/).

[2] From T. S. Eliot, 'Ash Wednesday', in *Collected Poems 1909–1962*. London: Faber & Faber, 2002.

[3] John Brook, *The School of Prayer: An Introduction to the Divine Office for All Christians*. Collegeville, Minnesota: Liturgical Press, 1992.

Bibliography

Primary Sources

All items listed under Primary Sources are by George Mackay Brown, unless stated otherwise.

Manuscript Collections

ORKNEY ARCHIVE

'Kirk Elder', March 1943. D31/30/2

'Christ Poem', July 1944. D31/30/2

'The House of Death', March 1945. D31/30/2

'Dream of Winter', March 1946. D31/30/2

'Man into Oak', June 1946. D31/30/2

'The Prisoner', August 1947. D31/30/2

'Summer Day', 1947. D31/20/3

'Landscapes from Memory', 1953, typed manuscript signed 'Hjal'. D1/296/1, p. 11

'Ernest, today our sky is lowering', 19 January 1954, from Eastbank Hospital. D31/30/4

'Profile of George Mackay Brown', 1965. D31/30/4

'Why Live in Orkney', 1966. D31/TR/68

Good Morning Scotland (1 January 1974), BBC transcript, preparatory comment for recording, dated 24 December 1973. D31/30/4

'Thoughts of an Old Age Pensioner', August 1986. D124/2/5, p. 9

'The Story of Scotland. Edwin Muir', 21 November 1988. D124/2/2/12, p. 2

Letters to Ernest Marwick. D31/30/4

'George Mackay Brown'. D31/30/4, p. 6

EDINBURGH UNIVERSITY SPECIAL COLLECTIONS

Fragment (note) in Essays and Articles, 2 May 1983. MS 2844.1

St John's Kirk 750th anniversary 1991 booklet. MS 3119, 1986–94

'The Architect. A Story', October 1993. MS 3118.27

NATIONAL LIBRARY OF SCOTLAND, GEORGE MACKAY BROWN
ARCHIVE

Robert Rendall, letter to George Mackay Brown, 8 April 1948. Acc.
4864/15–30

'The Poet Speaks', typescript, 3 May 1965, of interview by Peter Orr
of the British Council, 14 October 1964 (National Sound Archive).
Acc.1020/6

Comment on Paul Butter's book *Edwin Muir* (London: Oliver & Boyd,
1962) in letter to Willa Muir, 17 November 1966. Acc. 51/5

'The Resurrection', in letter to Stewart Conn concerning the play *Spell
for Green Corn*, 16 July 1967. Acc. 4864/15

Letter to Stewart Conn concerning the play *Spell for Green Corn*, 16
July 1967. Acc. 4864/19

A 200 word summary of the novel *Greenvoe* for the publisher, Harcourt
Brace, 22 March 1973. Acc. 10209/8.

Published Works

'Billy Graham', Island Diary, *Orkney Herald*, 1 Feb. 1955. Copy also held
in Orkney Archive, D31/30/1)

The Collected Poems of George Mackay Brown, ed. Archie Bevan and
Brian Murray. London: John Murray, 2005

'Edwin Muir', *Glasgow Herald*, 15 June 1985. Copy also held in Orkney
Archive, D124/2/1/2

'Enchantment of the Islands. A Poet's Sources', *Flightpath* (Loganair
magazine), 1993. Copy also held in Edinburgh University Library,
George Mackay Brown Collection, MS 3118.16

For the Islands I Sing. An Autobiography. London: John Murray, 1997

'Go Down Moses', Island Diary, *Orkney Herald*, 25 Sept 1956. Copy
also held in Orkney Archive, D31/30/1

Greenvoe. Edinburgh: Birlinn, 2004

'Living in Orkney', *Saltire Review* 2/6 (1955), pp. 55–8

Magnus. Edinburgh: Cannongate Classics, 2000

Northern Lights. A Poet's Sources. London: John Murray, 1999

The Orkney Tapestry. London: Quartet Books, 1973

'Poetry Keeping the Flame Alive', *Spotlight* (1988), p. 49. Copy also held in Orkney Archive, D124/2/4/27

'Predicament of the Writer', *The Scotsman*, 22 February 1986. Copy also held in Orkney Archive, D124/2/2/4

'Rooted in One Dear Familiar Place', in the 'Letters' section, Royal Society of Literature quarterly, 15 September 1994. Copy also held in Edinburgh University Library, George Mackay Brown Collection. Photocopy, MS 3118.16

Spell for Green Corn. London: The Hogarth Press, 1970

'Suddenly there were Penguins', *The Scotsman*, 11 August 1985. Copy also held in Orkney Archive, D124/2/1/1

Time in a Red Coat. Harmondsworth: Penguin, 1986

A Time to Keep and Other Stories. Edinburgh: Polygon, 2006

'Transformation', Island Diary, *Orkney Herald*, 3 May 1955. Copy also held in Orkney Archive, D31/30/1)

'Treasures beyond Price', in *The Sunday Mail Story of Scotland*, vol. 4. Glasgow: R. Maxwell, 1988, p. 48. Copy also held in Orkney Archive, D124/2/2/13

Vinland. Edinburgh: Polygon, 2005

'The Voice', Island Diary, *Orkney Herald*, 5 April 1955. Copy also held in Orkney Archive, D31/30/1

Secondary Works

Aquinas, Thomas, *Summa Theologica* as translated by the Fathers of the English Dominican Province, and from the works of Blessed John Duns Scotus as selected and arranged by Jerome of Montefortino and as translated by Peter L. P. Simpson. Texts are taken from the *Opus Oxoniense* and the *Reportata Parisiensia* of the Wadding edition of Scotus's works. http://www.franciscan-archive.org/scotus/opera/Monte-ST3–27.pdf

Ascherson, Neil, *Seven Poets. Hugh MacDiarmid, Norman MacCaig, Iain Crichton Smith, George Mackay Brown, Robert Garioch, Sorley MacLean, Edwin Morgan*. Glasgow: Third Eye Centre, 1981

Balthasar, Hans Urs von, *The Glory of the Lord. A Theological Aesthetics. I. Seeing the Form.* San Francisco: Ignatius Press, 1982

Balthasar, Hans Urs von, *The Glory of the Lord. A Theological Aesthetics. II. Studies in Theological Styles: Clerical Styles.* San Francisco: Ignatius Press, 2006

Balthasar, Hans Urs von, *The Glory of the Lord. A Theological Aesthetics. III. Studies in Theological Style: Lay Styles.* San Francisco: Ignatius Press, 1986

Benedict XVI, Pope, General Audience , 7 July 2010. http://w2.vatican.va/content/benedict-xvi/en/audiences/2010/documents/hf_ben-xvi_aud_20100707.html

BBC Scotland, *George Mackay Brown 70th Birthday. One Star in the West.* Broadcast on BBC Scotland, April 1996

Benedict XVI, Pope, 'John Duns Scotus', in General Audience, 7 July 2010. http://w2.vatican.va/content/benedict-xvi/en/audiences/2010/documents/hf_ben-xvi_aud_20100707.html

Bede, *Ecclesiastical History of the English People*, ed. B. Colgrave and R. A. B. Mynors. Oxford: Clarendon Press, 1969

Boethius, *The Consolation of Philosophy*, trans. W. V. Cooper. London: Dent, 1902

Broadie, Alexander, *The Shadow of Scotus. Philosophy and Faith in Pre-Reformation Scotland.* Edinburgh: T&T Clarke, 1995

Brook, John, *The School of Prayer: An Introduction to the Divine Office for All Christians.* Collegeville, Minnesota: Liturgical Press, 1992

Butter, Paul, *Edwin Muir.* London and Edinburgh: Oliver & Boyd, 1962

Cairns, Craig, ed., *The History of Scottish Literature.* 4 vols. Aberdeen: Aberdeen University Press, 1987–8

Carruthers, G., and L. McIlvaney, eds., *The Cambridge Companion to Scottish Literature.* Cambridge: Cambridge University Press, 2012

The Catholic Encyclopedia. New York: Robert Appleton Company. New Advent:http://www.newadvent.org/cathen/15362a.htm

Chesterton, G. K., 'The World Inside Out', in *The Wisdom of Catholicism*, ed. Pegis.

Clancy, Thomas, 'Scottish Literature before Scottish Literature', in *Cambridge Companion to Scottish Literature*, ed. Carruthers and McIlvaney.

Conti, Bishop Mario, 'Sermon at St Magnus Cathedral on St Magnus Day, 16 April 1996, Funeral of George Mackay Brown'. Reproduced in Appendix 2 of Gray, *Circle of Light*

Crawford, Barbara E., *The Northern Earldoms. Orkney and Caithness from AD 870 to 1470*. Edinburgh: Birlinn, 2013

Davidson, Thomas, 'Plough Rituals in England and Scotland', *The Agricultural History Review* 7 (1959), pp. 27–37

Dickson, Neil, *An Island Shore. The Life and Work of Robert Rendall*. Kirkwall: Orkney Press, 1990

Duffy, Eamon, *The Stripping of the Altars. Traditional Religion in England 1400–1580*. London: Yale University Press, 1999

Duffy, Eamon, 'The English Reformation after Revisionism', *Renaissance Quarterly*, 59 (2006), pp. 720–31

Eliot, T. S., *Collected Poems 1909–1962* London: Faber & Faber, 2002

Eyston, Edward Frances, 'A cleer looking glass for all wandering sinners', cited in Shell, *Oral Culture and Catholicism in Early Modern England*.

Fergusson, Maggie, *George Mackay Brown. The Life*. London: John Murray, 2006

Gray, Alison, *Circle of Light. The Catholic Church in Orkney since 1560*. Edinburgh: John Donald, 2000

Hall, Simon W., *The History of Orkney Literature*. Edinburgh: John Donald, 2010

Hopkins, Gerard Manley, *The Journals and Papers of Gerard Manley Hopkins*, ed. Humphrey House and Graham Story. London: Oxford University Press, 1966

Hopkins, Gerard Manley, *The Note-Books and Papers of Gerard Manley Hopkins*, ed. Humphrey House. London: Oxford University Press, 1937

Hopkins, Gerard Manley, *Poems and Prose*, ed W. H. Gardner. London: Penguin, 1971

Hossack, B. H., *Kirkwall in the Orkneys*. Kirkwall: William & Son, 1900

Hume, David, *Dialogues concerning Natural Religion*. London, 1779. http://www.davidhume.org/texts/dnr.html

James, William, *The Varieties of Religious Experience*. New York: Penguin, 1985

John Paul II, Pope, Address at Blessed Scotus Beatification Ceremony, 20 March 1993. http://w2.vatican.va/content/john-paul-ii/en/homilies/1993.index.4.html

Jones, Norman, *The English Reformation: Religion and Cultural Adaptation*. Oxford: Blackwell, 2002

Ker, Ian, *The Catholic Revival in English Literature, 1845–1961*. Leominster: Gracewing, 2003

Kerr, Fergus, *Twentieth-Century Catholic Theologians. From Neoscholasticism to Nuptial Mysticism*. Oxford: Blackwell Publishing, 2007

Komonchak, J. A, M. Collins and D. A. Lane, ed., *The New Dictionary of Theology*. Dublin: Gill & MacMillan.

Langland, William, *Piers Plowman with Sir Gawain and the Green Knight, Pearl, Sir Orfeo*. The Millennium Library. London: Everyman, 2001

Lynch, Michael, *Scotland: A New History*. London: Century, 1991

Muir, Edwin, *The Story and the Fable: An Autobiography*. London: Harrap, 1940

Muir, Edwin, *An Autobiography*. London: Hogarth Press, 1954

Murray, Rowena and Brian, *Interrogation of Silence. The Writings of George Mackay Brown*. Edinburgh: Savage, 2008

Newman, John Henry, *The Idea of a University*, ed. F. Turner. New Haven and London: Yale University Press, 1996

Newman, John Henry, *Fifteen Sermons Preached before the University of Oxford between A.D. 1826 and 1843*. Notre Dame: University of Notre Dame Press, 1997

Newman, John Henry, *Apologia Pro Vita Sua*. London: Penguin, 1994

Newman, John Henry, 'English Catholic Literature', in *The Idea of a University*, ed. F. Turner.

Nicholson, D. H. S., and A. H. E. Lee, eds., *The Oxford Book of English Mystical Verse*. Oxford: Clarendon Press, 1917

Pegis, Anton C., *The Wisdom of Catholicism*. London: Michael Joseph, 1950

Pius IX, Pope, 'Constitution', in *Ineffabilis Deus*, 8 December 1854: http:// www.papalencyclicals.net/Pius09/p. 9ineff.htm.

Rendall, Robert, *Collected Poems*. Edinburgh: Savage, 2012

Robertson, Ritchie, 'Edwin Muir', in *The History of Scottish Literature*, ed. Cairns

Schmid, Sabine, *Keeping the Sources Pure. The Making of George Mackay Brown*. Bern: Peter Lang, 2003

Schumacher, Michele M., *A Trinitarian Anthropology. Adrienne von Speyr and Hans Urs von Balthasar in Dialogue with Thomas Aquinas*. Washington, DC: The Catholic University of America Press, 2014

Scola, Angelo Cardinal, *The Nuptial Mystery*. Cambridge: Eerdmans, 2005

Shell, Alison, *Oral Culture and Catholicism in Early Modern England*. Cambridge: Cambride University Press, 2008

Sherry, Vincent B., ed., *The Dictionary of Literary Biography*, vol. 27. *Poets of Great Britain and Ireland, 1945–1960*. Michigan: Gale, 1984

Thomson, William P. L., *Orkney Land and People*. Kirkwall: Kirkwall Press, 2008

Whyte, Christopher, *Modern Scottish Poetry*. Edinburgh: Edinburgh University Press, 2004

Index